GIVING
SORROW
WORDS

GIVING SORROW WORDS

How to Cope with Grief and Get On with Your Life

Candy Lightner & Nancy Hathaway

WARNER BOOKS

A Time Warner Company

Warner Books, Inc., 666 Fifth Avenue, New York, NY 10103
W A Time Warner Company

Printed in the United States of America
First printing: September 1990
10 9 8 7 6 5 4 3 2 1

Library of Congress Cataloging-in-Publication Data

Lightner, Candy.
    Giving sorrow words : how to cope with grief and get on with your
life / by Candy Lightner and Nancy Hathaway.
        p.   cm.
    ISBN 0-446-51509-4
    1. Bereavement—Psychological aspects.   2. Self-help techniques.
3. Lightner, Candy.   4. Lightner, Candy—Family.   I. Hathaway,
Nancy, 1946–   II. Title.
BF575.G7L54   1990
155.9'37—dc20   90-50292
                                                                      CIP

Designed by Giorgetta Bell McRee

For Serena and Travis
and in memory of my mom and dad,
my friend Joe Nall,
and my daughter Cari.
"She blossomed on earth; she blooms in heaven."
—CANDY

For my mother, Hannah Berman,
and in memory of my father, Alan Berman.
—NANCY

CONTENTS

ACKNOWLEDGMENTS

Writing a book is very much like starting an organization. Although one person may have the initial dream, it takes many to turn that dream into reality. So it went with MADD and so it goes with this book.

This has been my dream for the past four years but without the support and encouragement of my manager, Arlene Dayton, there would be no book. Rachel Ballon's review and comments were extremely helpful, as was Judy Tatelbaum's wonderful insight into the grieving process. Several organizations were generous with their time and their resources, including ADEC (Association for Death Education and Counseling), Center for Living, the Centering Corporation, the Saint Francis Center for Bereavement, and Resolve Through Sharing. My secretary, Elizabeth Trafford, deserves more than just thanks for her contribution to the nuts and bolts of this project.

I can never fully express my appreciation to Connie Zweig, for bringing Nancy and me together.

I am especially grateful to Jeanne Tiedge, our editor, and Warner Books, for confirming our belief in *Giving Sorrow Words*.

A special thanks to friends, too numerous to mention, who tolerated my hysteria and held my hand when the crunch was on and to Serena and Travis for sharing my enthusiasm.

The individuals who contributed to this book are too numerous to mention but their involvement shows on every page. The people we interviewed spoke from their hearts, sharing their sadness and their triumphs in the hope that our readers will benefit from their experience. It is these mourners who truly "give sorrow words." Thank you.

—CANDY LIGHTNER

Many people contributed to this book by telling us about the most painful experiences of their lives. To those people, named and unnamed in these pages, I owe an enormous debt of gratitude.

Many professionals gave freely of their time and expertise. Psychiatrist Dr. Barry Kerner, M.D., and Karen Shannon, Ph.D., submitted to countless last-minute interviews and provided important insights, hard-to-find psychiatric volumes, and warm friendship. The professionals and mourners at the conference on Growing Through Loss sponsored by the Institute for Religion and Wholeness in Claremont, California, were also very helpful. Jo Warner's contribution was particularly valuable.

Jeanne Tiedge of Warner Books, our editor, deserves heartfelt thanks, as do Artie and Richard Pine, my agents.

Throughout the process of writing this book, my friends and family have been exceptionally understanding and considerate. I especially want to thank Helen Abbott, Betsy Amster, Chris Beach, Paul Berman, Candy Borland, Sharon Bronte, Carolyn Fank, Bob Frysinger, Barry Glassner, Carol Hofmann, Peggy Kaye, Joy Manesiotis, Diana Rico, Sigrid Solheim, John Winokur, Jennie Yamasaki, and Connie Zweig. My mother, Hannah Berman, has been encouraging and helpful. Sharon Budge, Nina Jacob, and Steven Benedict offered solid support and excellent advice. I am grateful, too, to Steve Ward, who was dying while I was working on this book, and who helped nonetheless, in more ways than he knew. Finally, Mary Goodfader, Terry Baker, Diane Williams, Blake Latimer, Bonnie Reynolds, and the staff of Small World Books in Venice, California, have been flexible, forbearing, and unfailingly generous. They ordered books for me, gave me bound galleys of new ones, allowed me full access to the laser printer, and supplied ultimate proof that every writer should work at a bookstore.

—NANCY HATHAWAY

Give sorrow words; the grief that does not speak
Whispers the o'er-fraught heart and bids it break.
　　　　　—SHAKESPEARE, *Macbeth* (IV, iii)

CHAPTER 1 | Crying for Cari

I have a large collection of family photographs that for many years I kept hidden in a drawer. Those snapshots of a world gone by offered a glimpse into the past that was too painful to bear. But I must have looked at one photograph a thousand times. It's my thirteen-year-old daughter Cari's softball picture. Whenever I look at her freckled face gazing with such determination at the photographer, and at me, I remember the sunny Saturday when the picture was taken. It was May 3, 1980.

On that day, Cari walked down a quiet suburban street on her way to a school carnival and was killed by a hit-and-run drunk driver.

The night before, she told me at the last minute that she wanted to sleep at a friend's house. I was very irritated! I'd been trying to teach my kids—without success—to plan ahead. If you want to spend the night with a friend, I told them, let me know in advance so we can mark it on the calendar. But the message obviously didn't penetrate. So that night when Cari asked me to drive her to her friend's, I was angry. All the way over in the car, I yelled at her about always doing things at the last minute.

As she got out of the car, it dawned on me that I was acting like a shrew. I said, "Cari, you know that I love you, don't you?" She looked at me and said, "Oh, Mother, don't be so mushy." And she went off to be with her friend.

Those were the last words we ever spoke to each other. I never saw her alive again.

Cari was a sturdy, healthy kid (despite infant epilepsy) with a feisty personality. She spent hours talking on the phone and she liked to cook. She was always the one who baked the cookies for Santa Claus. She loved to imitate people, and she was good at it. We were always giving her the Oscar! She and her identical twin, Serena, were also athletes. They played basketball and softball after school through the Department of Parks and Recreation. That day, the girls were going to have their

1

softball pictures taken at the John Holst Grammar School in Fair Oaks, California. Afterward, with their younger brother, Travis, they planned to attend the annual school carnival at Saint Mel's.

Serena and Travis already had rides to the carnival, but I had been planning to take Cari. Waiting for her, I was irritated once more because she didn't show up on time. I waited and waited. Finally, I decided to let her walk and to go ahead with my own plans to meet my friend Jill Bailey. I knew that later that day, my ex-husband, Steve, was coming to take the kids to his place for the night. I remember looking forward to a weekend by myself. It was not something that happened all that often.

So Jill and I went shopping. When I arrived back home, I saw my dad and Steve sitting in lawn chairs in the front yard. I'll never forget them sitting far apart—too far apart, it seemed to me. I don't know why details like that stick in the mind, but they do.

I had no inkling of what had happened. In fact, as I pulled into the driveway, I was worried that Steve was going to be angry at me. I thought the kids were probably not there on time for him to pick them up and so he was going to blame me as usual. I wondered how to deal with it. When I got out of the car, however, he and Dad approached me in a protective manner.

"What's wrong?" I asked.

Steve said, "Honey, we've lost Cari."

I patted him on the back and said, "It's all right, we'll find her." I was about to suggest that we check with the neighbors but he didn't let me continue.

"You don't understand," he said. "She's been killed. She was run over and she's dead."

I didn't pass out completely but I did collapse. They carried me into the house and I screamed all the way in. A few years before, in 1975, my four-year-old son, Travis, was run over by a car and critically injured. He was paralyzed on his right side for a while, his right leg was broken in several places, his lung collapsed, his ribs were broken, and he had a fractured skull. He was in a coma for five days and he needed multiple surgeries. He was in the hospital three different times. On several occasions we thought he was going to die. He pulled through, but it was a terrible time for us all. And less than two months later, my mother died of a heart attack following major surgery. Somehow, I survived.

But I couldn't believe such a horrible ordeal would happen again, not ever, not even in a million years. I didn't want to believe it. I *couldn't* believe it. I experienced a classic case of denial and shock. I kept repeating to Steve and Dad, "You're lying to me, you're telling me cruel lies, why do you hate me so much?" But even while I railed against the news, the possibility of its truth was seeping in. I could tell by the look on my father's face. My dad had very expressive eyes and I could see his pain.

Part of me was utterly numb. And part of me was buried in an avalanche of pain. I was filled with despair. I was filled with guilt. I was sure that if I had waited and driven her myself to the carnival, this would not have happened! After all, I had been out shopping with a friend while my daughter was being killed. If only I had been a little more patient, my daughter would be alive!

I was also filled with anger. I thought about how unfair it all was. My first reaction after I finished screaming was "Why her? Why not someone else?" I thought about a girl in Cari's school named Sarah who was always giving her mother an infinite amount of trouble. I remember thinking, Cari is a good kid. Why couldn't it have been Sarah?

Then I went into the bedroom and the phone rang. Ironically, the very first person to call me was Sarah's mother. She said, "I'm so sorry about Cari." It took tremendous willpower not to show my anger to someone who was reaching out in sympathy. When I hung up, the truth was beginning to filter through the confusion.

My little girl was dead.

I don't remember a lot of that day. I got a bottle of wine out of the refrigerator and began drinking. I had quit smoking a few months earlier but someone went out that day and brought me a pack of cigarettes and I started smoking again. I called my friends, including my girlfriend Leslie Hidley, who was living in Ojai with her husband. I told her I needed her and she flew up the next night. I called my girlfriend Bunny Corbin in Texas and told her husband, Joe. About an hour later she got on the phone and couldn't talk because she was crying so hard. By then, a lot of people were calling and coming over. I remember Serena wandering in and out, holding me, and putting her arm around me, a look of utter disbelief on her face. And I remember my nine-year-old son, Travis. In the living room crowded with people, he turned to me and said, "I guess she wasn't as lucky as me."

All of us were talking. Because Cari was killed going to a Catholic school carnival and I was at one time a practicing Catholic, a neighbor thought the priest from Saint Mel's might be of some comfort to me. When he arrived, he offered no comfort at all. I asked over and over again, "Why her?" He simply sat on the couch and said, "This is God's way."

I was already angry and perhaps he noticed. He repeated, "You should remember when things like this happen, it's God's will."

"What do you mean God's will?" I said. "God's will isn't to run down children in the street and leave them there to die." And I got him up from the couch and physically shoved him out the door.

Soon my psychiatrist, Dr. Jean Warren, came over. Two weeks before, we had mutually ended therapy. That terrible day, I called him and told him that it was more than I could bear, there had been too much trauma in my life, and I didn't think I was going to make it through this. He reassured me. "You will make it through this," he said. "I know you will." He asked if I wanted him to come over, and I did. Very much. He arrived with a bottle of Librium or some other tranquilizer. But as soon as he glanced at the almost-empty bottle of wine, he said, "I don't think you need these." And he put the pills in his pocket.

People started to drift out, until only my friends Cheryl Hart and her sister Nancy Lemmon were left. Finally, Cheryl had to leave but Nancy stayed the night. By this time, I was miserably hung over with a throbbing headache. I was frustrated, and I kept repeating to myself, this is so senseless.

My philosophy in life had always been that you could get something positive out of everything negative. In trying to retain some sense of normalcy, I began to think this way. What could I do that would be positive? It occurred to me that I could donate her organs so that someone else might live or see or function better as a result of her death. At least then perhaps my daughter's death would have some meaning.

It was eleven o'clock at night when I called the hospital and asked if there was a way I could donate her organs.

That's when I learned the reality of what had happened to my child. Oh, I knew she had been hit. But somehow I had this image of her being hit and looking perfect afterward. That idea was quickly dispelled. Cari had been thrown 125 feet. They informed me that she was so badly mutilated, there was nothing they could save, and we had waited too long for the eyes. I hung up feeling completely hopeless—and helpless.

That night, one thought was particularly persistent. I kept thinking, I really want to see her one more time. It isn't fair that I didn't get to see her. So I went into her room and touched all of her things: her bed, her toys, her pillows, her stuffed animals. I walked around that little room touching everything and crying. The pain was unbearable—beyond imagination.

Eventually, I lay down on my bed. Serena was beside me. Originally, she had planned to spend the night elsewhere but ultimately she decided to come home and be with me. Instead of sleeping in her own room, she got into my bed and fell asleep.

I remained wide awake. I put my hand over my eyes and something happened which I know was not a dream. I saw Cari standing at the corner of my bed. She was wearing shorty pajamas and had a look that was literally ageless. She silently communicated to me that she was okay. I felt comforted but I was also reluctant to move. My fear was that if I moved, I'd lose her. So I stayed still for as long as possible. And in time she was gone. I felt better having seen her.

That night, I couldn't sleep. I got out of bed before dawn at some ungodly hour. Later that day, Sunday, Steve and I picked out the casket. Steve had said to me on the day she died, "We're not going to have an expensive funeral. She's dead and we can't afford it." And in the car on the way to the funeral home, he kept repeating the same line. "We're not going to overdo this," he said. "We're not going to pay a lot." He couldn't stand to think about it; at one point, he even announced that he wasn't going to attend the funeral. In the end, of course, he did. But he wasn't having an easy time, and talking about the expense of Cari's funeral was one way of not dealing with the reality of her death.

His financial caution turned out to be just a lot of talk. The moment we went into the room where the caskets were on display, we both saw the one we wanted. It was beautiful, white with pink lining. And that's how we ended up with the most expensive casket there. Much later on, we laughed about it. At the time, we looked at each other and wondered, why are we doing this? The answer was clear: because she's our daughter and we wanted to do our best, even in death.

I was also concerned about the dress in which she would be buried. I envisioned it clearly: it would be pink, flowered, long, and lacy. Nancy Lemmon offered to go out and find a dress, and she asked me what I had in mind. I told her I wanted something very feminine, but I didn't specify a color or pattern. Nancy came back with exactly the dress I had pictured: pink flowers, long sleeves, a lacy collar. I found some satisfaction in that dress. It was one of the last presents I was able to give my daughter, and I wanted it to be right.

On Monday, they did the autopsy—a necessity, because she had been a crime victim. I talked to the funeral director at Mt. Vernon Mortuary in Fair Oaks. "I don't know what she's like," I said. "But you have got to fix her up so I can see her. I really need to see her."

"Mrs. Lightner, do you know how badly injured she was?" he asked. "I need to be honest with you. I'm not sure that she can be fixed."

I said, "You don't understand. I have *got* to see her."

He was aware of the extent of the injuries, although he had not actually seen her. So he said, "I'll tell you what. If I can fix her right, the way she should be, I will open up the casket for the viewing. But if I can't, I'll drape a gauzy scarf over the casket. You'll be able to peek through it and see her—but not clearly. If I can fix her up, there'll be no scarf."

I agreed. By Monday night my friends had arrived from out of town and we went to view her. I believe in open-casket funerals whenever possible because I think that in order for most people to realize and accept that someone is dead, they actually need to see the dead body. As long as the casket is closed, there's always that distant thought: is the body in there?

When my mother died on May 28, 1975, we debated about whether to have an open or a closed casket. We decided on an open one so that friends could pay their last respects. When the funeral services started, we closed the casket. But I remember that having an opportunity to see her one more time was very meaningful to me and to others. When I planned Cari's funeral, that came to mind. Since Cari and her friends were so young, I was concerned that many of them might wonder if she was really dead. I wanted to make sure that they would never have to wrestle with that worry.

This is not to say that I wasn't apprehensive. I was. I agonized over whether the funeral director would be able to make her presentable without the gauze scarf. I asked my girlfriend Leslie to go up before me and if she saw the scarf, to come and tell me so that I could prepare myself. But as we were walking up the stairs, I pushed in front of her because I *knew* there would be no scarf. And there wasn't. (Afterward, the funeral director told me that he had worked so hard because Cari reminded him of his daughter, who also had auburn hair and freckles.) At the casket, I took a ring I had saved for her and put it on her finger. I kissed her and touched her hands and her body, and I asked Serena and Travis if they wanted to also. I seem to recall that they both touched her and kissed her. But I also remember being struck by Serena's expression as she looked at Cari in the casket. She looked very confused. I was concerned.

Looking back, I can see that I was still in shock, still in denial. I had a dead child in there but the unimaginable reality of that was more than I could bear. So instead of dealing with it, I concentrated on the details. For an obsessive-compulsive like myself, the whole process of arranging a funeral offered a certain relief. Is she suitably fixed up for viewing? Is the casket right? Are the flowers nicely arranged around the room? Is everybody being taken care of? Who sent the flowers, and to whom do I have to send thank-you notes? In the beginning, I focused more on those details than on the loss. I was crying but I was also making sure we got the right dress and flowers to match the casket, and I was thinking about seating arrangements and where I would sleep out-of-town relatives: busywork. It was a good way for me not to deal with reality.

The funeral was Tuesday and the place was mobbed. Steve sat with Serena, Travis, and me, and his new wife sat elsewhere. Most of my close friends were with me. I didn't want a religious service. I do not have a particular religious affiliation and my children have always been free to choose their own religion. My friend Nancy Lemmon found a Unitarian minister and he was wonderful. He really spoke well. As he looked at Serena he talked about how beautiful Cari must have been. I had told him I wanted nothing from the Bible, nothing referring to God.

He had a hard time with that, but I was adamant. Instead, we had him read from *The Little Prince*, by Antoine de Saint-Exupéry. There are about two pages in that book that I think are appropriate for death. It's when the Little Prince is about to die and he talks about going up into the sky and becoming a star:

> In one of the stars I shall be living. In one of them I shall be laughing. And so it will be as if all the stars were laughing, when you look at the sky at night. . . . And when your sorrow is comforted (time soothes all sorrows) you will be content that you have known me. You will always be my friend. You will want to laugh with me. . . . And your friends will be properly astonished to see you laughing as you look up at the sky!

I also had them play songs that Cari loved, like "Puff the Magic Dragon" and "Somewhere over the Rainbow." It was terribly emotional; everyone was sobbing. Although it may sound strange, at one point Steve leaned over to me and whispered, "I would give anything if I had the Kleenex concession." We chuckled silently. I knew then that I would get through this ordeal. The knowledge that I still had the ability to laugh was my salvation.

But I also felt it was necessary to control myself. The role model in my mind was Jacqueline Kennedy. I had to be strong—don't ask me for what or for whom. I just had to be strong. It was easy to say, but hard to do, when attending your child's funeral. I broke down when the children from Cari's class paraded past that pink and white casket. One by one, those kids came up and laid a rose across the top of her casket. That did it. I fell apart. I wept.

I was also touched by another encounter with a classmate of Cari's. At Fair Oaks Cemetery, Cari's friend Jerome came up to me with a brown paper lunch bag full of money and said, "We took this collection up at school to help pay for her funeral." The sight of this thirteen-year-old boy, so earnest and concerned, brought tears to my eyes. I hugged him and said, "I don't need money for her funeral. But how would you like to use this as a reward to catch the driver who killed her?" He agreed right away.

At the grave site I met Steve's wife for the first time. Her name is also Candy. After the service, I said, "This is a hell of a way to meet but I'm glad I finally got to meet you." It was obvious that she was uncomfortable, and she was not receptive to me. I didn't understand her reaction but I had other problems and couldn't dwell on it.

One of those problems concerned the driver of the car. He hadn't been caught yet. At the time, I was selling real estate, and in those few days after Cari's death, I developed a morbid fear that they might never catch him and one day, inadvertently, I might sell him a house. There he would be, the man who killed my daughter, and I, in my ignorance, would be civil to him! I imagined how awful that would be! So I determined that he had to be found.

I didn't have long to wait. The next day, I was in a lethargy. I could barely move. My friend Frank Walker was with me along with Leslie, Bunny, my sister Kathy Cockman, and a few other friends. Frank offered to take us to dinner, and I was forcing myself to get dressed when the phone rang. It was the California Highway Patrol.

The man on the other end of the phone said he wanted me to know that they caught the alleged driver. His name was Clarence William Busch, and his car fit the description they had been given. At the time, I had some competing images in my mind of the driver. In one image, he was a smoker who had dropped his cigarette and while trying to retrieve it, hit my daughter. I guess I thought of him as a responsible individual, a grown-up man, who made a horrible mistake. But that didn't fit with the fact that her death had been a hit-and-run.

So in another image, I imagined a drug-crazed youth. It never occurred to me that it could have been a woman. I could never picture a woman leaving a child in the road to die.

When I asked the man from the Highway Patrol about the driver of the car, I was told he was in his late thirties or early forties, and married. I also asked if he had children. I was told that he did: a boy the same age as Cari and a girl a few years younger.

I asked how his family was doing. Years earlier, when Travis was run over, I had done the same thing. Once I knew that my son was alive, I looked to see how the driver was. She had several children, including a baby, in the car. She was an unlicensed driver. But she was very concerned and called several times to find out how Travis was doing. I also knew from all reports that as a result of the accident she was a wreck—an absolute basket case. That seemed like the normal response.

But that wasn't what I was hearing now. When I asked the highway patrolman how the driver's family was doing, I was told, "His wife's upset." Something about the response disturbed me. The words were too understated and I had the feeling that something wasn't right.

Still, I was glad to report to Frank and Leslie and my other friends that the police had caught the driver. We piled into two cars and drove to Chuck's Steak House, my favorite restaurant in Sacramento. On the way to the restaurant, I noticed two highway patrolmen measuring something in the road where Cari was killed. I pulled over, jumped out of the car, and walked over to them.

"Are you investigating the death of Cari Lightner?" I asked. They nodded and I said, "I'm her mother."

They extended their sympathies. One of them said, "I guess you know the whole story."

"Yes," I replied, without having any idea what they were talking about. Something just told me to say yes.

And he said, "I guess you know he was drunk at the time he killed your daughter."

"Yes." I nodded, wanting to hear more.

They continued, "You know he's got four prior arrests," and I again responded, "Yes."

"I guess you also know he had one just two days before he hit your daughter," and I agreed as if I'd known this all along. Inside, I was furious. But where do you vent your anger?

"He killed my child. So now he'll go to prison, won't he?" I asked.

The highway patrolman looked at me in a funny way and said, "Lady, you'll be lucky if he sees any jail time at all, much less prison. That's the way the system works."

I was furious. I got in the car and I gave this information to my friends. All the way to the restaurant I couldn't concentrate on anything they were saying because I was so angry that this could happen in a civilized society. My friends felt the same way; nobody could believe that that's the way the laws worked. I was fuming. I felt enraged and helpless.

When we reached the restaurant, we sat in the bar waiting for a table and I kept asking, "What am I going to do? What am I going to do?"

Finally, my sister said, "I don't know what you're going to do, but I know you're not going to let this go. You're going to do something."

"You're right," I said. "I'm going to start an organization because people need to know about this."

Leslie immediately added, "And you're going to call it MADD, Mothers Against Drunk Driving."

I knew the moment I heard those words that that was exactly what I was going to do.

And that's how MADD started. There was no sense in thinking about it. My decision was made. I simply had no choice.

And so, ironically, MADD began in a bar—in Chuck's Steak House, where we were waiting for a table. Through MADD, I found a way to deal with my anger, a way to address a serious social problem that had taken my daughter from me, and a way to fill my time for many years to come. Cari's death plunged me into the worst pain I had ever imagined, and it turned my life around. Before her death, I was a divorced mother raising three children and selling real estate. Within a few months after her death, I had become a public personality and a crusader with a cause. The texture of my days changed enormously.

For one thing, the nitty-gritty business of starting an organization was incredibly complicated. My girlfriend Sue LeBrun suggested I see the state attorney general. I was an innocent then. I was not even a registered voter. I had never been political and I had no idea who the attorney general was or what he did. But I went ahead and made an appointment with Steve Blankenship, one of his aides. Then things started to snowball. Before long, I was reading books, attending meetings, making phone calls, working with the media, writing letters, doing research, and talking to people. I was working all the time.

In the meantime, Clarence William Busch was going through preliminary hearings. His case came up later that summer. By then, MADD had gone public. For killing my daughter, he was sentenced to two years imprisonment, of which he eventually served sixteen months before being released.

I was in such pain. I cried in the car. Some days, I couldn't get out of bed. I also suffered from the insomnia that is so often part of the mourning process. Although I had no problem falling asleep, I'd wake up every morning at four o'clock. My way of dealing with that was to read the California Vehicle Code, which usually put me back to sleep right away. Still, there were days when I could not function, days when I felt as if I had a five-hundred-pound weight sitting on my chest.

It was the right time to grieve, and I thought I did grieve. I believed my work with MADD was a great way to do that. But I was wrong. As an activist, I was far more attuned to the legislative process than I was to the grieving process. MADD was effective as a political tool but not as a personal one, with one important exception: it gave me an outlet for my anger.

Cari's death was the immediate source of my anger, but before that, I had encountered other drunk drivers. When the girls were eighteen months old, they were in my mother's station wagon when her car was rear-ended by a drunk driver. Cari, strapped into the front seat between two adults, was unhurt. But Serena was sitting in an old-fashioned car seat that hooked over the back of the seat (the new ones are more safely designed). When the car was hit, it accordioned, the rear window shattered, and Serena's car seat flipped over. Serena was lacerated with glass. They all were taken in an ambulance to a hospital where, coincidentally, I was working as a Red Cross volunteer, and I saw them arrive. The glass was removed and two days later, Serena's little body was black and blue all over. It was terrifying, but she recovered. Because my attentions were focused on her injuries, however, I did not pursue the case and I'm not sure what happened to the driver.

Then, a few years later, when Travis was four years old, he was run over. The driver of the car, according to my attorney, was unlicensed and on tranquilizers. She wasn't arrested. The policeman said it was Travis' fault because he had run out into the street. They even refused to issue a ticket. Those two incidents fueled my fury over Cari's death.

I was filled with rage, so fired up about my cause that I was unstoppable. MADD became a twenty-four-hour-a-day, seven-day-a-week job. As a result, I was able to avoid a large part of the grieving process. My attention as a mother should have gone to my other two children, but I avoided that too. Much later on, Serena and Travis told me how much they resented my involvement. They were right: I did put MADD first, and I shouldn't have, although I didn't realize it at the time. I was so obsessed that, in many ways, I did not permit life to go on outside of MADD.

Looking back, I can see that I was afraid to stop for even a moment because I imagined that if I did, I would drown in my grief. I thought I would never stop crying. So I kept busy virtually all the time. My activity had a purpose: avoidance. I didn't set out to make MADD the force that it became; that was a beneficial by-product of my avoidance. I know today that keeping busy is an important way to gain temporary respite from grief; but the danger of total preoccupation is that one does not deal with the grief. It's a distinction I've learned to appreciate, and one that I'll discuss more in another chapter.

As a result of my avoidance, I got stuck. Rather than accepting her death, I kept her alive. I would take Cari's picture to TV stations and public events. Every time that picture was on a brochure, in the newspaper, or on television, I was able to postpone certain aspects of my grieving. As long as I had MADD, I was able to keep her very much a part of my life. For five and a half years, instead of focusing on my grieving, I concentrated on the manner in which she died. Practically everything I did was centered on the fact that she was killed by a drunk driver rather than the fact that she was dead.

I put her death on an impersonal level. Although I'd take her picture to TV studios, it was not on display in my home until recently. I couldn't bear it. I thought about her constantly and talked about her every day, but I had to act as if her death had happened to someone else; I had to pretend I was not talking about my child. I learned to talk about her without thinking about her. It was like going on automatic pilot.

For instance, I remember the first speech I ever wrote and gave on my own. It was at the Traffic Safety Conference in Oregon. My friend Sue and I worked all night on this speech. I began talking about a freckle-faced, auburn-haired young girl, and how the drunk driver hit her from behind and threw her 125 feet, and how the impact knocked her shoes off and so forth. It was a dramatic introduction and everybody was completely silent. I knew that they didn't know who I was because I'd had no publicity in Oregon. So when I said, "That little girl was my daughter," the audience gasped. The press jumped up and ran out the door to call the photographers. Pandemonium broke out.

But I couldn't have given that speech if I had faced the reality of the situation, because I had to say it without any real emotion. I couldn't sob on the podium. I couldn't break down. I realized that if I cried every time I talked about Cari publicly, I would lose credibility. The audience would think I was just an emotional, overwrought mother rather than someone who was truly concerned about a social issue. So I had to learn to talk about my daughter as if she were somebody else's child. And because I did that *so well*, I denied myself the luxury and the necessity of actively grieving. In a sense I had to. I don't think I could have grieved and put my energies into MADD at the same time.

For over five years of my life, MADD was my passion. It was my mistress, my mister, my husband, my wife, my kids, my family. When we moved the national headquarters to Texas, I moved too. MADD was my life. I was a crusader and I'm pleased with what I was able to accomplish during that time. Roughly 25,000 people die every year as a result of drunk driving. It's a horrifying statistic, and during those years with MADD, I was able to change public attitudes toward drunk driving so that today most people understand that it's not something to joke about; it's not macho; it's not cool; it's not funny. It's a crime.

During the years with MADD, I met with legislators and politicians across the nation to help enact stiffer legislation and reduce the number of needless deaths that happen every year. I am proud that I have been able to make a difference and save thousands of lives.

Through MADD, I have benefited in other ways too. I have made many good friends, come to know some of the most interesting and influential people of our time, traveled widely, and become a savvy businesswoman. I have grown in experience and, more important, in empathy. I am grateful for all of that. But it does nothing to assuage the pain of losing my child. I would throw it all back in an instant if only my daughter could be with me still.

Throughout this period, there were times when I thought I had come to accept her death, when I thought I had let go in some way or experienced some form of closure. Inevitably, three months later or six months later, I would realize that I hadn't.

I didn't truly begin grieving until December 1985, two months after I left MADD. For the first time, I could no longer evade the reality of my daughter's death by focusing on my anger or the legislative process. This time, I had to face the pain.

The process of leaving MADD wasn't an easy one, even though I knew the time was right for me to leave. There was conflict between the board and me. I was upset. One morning, I had breakfast with a friend. I was describing the situation to him when he suddenly said, "You know what your problem is—"

I interrupted. "I know what you're going to say. You're going to say I can't say good-bye to her."

Only that wasn't what I had intended to say. I *meant* to say, "I can't say good-bye to MADD." I started crying. "That's my problem," I said. "I can't say good-bye to Cari."

As soon as I could, I called my former psychiatrist, Dr. Warren, in Sacramento—the one I had stopped seeing two weeks before Cari died. I realized that this moment had been coming for at least a year. In a bereavement group that I initiated for MADD, I had become weepy. At the time I thought the reasons for my tears were only slightly connected to Cari. Clarence William Busch had just been rearrested, which was upsetting. I was having problems with my son. And leaving MADD was traumatic. I tried hard to attribute my weepiness, depression, and lack of motivation to my need to leave MADD. I even discussed it with Ann Seymour, my assistant, and a few close friends. I knew it was time to leave. The same passion was simply not there and I knew something was very wrong.

I called Dr. Warren, and he understood right away. "It sounds to me like you're grieving," he said.

"I thought I did this five years ago," I responded.

"You dealt with your anger. Now you have to deal with your pain," he told me. He recommended that I make an appointment with a psychologist and explain that I needed help with my grieving.

I did just that. I found a wonderful psychologist named Dr. Joyce Buckner, Ph.D., and I told her, "I'm here because I want to grieve for my daughter. I've been avoiding it for some time and I want to do it now." This was during Christmas—never an easy season, but particularly rough for those in mourning. My therapist suggested I put everything aside, and I took her advice. By then, I didn't have much choice; I was filled with repressed mourning. It had to come out.

And it did. The pain was incredible. That Christmas, I felt as if my little girl had died the day before. And during that year, on every holiday, every anniversary, New Year's, Easter, all of it, I felt tossed once more into that inconceivable void. It might as well have been the first year. I cried constantly.

I began by mourning for Cari but soon realized I was mourning for more than my daughter. She was the heart of my grief and the catalyst. But I had to deal with other losses too. One of them was the death of my mother. I hadn't grieved for her either, because Travis had been run over less than two months before she died, and he required my total attention for quite a while. So I grieved for my mom. I grieved for my son and his losses. I grieved for the family I used to have, for that brief moment when I was a happily married mother of three. And I grieved for my loss of MADD and my changing role. MADD had been the center and the purpose of my life for so long: without it, I grieved for my identity.

I had an awful lot of grieving to do and I didn't want to do it in Texas. I had moved to Texas for MADD but I didn't want to be there any longer because, although I was constantly surrounded by people while I was with MADD, I was also strangely isolated. When I started MADD, I was fixated on the inequity of the laws regarding drunk driving and I became a crusader determined to change them. The idea of heading an organization with all its attendant problems was not in my mind. As MADD grew—and it grew fast—I was catapulted to the top of a far-flung organization with chapters in every state, dozens of employees, and hundreds of volunteers. My concerns were suddenly completely unlike those of my friends, and I believe they were uncomfortable with me. It was partially due to my activities; I was tremendously busy and passionately focused, and I no longer had much interest in long, lazy lunches or afternoons at the mall. They were also uncomfortable, I believe, because I had become a public personality. Celebrity was not something I had ever expected in my life, and I still find it somewhat awkward. I have a peculiar sort of celebrity, for I am less well known as Candy Lightner than as "the founder of Mothers Against Drunk Driving." In that capacity, I was on presidential commissions; I was interviewed by everyone from reporters for the *Sacramento Bee* and the *Sacramento Union* to Ted Koppel on *Nightline*; I met many famous people. I have to admit that I was excited about that, but when I talked about it, some of my friends just froze. I didn't know what to do.

But there was yet another reason why people were ill at ease in my presence, and it's something I'm still conscious of today. It has to do with drinking and driving. Even today, drunk driving is socially acceptable. Oh, people claim otherwise. But when they're at a party and have had a few drinks, they usually believe *they're* perfectly capable of driving home safely; it's just other people who need to be cautious. I think otherwise. My vigilance on the topic—my insistence that people who are drinking should not drive—made me a latter-day Carrie Nation in people's minds. I was no fun at all.

Within the context of MADD, I felt isolated for other reasons. The ultimate responsibility for decisions was mine. When things went well, I got the credit, and when things went wrong, I got the blame. The burden was enormous, and I lacked a real support system. I understood the phrase "lonely at the top."

By the time I left MADD, I was also ready to leave Texas. I wanted to move back to California and live on the beach because the ocean to me is very healing. When I gaze out at that vast magnitude of water, my problems seem minute in comparison. I found a wonderful condominium in Malibu on a hill overlooking the Pacific. Many mornings, I would climb down that hill and walk along the shore, and many evenings I would stand in my living room and watch the sun set over the water, and I felt soothed.

I spent a great deal of time alone there, and by doing so I discovered the difference between isolation and solitude. My son had decided to stay in Texas; Serena had moved to New York. This was the first time in my life that I had ever lived alone, and to my surprise, I loved it. I no longer had that awful sense of being alone in a crowd that I felt so strongly during my years with MADD. Instead, I luxuriated in my solitude because it gave me the opportunity I needed to grieve, to relax, and to be replenished.

I found much of what I needed in nature. I frequently walked down to the beach, where I listened to the waves, watched the dolphins play, and lay on the sand getting tan. I spent hours wandering around the landscaped grounds of my apartment complex. I needed to see earth again, to listen to the birds and to gaze at the trees and the flowers that grew there in profusion.

I also devoted myself to my health. I exercised every day, power-walking or working out to videotapes in my living room, where I could look past the television set to the ocean. I was careful about my diet; I ate a lot of vegetables, I cut back on red meat, and I gradually weaned myself completely off the medication I'd been given for headaches and irritable bowel syndrome.

I pampered myself in other ways, too. I got facials and on occasion I treated myself to a massage, and I spent many evenings curled up on my couch, reading novels or watching television—something I had not done since before Cari was killed.

Throughout that period, I actively grieved, by which I mean that when I felt pain, I gave in to it; I allowed it precedence over everything. It had been there all along, of course, but for the most part, I pushed it back. I'm pretty good at holding back tears. This time, I wanted to let them come through.

That initial painful period lasted about a year and a half before it began to taper. As the months passed, I felt increasingly calm and centered. And I slowly came to a sense of myself as an individual, not as an advocate or an activist or a real estate salesperson or a wife or even a mother. I felt at ease, content with who I was. While I was with MADD, I felt incredibly strong because I was fueled by anger. Now I began to feel powerful from a sense of peace within myself.

Throughout that time, I was fortunate to be able to live in a beautiful area. The presence of nature opened me up to other things in life. If I had lived in the heart of a city, surrounded by the same tension and pressure that I felt at MADD, I doubt that I would have found such peace. I still cry. I still miss Cari. It still hurts. There are times—

Christmas is one of them—when the pain reappears. But it is no longer unendurable. I'm sad, but the sadness doesn't last long. When I remember her now, I think about how she lived, not how she died. Dr. Warren told me that I tend to postpone pain and he was right. That is what I used to do. But not anymore.

I've found out too much about grieving to do that any longer. Nothing is more painful than grief, which is why it cannot be ignored. So I've learned to express my grief. Grief, I have discovered, ebbs and flows, and I've learned to ride those waves. When I feel it, I'll go into my room as soon as I can and immerse myself in it. I kept a few of Cari's things: her baby book, a necklace, a lipstick, a little pillow she made and one somebody gave her, and several recipes with her handwriting on them: that's about it. There are times when I just want to look at these things and hold them. For many years I kept them packed away. Now, looking at them brings me comfort. When I need to, I call a friend. Or I walk down to the beach and watch the tide come in. Sometimes, I just lie on the bed and cry. And then I can go on. It's all part of the process.

This book is also part of the process. When Cari was killed, I knew how to organize but I didn't know how to mourn. I didn't know what was normal or what to expect. I didn't know how others grieved or even how I ought to grieve myself. But I have learned. This book is the result of a journey I never wanted to take.

Many people agreed to be interviewed for this book, including psychologists, psychiatrists, and more than one hundred people whose lives were forever changed by the death of someone they loved. When requested, names have been changed for reasons of confidentiality. All we spoke with, however, were willing to give sorrow words in the hope that someone else's passage through grief might be eased. That is my hope as well. The road through grief is a rocky one. Traveling along it requires courage, patience, wisdom, and hope. It is my wish that this book will help you to find those qualities within yourself.

CHAPTER 2 | The Cycle of Sorrow

Grief is a cyclic thing. It goes off by itself, the way earthquakes do. They need to happen to keep the earth stable but they're still overwhelming. Yet afterward you feel calmer.

—ROSEANNE LURIE

The price of life is loss. From the moment of birth when we leave the womb forever, we face loss in many ways. We move and never see our childhood home again; friendships fade; we may lose money, possessions, hope; we change jobs; we graduate; we marry and divorce. Every change, desired or not, large or small, involves loss. Losses shape our lives. And of these, the most universal, inevitable, and serious loss is the death of someone we love. Yet death is the loss for which most of us are least prepared.

Once, when most people lived in small communities and closely knit family groups, death was woven into the fabric of our lives. Babies died in infancy; children were swept away by disease; mothers died in childbirth; and dead bodies were displayed in the parlor. For most of human existence, young people died with a frequency hard for us to imagine. As late as the turn of the century, more than half the people who died in the United States were under fifteen years old. Only 17 percent were over the age of sixty-five. By the late 1960s, more than two thirds of recorded deaths were of people over the age of sixty-five. As a result, many people today are well into middle age before they experience the death of a loved one.

Our difficulty in dealing with death is compounded by the fact that we live in a death-denying society. To deny its existence, we use a symphony of euphemisms. Instead of admitting that people we love have actually *died*, we say they are "no longer with us," that they have "departed," "expired," "passed away," "gone." We say we have "lost" them as if they might be found. And rather than using the word *dead*, we say they are "late"—of all euphemisms, surely the one of greatest denial, since it seems to imply that any moment now the late John Doe might show up—tardy again!

In recent years, the silence surrounding death has started to lift, thanks in part to pioneers such as Herman Feifel, Colin Murray Parkes, Phyllis Silverman, and Elisabeth Kübler-Ross. Many books have been written on the topic. College students take courses in death and dying. But while working on this book, Nancy and I discovered that even *discussing* death still makes some people tense. Most mourners were glad—and often grateful—to talk with us. But in general conversation, people who had not experienced the death of a loved one were sometimes edgy, happy to change the subject.

Grief is also a topic about which we know very little. Even doctors and members of the clergy are often uneducated about it. And in a mobile age characterized by the fragmentation of the family, many of us have literally never seen another human being grieve—not up close anyway. With little knowledge and few role models, we are unprepared for grief and so frightened by it that we don't even want to see other people experiencing it. That's one reason why Jacqueline Kennedy's dignified, shocked demeanor during President Kennedy's funeral was so moving and reassuring to us; stoicism is something we admire. Tears and lamentation, on the other hand, make us uncomfortable. Other people's grief stirs up our fears of death, of pain, and of the unknown. It reminds us of our own mortality. No wonder that, when it comes to grieving, most people prefer it to be invisible.

As a result, mourners often have difficulty finding people to validate their feelings. For example, at a bereavement meeting recently, we met a woman who was grieving the death of her mother. One day she made the mistake of crying in front of her sister. "What's wrong with you?" her sister asked. "It's been three weeks!" That attitude is all too common. People want grief to be over fast. The figure of one year has long been bandied about as a typical length of mourning. Yet grief has no timetable; that idea is a myth. Some people find that it diminishes more quickly than they expected. For many other perfectly healthy people, intense grief lasts far longer. Yet mourners are often allowed no more than a couple of months, a few weeks, or less. And at many corporations, when a loved one dies, an employee gets only three days off. After that, it's back to work!

Whether it comes suddenly or slowly, early or late, violently or serenely, the death of a person we love changes our world and ourselves in a way that nothing else can. First-time mourners, stunned by the depth of their own grief, are often disturbed when, very early on, other people begin to suggest that they are not responding well, that they ought to pull themselves together, that their responses are unhealthy. Many grievers wonder if those criticisms are valid. Am I normal? Am I going crazy? Am I becoming senile? Do other people react this way? And how "should" I feel? Sad? Lonely? Unable to think about anything else? The people interviewed for this book asked themselves these same questions, felt these same emotions—along with anger, guilt, fear, confusion, depression, vulnerability, despair. They experienced grief in all its complexity. Their stories illustrate its reality.

One of those realities has to do with the intensity of feeling. "After my baby died, my emotions were like an avalanche going down a mountain and I could no longer control them," a bereaved young mother reported. People are often surprised by how powerful those feelings are. "It just pours out," a bereaved father said. "It's like a dam that breaks. It keeps coming and it keeps coming and you wonder, is this ever going to end?" Despite what people think, those feelings may not completely disappear. But that torrential flood of grief eventually forms a river, and the river imperceptibly becomes a stream, and although that stream narrows, it could meander through your life forever.

Inextricably mingled with emotions is a variety of physiological responses to grief. "I felt deep constant chest pressure and headaches," said the mother quoted above. "I was forgetful and unable to do a simple task. I felt sick to my stomach. I felt insomnia and dizziness. I felt tired all the time. I had contractions in my uterus like I was in labor." The impact of grief can also cause difficulty breathing, frequent sighing, heart palpitations, hyperventilation, tension, blurred vision, skin rashes, nervousness, weakness, exhaustion, agitation, difficulty swallowing, digestive problems, an altered appetite, a decreased or increased interest in sexuality, and the feeling that you're losing your mind.

Yet even doctors are often unaware of these patterns, as I learned. After Cari died, I lost twenty-one pounds in three weeks. The only food I could hold down was yogurt, so I went to see my doctor. He asked why I thought I had lost that weight. I was surprised, since I knew that he had heard about Cari, and I suggested that it might be a reaction to my daughter's death. "Gee," he replied. "I didn't know you were taking it so hard." I walked out.

Grief is not solely an emotional crisis; it lives in the body. Spotty and contradictory though it sometimes is, scientific research indicates that grief can depress the immune system, alter endocrine functioning, and weaken the cardiovascular system. It can even affect mortality; widowers and young people who have experienced the death of a family member are actually more likely to die following a death than are nonbereaved people of the same age. And several studies link bereavement to an increase in lung, cervical, and breast tumors. Fortunately, most people who suffer from health problems after a death recover quickly. Indeed, a 1988 study conducted at the University of Louisville in Kentucky among people fifty-five and older who had experienced a bereavement or other serious loss (such as divorce) indicated a slight decline in health during the first year and a half, followed by an improvement. Most people really do recover, both physically and emotionally.

It helps to know what other people who have traveled through grief have found there. The purpose of this book is to explore grief through the eyes of experts who have studied it and through the words of real human beings who have experienced the death of a loved one and who have learned to go on with their lives with renewed strength, hope, and direction.

THE PHASES OF GRIEF

It begins when we hear about the death. Perhaps a grim-faced doctor announces the bad news in advance of the actual event. Or maybe the worst of all possible moments arrives without warning: the telephone rings, the policeman knocks at the door, and the world shatters about us.

Once the death has occurred, everyone reacts differently. Some people plummet into grief; others, numbed, postpone the pain. Some people spend years submerged beneath the weight of sorrow; others balance precariously on the edge of anger. Reactions depend on our personalities, the manner of death, previous losses, the social support we receive, and the nature of our relationship with the deceased. (Paradoxically, the more ambivalent the relationship, the more difficult the mourning process may be.) Grief cannot be reduced to a formula, any more than love can. Every story is unique.

Beneath the sobbing or the stoicism, the anger or the acquiescence, the guilt or even the gratitude, there lies a pattern. Experts agree on that. But exactly what *is* that pattern? Prominent researcher Phyllis Silverman, Ph.D., developer of the Widow to Widow program, believes there are three phases: impact, recoil, and accommodation. Therese A. Rando, Ph.D., another leader in the study of bereavement, also describes three phrases, which she calls avoidance, confrontation, and reestablishment. Psychoanalyst Dr. John Bowlby, author of a three-volume work on loss, decided that there were three stages and then changed his mind and announced that there were four: numbing, yearning and searching, disorganization and despair, and finally reorganization.

But by far the best-known pattern is the one described by Elisabeth Kübler-Ross. In her widely read and highly influential book, *On Death and Dying*, she distinguished five phases of dying: denial and isolation, anger, bargaining, depression, and acceptance. Kübler-Ross originally used those phrases to describe how people with life-threatening illnesses deal with their own mortality; the phases she named were aspects of dying, not of grieving. Nonetheless, they quickly lodged themselves in the popular imagination as phases not only of dying but of mourning. Thus the concept of five stages of grief entered the culture.

Many organizations and individuals adapted these stages into their literature and practice. MADD is a good example. One MADD pamphlet carefully lays out the pattern of mourning. "The initial response is that of *denial*," this brochure states. Through the many grievers I have known, including people I met through MADD and people interviewed for this book, I have seen that frequently the initial response *is* denial—but not always. "Most commonly, *anger* is the next feeling to surface, although for some this will come much later," the brochure explains. Well, sometimes anger surfaces next and sometimes it doesn't. Sometimes it doesn't surface at all.

"In anticipatory grief or in the case of injury, *bargaining* may follow," the brochure continues. In fact, bargaining can occur even with sudden death. I did it. I knew Cari was dead, but the night she died, I went into her room and kept touching her things and bargaining to see her one more time. I negotiated with God. I promised to go to church—and then I took that back, because I remembered that when Travis was run over, I made the same promise and didn't keep it. It was very important to me this time to keep my part of the bargain. So I promised to be a more active parent, a more caring neighbor, a more supportive friend, a better person in every way. Maybe that would bring my daughter back!

Philadelphia poet Marion Cohen also bargained when her baby died. Her bargain? "If I look dreamy enough, it will turn out to have all been a dream." That didn't work any more than my bargain did.

And some people don't bargain at all.

The same MADD brochure states conclusively: "In *normal grief* these stages take approximately three to twenty-four months, depending upon a number of circumstances." Does that mean that if you're normal, you'll be done grieving after two years? It all depends. Some people take two years. Some people take longer. Some people take less time. And however long or short that time may be, emotions within it can be chaotic and unpredictable.

The idea of grieving on schedule has added an unachievable goal to the difficulties of mourning. The unhappy mourner, on top of everything else, has to worry about grieving right! And mourners do worry about whether they are progressing through the stages appropriately. Los Angeles speech therapist Joni Schaap had that concern when her son Jeremy, the second of her four children, was murdered at age sixteen:

> I had read about the stages of grief, and I thought, how come I'm not doing it in the order they say? I haven't felt angry yet. Am I doing something wrong? Or, ah, today I forgot that he was dead—and I thought I was past denial! It didn't go in the right order. I thought I was losing my mind. My therapist said, "No, this is normal. I would worry if you weren't feeling that way." So I felt crazy but I knew that was a normal reaction.

Many psychologists and psychiatrists untrained in the specifics of mourning have totally unrealistic ideas about its patterns. Less than a year after her husband and daughter were killed in an airplane crash, one grief-stricken woman consulted a highly recommended psychiatrist. "He told me that at eight months I should be looking back with fond, happy memories," she said. Yet mourning a sudden, double death is likely to take far, far longer. Think in terms of years.

The truth is, grief is messy. One phase overlaps the other; emotions we thought were gone for good can reappear for no apparent reason. Some people are overwhelmed by emotions other people barely notice. Yet although the concept of grieving in phases is not an accurate one, it does provide a way to think about the process. In my view, the simplest division is the best: the beginning, the middle, and the rest of your life.

THE BEGINNING:
SHOCK, NUMBNESS, AND DENIAL

Shock, numbness, and denial are common reactions in the beginning. Shock is most severe when death comes without warning, as it did with California illustrator Rae Ecklund's older brother, who was forty-four when he died as a result of auto mechanical failure. She describes her relationship with him in two words—hero worship:

> The phone call came from my sister, Jo Beth, in the early morning hours. She said Ted had been returning to his ranch house in Texas when he was catapulted from the car. His seventeen-year-old son found him in a fetal position, carried him to the car, and drove him to the hospital. Jo Beth said, "It looks like brain damage. Can you come right away?"
> I bolted from bed and made a series of strange sounds, little

screams and shrieks, and I ran in circles. I wound up on the stairway curled in a ball and I started to convulse. I was shaking uncontrollably. It frightened me so much. I had no clue to that being a symptom of shock.

Shock can also occur even when the person was known to be dying, for as long as there is a smidgen of hope—perhaps due to a remission, perhaps simply because the person's mood was brighter—death can take people by surprise. A widow explained: "I knew my husband was ill but everybody kept telling me that prostate cancer moved very slowly. He had had heart trouble for quite a while too. I look back and I think I should have been prepared. But I wasn't. It was a great shock to me when he just went."

Shock can make people feel as if they are watching themselves, inhabiting some far corner of the room apart from their bodies. Shock can make them shiver. It can make them sigh. It can make them feel empty. It can make them feel utterly and completely numb; many people describe it as feeling "like a zombie."

That numbness anesthetizes the pain, allowing the psyche a little time to absorb the magnitude of what has happened. Numbness can come and go. Bennett Sloan, an engineer whose son committed suicide with a gun, put it this way: "I was stunned and shocked over and over again by the finality of Justin's death as well as the way in which his death occurred. Between bouts of tears and grieving, I slipped into states of numbness. Perhaps it was nature's way of calling a truce to the battle raging within."

In addition to dulling the pain, however temporarily, numbness can furnish a little of the wherewithal necessary to accomplish tasks such as arranging the funeral or calling friends and relatives. Numbness can also fool people into assuming that the bereaved feel calm. "I felt like I was outside the world looking in," one widow said. "I smiled and I talked and I pretended I wasn't shattered. Outwardly, I was adjusting well. Inwardly, I was not."

Another common reaction in the beginning is denial. For many people, this is the first reaction. "I can't believe it!" is a typical response. "I can't believe I'll never get to talk to him again."

Denial gets a bad press these days. Many mourners have actually felt accused of denial, as if it were a bad thing, something that needed to be overcome fast. But denial helps us function. As a defense mechanism, it keeps fear and anxiety at bay.

Like every aspect of grief, denial fluctuates in intensity. In the beginning, it can mean the literal refusal to believe. One person who experienced that was Joan Conley, a Georgia homemaker whose twenty-one-year-old son, Kirk, was killed in a drunk-driving crash in Chattanooga, Tennessee. "At first I was in total disbelief. Kirk died early Sunday morning and we didn't see him until Monday afternoon. I went to the funeral home knowing I was going to see someone else. I could not believe this happened."

Denial is a form of wishful thinking, and its symptoms can be subtle. Forgetting that the person is dead is typical. In a moment of denial, the bereaved reaches for the phone to call Mother—and only then realizes that she's dead. And many people who know that the person is dead may find themselves scanning faces in a crowd, searching for Dad, thinking maybe he's not dead! When one woman's ex-husband died, she searched for him while she was driving. "I think I recognize him in cars, and it flashes on me, Oh my God, that's just like him. I actually turned around and went after a car once, it was so much like him." These reactions can continue for a long time; the mind knows better but the heart still hopes.

Denial can also be dramatic, especially in the beginning. At her husband's funeral, one widow said, "Our grown daughter called out and told her father to *get up, get up*, and quit playing games with her!" The daughter may have been as surprised as anyone else at her own behavior.

A woman whose husband died when their house burned down was able to save herself and a child. At the funeral, she comforted everybody else. "I was in shock. It was three months before I realized that I was the one who lost something." By then she was in such deep denial that she actually went shopping for her husband and bought hundreds of dollars worth of merchandise for him before she passed out.

Denial is most noticeable when death is untimely, but it arises even with death in old age. Gene Brody, an educational psychologist, described denial as his most powerful emotion after his mother died at the age of eighty. "When she was alive, not a day went by that I didn't speak with her. Even when traveling in China and Brazil, I called her. After she wasn't here anymore, I began driving past her house. Perhaps she wasn't dead, I'd say to myself. Perhaps she's still here. It's been two years and even today I have this terribly strong attachment."

Keeping the loved one's room exactly as it was for longer than a few months—a process known to psychologists as mummification—is usually an attempt at denial. Yet even this can serve a useful purpose. Often a griever is not denying the death, but evading it. After her son was murdered, for example, Joni Schaap could not enter his room. "I didn't go in it for a year. I didn't even empty the garbage. I couldn't do anything," she said. "Then, around the anniversary of his death, I went in and cleaned everything out. It was a pigsty! Clothes were all over. It was hard to see the stuff again. But after a year it was time." Was she denying reality during that year of mummification? Maybe a little. But so what? She knew full well what had happened; she was even seeing a therapist to deal with it. The fact that she couldn't face all of it at once is normal.

And finally, there's the unconscious denial that appears in dreams. My aunt Hazel Haydon recounted a dream she has had since her mother died approximately forty years ago. "I still dream that Mother's alive and that she's down South somewhere and I can't find her. I'm always dreaming that—time after time after time." Another woman described the dreams she had after a close friend died. "I used to dream she'd call me on the phone. I'd say, 'I thought you were dead.' And she'd say, 'It was a mistake,' and I'd be so happy. But then I'd wake up crying."

Another, more insidious form of denial is a turning away from grief. You might suspect this type of denial when you meet recently bereaved people who claim to have gotten over it. Sure, they used to be in grief, they'll tell you—but no longer! *What good does it do? Life is for the living. You put it behind you.* When you hear someone talking like that, especially in the first few months after a death, you are in the presence of a world-class denier. They are terrified by the power of grief. They don't want to talk about it or think about it because they are afraid that once they stop denying what they feel, the lid will be lifted on an emotional tornado. "I just can't handle grieving," said Alice McCarty, another one of my aunts. "After my mother died, I thought I'd cry my eyes out. And then I'd probably have gotten sick. I'm sure I would have." I'm certain she wouldn't have.

Denial of mourning is born out of the desire to feel better fast, to be done with the pain. It is a normal reaction that allows the pain to be put off until we are ready to handle it, and as such, it is a useful psychological tool. But sooner or later those feelings come flooding back, as Sara Grisanti learned. She is a real estate saleswoman in Malibu, California, whose son Alexander Samuel Hercules Grisanti, the youngest of her four children, died within twenty-four hours of birth. The emotional components of her grief were difficult for her to acknowledge and, despite her concerted effort, impossible to avoid:

> I know that the theory is that you should get it all out, like it's a wound you should pick and let ooze until it heals over. I don't think that's necessarily true. I think it's very fine to try not to think about it and to try to do other things to avoid dealing with it constantly.
>
> But you know what? It catches you by surprise. I really thought I was over it. Then two Sundays ago I was in church and now I don't think I can ever go back. This little girl spoke. She was the March of Dimes poster child of the year. She had spina bifida and she was on crutches. She was seven, very little for her age, with a beautiful face, and her mother had taken her on tour. She was so cute. She was telling how she has problems but it's okay because she has a wonderful life.

I don't know why, but it really hit me. The doctors said that Alex would have never been normal and to keep in mind that maybe it was for the best. But when I saw that little girl, that theory went down the drain. I cried like a baby. Finally, I had to get up in the middle of church and walk down the aisle, feeling like an idiot.

The main task at the beginning of mourning is to accept the reality of the death. One way to do that is to talk about what happened, including the exact circumstances of the death. Although focusing obsessively on the details can become a trap that keeps us from other aspects of our grief, in the beginning we need to tell the whole story. By giving sorrow words, we start to accept what has happened and to release some of the pain of it.

THE MIDDLE PERIOD: ANGER, DEPRESSION, FEAR, GUILT, AND OTHER REACTIONS

After the funeral, when the shock has worn off and the guests are gone, grievers are often bombarded with emotions. During the middle period of grief, the loss sinks in. The bereaved typically feel ambushed by a mixture of sadness, fear, anxiety, agitation, anger, guilt, depression, despair, and confusion.

Roseanne Lurie, a thirty-five-year-old nurse in Venice, California, captured many of those feelings in a journal she kept after her thirteen-month-old baby, Joshua, the younger of her two children, died as a result of febrile seizures. Here are some excerpts from her journal:

May 21, 1988: It has been eight or nine days since Joshua died. Sometimes I still can't believe it. My heart is broken that I will never again hold my Ja-Ja, bite his fat little face, play our games. My life is empty. I'm lonely. I am in tremendous pain. It comes in waves. I want to be mothered. I can't take care of myself.

May 26, 1988: Tomorrow it will be two weeks since Joshua died. I feel overwhelmed by despair, loneliness, and emptiness. I hear him crying in a dream. I think of his little body in the blue coffin. I am only going through the motions of life. I need God. I need to believe that we will be together again when I die. I see my Jonathon lonely for his little brother. Joshua is dead. I miss him. I'm hit with waves of anxiety, depression. I see his little face so clearly—being happy, laughing, playing with the cat. And then I see his face so clearly brain-damaged—his limbs so distorted, the huge beautiful blue eyes fixed to the side. Oh, my little boy. If only we could be a family again. If only Mommy could get over this loss and be able to live again. A piece of myself is in that casket—a very important piece. I want to go to his grave. I want to be able to say good-bye. I want to dig up his body and hold it close to mine. I'm deeply disturbed by my feelings.

May 27, 1988: I went with Mona to see Ja-Ja's grave. I lay like an infant curled up on the marble. I spoke to Joshua and said, "I miss you. I love you. Are you feeling comfortable?" I sing our songs. I feel empty. He is so gone. Only the shell of his person lay there. If only I could stroke his head, hold his hand. My longing for him increases.

June 12, 1988: It has been a month since Ja-Ja died. It still feels like yesterday. I cry hysterically three or four times daily. I see his face in the crowd. I catch a glimpse of him in my memory. Life seems so pointless. Scott and I are stressed. It is hard to see your spouse suffer. I want to go away, start a new life, be in another person's life. My tears pour out silently no matter where I am. How could it be? To never again hold my sweet baby. To never again watch them grow together. Never again the twin stroller, the matching cribs, the beach park, the special games. I whisper outloud: "Ja-Ja. I miss you. I love you." So slow is recovery as to almost seem to remain still. Just a flicker of sunlight here, a laugh with Jonathon there, the beauty of a flower, and thinking that all that comes from the earth is part of Joshua since he is part of the earth now. How much time will have to pass to heal us? It is as slow as a turtle crawling up a hill.

Grief is slow, hard work for a simple reason: when we grieve, we mourn for many things. We mourn the relationship. We mourn the daily activities that were so unremarkable we never stopped to appreciate them. We remember special moments and play them back to ourselves until they form an idealized portrait. We mourn the best of times.

But to mourn fully, we must also admit to the difficulties and disappointments in the relationship. We remember disagreements, dreadful silences, injured feelings; we recall the times we were furious, frustrated, embarrassed, hurt. You might think that the better the relationship was, the worse the pain will be. But a turbulent relationship can also be difficult to mourn, because there's more guilt, exasperation, and anger. We mourn the relationship we had and the one we wish we'd had. We mourn the worst of times.

We also mourn our social role. An adult whose parents are dead is an orphan at any age: nobody's child. A widow is a wife no longer. A parent whose only child dies may feel like a parent no more. And even a parent who has other children is still no longer a parent to that particular one. That role—mother to Joshua, mother to Cari—is gone. In my case, I was no longer the twins' mother. That special role was gone forever.

Outside the family, roles also change. Widows and widowers can discover to their astonishment that their social circle is only for couples. The death of a spouse can mean the loss of friends, activities, status, and income. When a child dies, the bereaved parents may find that other parents are so uncomfortable in their presence that they literally turn away. And many grievers note that they feel jealous of everyone who still possesses what they no longer have. "I feel envious of complete families," said Joni Schaap after her son's death. "I stare at teenage boys."

Another loss that needs to be mourned is the loss of the future as we had imagined it: the trip to Europe we hoped to take, the retirement, the anniversary we once dreamed about, the graduation that never came.

You'd think that would be enough. But every death also reopens old wounds. One loss inevitably reminds us of others: so the newly bereaved widow may find herself crying for the parent who died a quarter of a century before, and the man who has buried his child may mourn his mother as well. Bruce Reynolds is a rock-and-roll singer from South Carolina. Her father died in 1981, the same year she got divorced; in 1985 her boyfriend was killed by a truck; twenty-three days later, her house burned down; and in 1989 her cat was killed by a hit-and-run driver. The death of her pet might seem small, but her grief for her cat revived other feelings:

> I came home and my neighbor met me at the door. She was sobbing, and she told me Miko was killed. She put him in a box in the garage so I went and I stroked him and then I walked into the house, ripped his scratching post off the wall, and went striding outside to throw it away. Cars were speeding by and I went red. I grabbed a broom handle and was holding it as if it were a javelin and yelling, "Slow the fuck down!" People looking at me through the windshield must have thought I was a crazy person. Then I went back and lifted him up, and I knew he wouldn't come to me to be held again. He used to come to

me to be held every morning and every nighttime, and his coat felt like a seal's, sleek and soft.

I put him back in the box and broke down. Huge, cracking sobs came pouring out. All of those earlier losses—being abandoned, being alone—all those feelings were pouring up and up and up. The sobs immediately were for Miko, and from that I went to the earlier losses: the loss when Darren was killed, not ever being able to finish conversations we'd started or apologize for things or thank him for things; and all the times I picked up the phone to ask my father something and realized I can never ask him again. Maybe he's in a wonderful place, but I'm left behind. What do I do now? Who is going to take care of me? Who is going to love me when I hurt? Once you're in that mode, you just keep reeling on. On the night of my birthday, two weeks later, I heard myself voice the words, "I'm thirty-eight years old, I'm all alone, my cat is dead, nothing in my life has gone right." Three weeks later, I realized, hey, I'm getting better, it doesn't feel so bad. And I started crying again.

Many people cry a great deal during bereavement. "It was about ten months before I did not cry every day. Tears will come when I least expect them," said a sixty-eight-year-old widow. Some people worry that they are crying too much. But unless tears are significantly interfering with important functioning, crying is beneficial. It is a cathartic release that really does make people feel better, perhaps because tears are composed of more than just salt water. Some experts believe that by crying we bring our bodies into a better chemical balance. And although tears feel endless, the average crying session lasts only six minutes.

Other people have trouble crying at all. "I feel all this pressure in the center of my chest and I know it's grief but I can't get it out," one mourner said. Frequently, the dry-eyed mourners are men, whereas those who worry about crying too much are women. Women are usually tuned in to their feelings and willing to express them. Men generally avoid the murkiness of emotions and turn instead toward action. According to Pennsylvania psychologist Jeffrey A. Kauffman, Ph.D., "Being vulnerable is okay for a woman but for a man it is shameful. The shame inhibits their expression of grief." As a result, they often repress their grief and suffer the consequences of not getting through it. For no matter how hard you try—and some people try very, very hard—it is impossible to ignore grief. One way or another, it demands expression.

Does it seem too much to bear? Sometimes. The work of grief is long and arduous. Grief opens doors in the mind and in the heart that may have been shut for years. It reactivates the powerlessness and vulnerability we felt as children. And it's uncontrollable. As soon as we think we've mastered it, grief hits us again.

Anger

At some point after someone you love dies, you're going to feel angry. You might feel sputtering irritation; you might feel white-hot rage. Whatever its form, anger is an almost universal reaction to the death of a loved one. Many people, however, find it difficult to admit this. Anger makes many people so uneasy that they suppress it and feel depressed or guilty instead. It's not a good trade-off.

Some mourners get angry at people who have not experienced a similar loss. They explode at those who try to offer condolences (because what do *they* know?). They get angry at strangers who inadvertently remind them of the deceased, and they blow up at other family members. Widow Wanda Reid described her anger after her husband died:

> I've always been a little inclined to flash up, but I wasn't normally so horribly short-tempered. I used to have all sorts of patience with my grandchildren and also with other members of the family. Now I get angry over the silliest things. It embarrasses me to death.
>
> I haven't shown it, but I have felt really angry at women who complain about their husbands day after day. Why didn't their husbands go and leave mine here instead? We did all sorts of things together. We were each other's best friends.

That anger is a reaction not just to the death but to the changed circumstances of the mourner's life. Dvora Freeman, a Los Angeles therapist in her fifties, remembers her reactions after her husband died of lung cancer in 1984:

> Looking back, I realize I had this free-floating anger looking for a cause. I had to make a new life and new friends and I didn't like anybody. I was always irritated and angry. Even in a bereavement group I joined for a brief period, I was angry that all these dummies didn't really know what it was about. I was angry at my children. No matter how they came through for me, they reminded me of their father in so many ways that when they didn't do all the things that their father did, I was disappointed and angry. I think it's a way of not letting go of the person.

Some mourners get angry at God. Others get angry at the disease or the medical personnel, as Charlene Kelley Phillips did when her two-year-old son died during an examination following open-heart surgery. "I was angry at the pain he had to experience—and in vain! Only to die in the end!" she exclaimed. "And I was also mad at the doctors."

Mourners get angry at anyone who might have been even slightly responsible for the death. That's especially true when death has come as a result of a crime. People whose loved ones died as the result of a crime are very angry, not only at the killers but at the criminal justice system. For them, anger can be a far greater component of grief than it is for those whose loved ones die a natural death.

Many mourners get angry at the deceased. The anger may concern something that person did or didn't do while alive. "I have felt angry at my husband," said Wanda Reid. "He was a fix-it man. He would often do temporary repairs and never get back to doing them permanently. A couple of times, I've gotten really mad because he didn't fix the temporary repairs. Oh! Why didn't he finish that!"

But the main reason mourners get angry at the deceased is that they feel abandoned. Rational or not, it is a common reaction, one that Los Angeles resident Marcy De Jesus felt both before and after her husband died:

> The last week in the hospital, my husband was virtually in a coma and on life support. One day I got furious. I was screaming at him in the intensive-care unit about what a bastard he was for leaving me and cutting our plans short. I just lost it! After he died, I shoved a lot of feelings down. I would not let them surface. But then I would be driving in my car and suddenly I'd start screaming at him.

Fortunately, with time those feelings diminish—assuming they are expressed. (For ways to do that without taking it out on the people around you, see Chapter Twelve.)

Depression

For many mourners, grief manifests itself primarily as depression. "The sadness was intolerable," reports Dvora Freeman. "I was so depressed. I only recall wanting to die." Depression, which is a normal reaction to loss, can be the most difficult part of grieving, and the most long-lasting.

Depressed people, whether they are in mourning or not, feel withdrawn, apathetic, helpless, lonely, sad, and out of control. They have trouble concentrating, making decisions, and getting a good night's sleep.

But there are differences between regular depression and the depression associated with grieving. People who are depressed for reasons besides mourning focus on themselves; their minds are filled with self-denigrating and pessimistic thoughts, small problems loom large, and their depression tends to be a constant companion. People depressed after the death of a loved one focus on something other than themselves. Every object becomes a painful reminder, every moment alone a horrible proof. Life seems pointless, utterly joyless, and without hope because that person is dead. They yearn for the deceased. Nothing else commands their attention. Prior to his retirement, Lawrence Gadwa of Citrus Heights, California, was territory manager for a large corporation based in Michigan. He married his wife, Daphne, during World War II. He was eighteen and she was seventeen. When she died of Lou Gehrig's disease forty-four years later, he, like many mourners, found it difficult to get interested in anything, despite the core of friends who rallied around him:

> I have no ambition to do anything. I started working on my garage before all this happened. I have shelves that aren't complete. I've got cupboards I want to build and things to do in the house and with this yard. I water, but there's nobody to do it with and share it with. Why bother?

For some mourners, the depression is so strong that they want to die. "About a month after my wife was gone, I got really sick. It was the first time in my whole life that I was sick all by myself. Every night I would pray to God, 'Don't let me wake up in the morning,' " Lawrence Gadwa recalls.

"Suicidal thoughts—such as I have nothing to live for, or I wish I were with my mom—are normal. Eventually, you'll feel better," states therapist Paula Steinmetz of the Brotman Medical Center Bereavement Center in Los Angeles. Therapists who work with grievers often ask their clients to sign a contract, a promise not to kill themselves for a certain period of time. They know that such thoughts usually disappear as the mourner, in time, finds other reasons to live.

These feelings fade fitfully, for the progress of grief is never a straight-line graph. Like the Dow Jones average, it fluctuates wildly. Mourners may feel all right for a while, and then they plunge back into thoughts of the deceased. But with time the depression becomes milder and less frequent; there are moments of light in the midst of the general gloom. If that doesn't happen, and especially if you have difficulty with normal functioning, there may very well be a greater problem. "I just don't want to be here anymore. I used to be a voracious reader. I used to work for the Democratic Party. I used to love sailing. None of it means anything to me now," a fifty-year-old widow told us. "I gained fifty pounds. I smoke. Basically, I've been sitting around waiting to die. It's like a benign suicide. I try to handle it myself, which really isn't a good idea."

She's right: it isn't a good idea. If you feel similarly, seeing a therapist can bring understanding, comfort, the opportunity to explore your feelings and seek solutions. Therapy takes courage. That process may dredge up some pain. But you are in pain anyway—and it's affecting you every day of your life. If your depression is extreme, therapy can help.

Fear

"I never knew that grief felt so like fear," wrote C. S. Lewis in A *Grief Observed*. Fear is a natural component of grief; once you've experienced the death of a loved one, you *know* the world is not a safe place. Many people fear living alone, especially after the death of a spouse. They feel vulnerable and worried about the details of living. "I had never been alone in my life," a widow reported. "I went from my parents' house to my first marriage, directly into my second marriage. I was never alone for one minute and then my husband died and there I was. Then came the natural fear of what the hell am I going to do?"

The fear of losing another loved one is also common. After his newborn baby died, Paul Grisanti said, "I found I was looking at the world from a different perspective. I was afraid I would lose my wife as well. And I was afraid and guilty that it was somehow my fault." These fears can also appear in dreams. "I've had terrifying nightmares about funerals and mutilations that involved everyone in the family," said a woman whose father had recently died. "I even dreamed that someone was trying to break into my house to murder my husband and me."

Children who have buried a parent may wonder who will take care of them now. Their own safety seems at risk, both physically and emotionally. Adults may have similar feelings, especially after the death of the second parent. Not only are they orphaned, but they may be afraid that they're next.

The fear of dying is one that affects many bereaved people. It often appears in the form of hypochondriacal symptoms that mirror the loved one's fatal symptoms. Oncologist Dr. Heather Allen of Las Vegas, Nevada, observes:

> What people become aware of oftentimes is that when someone has died of cancer, it's because by the time it was diagnosed,

the cancer was too far along. They say, "She was fine. She had no symptoms." What absolutely frightens them is the realization that you can go for your Pap tests, you can go for your mammogram, and no matter how well you try to take care of yourself, things can happen that you have no control over. That realization is very difficult to deal with. Every time they turn around, it's "I've got cancer. I know I do."

I remember a woman I spoke with years ago when I was volunteering for the Red Cross at Mather Air Force Base Hospital. She was worried about lumps in her breast. During a six-month period, she repeatedly came to the doctor for a breast examination. Each time, he found no evidence of lumps. She would leave relieved, and then the fear would reassert itself and she would make another appointment. Only after this had happened several times did the reason become apparent: her mother had recently died of breast cancer, and having nursed her through the death, she was now convinced that she had the same symptoms.

Another woman whose father died of a heart attack developed pains in her chest. "I went to the emergency room and the doctor hooked me up to the EKG machine, looked at the tape, and told me that there was nothing wrong with me. I was very healthy and was going to live a long, long time—but had I considered therapy?"

These fears need to be faced: "Half a step at a time. One single thing at a time. And total concentration on that one single thing," a widower suggested. So if you are worried about your health, getting a checkup can reassure you that nothing is organically wrong. If you feel unprotected in your home, installing dead-bolt locks can calm some of your anxiety. Postpone major decisions made out of fear, because during this time, your judgment may not be the best. And remember that your fears *will* subside.

Guilt

Guilt is almost always a component of mourning. People feel guilty for not having been a wiser parent, a better husband, a more obedient child. They feel guilty for things they did and for things they didn't do.

A teenage girl felt guilty for not having told her deceased brother that she loved him—and for having been "irritated by his very existence."

A young widow felt guilty because she took a nap. Her husband had recently died of cancer. During his illness, she nursed him on a round-the-clock basis. One night, totally frazzled, she begged him to let her sleep for a couple of hours. He wanted to be held. Exhausted to the point of hysteria, she said no, and took a brief nap. While she was asleep, he died. Now she is filled with guilt, despite the fact that she loyally attended to his every need for months.

Most people are remarkably creative when it comes to finding reasons to feel guilty. They feel guilty about their actions and their thoughts. Sometimes they feel guilty merely because they are still alive and the other person is dead. This is called survivor's guilt. Originally identified among survivors of the Nazi holocaust and the bombing of Hiroshima, survivor's guilt particularly affects people who have lived through disasters in which others perished. It had recently been identified among gay men who are free of the HIV virus that causes AIDS. Psychologists now realize that anyone who has lost a loved one can feel it. Why did she die instead of me? It's a question without an answer.

And then there's the "if only" syndrome. Often this is an understandable attempt to rewrite the past. I certainly felt it. If only I had picked Cari up instead of letting her walk, I told myself, she would still be alive. Ann McArtor, director of marketing for Showtime, also had that reaction when a friend committed suicide:

> A close friend whom I had known since high school and had dated in college hung himself from the clothes rod in a closet in his apartment in Ann Arbor, Michigan. The rod was so low his feet touched the ground. He had been deeply depressed for months preceding his death and had even been hospitalized for a short period.
>
> I felt terrible remorse. Friends told me that he had mentioned me frequently in the weeks before his death, even though we had not been in close communication for some time. I felt an overwhelming sense of "If only I had been there . . . If only I had been in close touch with him, this wouldn't have happened. If only, if only. . . ." If only I had done something, I had the feeling that I could have stopped him.

Some people get stuck for years in a mine field of "if onlys." Talking to someone else can provide a more objective perspective on your actions. The chances are great that nothing you could have done would have prevented the death. By talking to a sympathetic friend, you may be able to see how unnecessary your guilt is. You're only human; the most important step when you're feeling guilty is to forgive yourself.

THE REST OF YOUR LIFE

During the middle period of mourning, every thought returns to the single overwhelming one. But eventually, other topics tempt the beleaguered mind. We cry less frequently. Life reasserts itself. We laugh. We adjust. And we learn to accept the death. "The whole experience of my wife's death strengthened my acceptance of death—even horrible deaths—as part of the natural process of life," a forty-year-old widower said. "It has been the most maturing experience of my life. After four years, I still occasionally experience moments of sadness or remorse. But I have come to accept those moments, and in some ways even to appreciate them, as a natural part of life."

Although the pain of grief does fade, grief is not something from which we recover. Nor do we heal. Many psychologists object to these terms because they imply that grief is an illness requiring a cure, rather than a natural, appropriate reaction to the death of a loved one. Bereavement, as Dr. Phyllis Silverman observes, "can best be seen not as an illness, but as a time of transition."

At first, we dwell primarily in the past. But gradually, we create new habits, find new ways of interacting, and reintegrate ourselves into the world. Slowly, we reach a point when we can feel the poignancy of the past without being overwhelmed by it. We look to the future.

By then, we have established a new relationship with the deceased. We neither say good-bye nor achieve closure because the relationship does not end. Instead, it is internalized, reevaluated, reimagined, remembered. The relationship does not disappear.

Grief does not entirely disappear either. It becomes incorporated into the psyche; it becomes a part of us. Occasionally, as on birthdays or anniversaries of the death, we feel a tinge of sadness. But grief no longer defines us. Having journeyed through it, we are no longer the same people. We know more about ourselves. And because we know more about death, we know more about life. Rae Ecklund recalls:

> I began to see that these "attacks" of pain come like waves, and the time between "attacks" begins to widen, making it more bearable. I had never been told this before. The first anniversary of my brother's death was met with early morning phone calls, quiet talk, more tears. By the second anniversary, there was easing back into using his name aloud, laughing a little, and lots of "remembering when." I decided to live with a few of his special things. His western hat hangs next to mine on a hall tree. I used to cry each time I passed it. Now I notice the dust!
>
> I have become aware of the gift that life is. I have a greater respect for time. I am more tolerant of others and I have learned, contrary to previous belief, that I can survive almost anything. Once you go through the process and come out the other side, you've been given something that others who have not been there do not have.

Mourners who have coped successfully are those who eventually found new activities, formed new relationships, and became more fully themselves. They sought purpose and pleasure in living and they generally found it. As a result of their contact with death, they have changed. Sometimes the changes seem small. A thirty-five-year-old woman, for instance, stopped putting things off after a close friend died. "I bought a beautiful piece of furniture for the first time in my life. What's the point of waiting? I've learned to seize the moment."

And sometimes the changes are large.

"I've become more active and more independent," one widow said. "I have more friends, I go more places, and I'm a much stronger person than ever before."

Another widow, a lifelong garden club member, became more adventurous after her husband's death. She moved to a new part of the country, made new friends, and finally decided to get serious about her hobby. She flew to Japan and lived there for almost a year studying flower arranging at a temple. It's something she would never have done before.

And Roseanne Lurie, having mourned for Joshua, gave birth to another baby. Her name is Hannah.

CHAPTER 3 | Good Grief, Bad Grief

My friend would force me to do things. Why don't I pick you up, she'd say, or why don't we go out for ice cream? Why don't we go shopping? I didn't want to shop . . . but it was nice just to walk around and be outside. I remember her taking me for these little outings. I'll never forget it.

—JENNIFER BLOCK

My friends said, "That part of your life is over. You need to forget about it." I was terribly disappointed by their lack of empathy. How do you forget about someone who was a part of your life for forty-five years?

—MARTHA COOPER

GOOD GRIEF

There is nothing like a death in the family to bring out the best in human nature—and the worst. When it brings out the best, mourners feel recognized and consoled, touched by the sympathy shown by others, shored up by their kindness and concern. Many people have found that the support they receive following a death strengthens their faith in humanity. Friends gather round doing things they normally never do. They cook for you; they cry with you; they connect from the heart. Under the best of circumstances, the attentions that come to a mourner act as a form of bonding, knitting together the griever with those who see the magnitude of the loss and understand its implications. Many mourners feel noticed, protected, loved, and even surprised by how caring people

38

can be. Zoe Schiff described how good her friends were after her husband died when she was forty-eight years old:

> People were unbelievably kind. I'll never get over that. There wasn't anyone who wasn't there. Barbara Medlin was absolutely devoted; I'd have dinner with her once a week on a regular basis because she was the only one I knew who was widowed and she understood. Marge Wolfe used to call at eleven o'clock at night to see how I was. And my neighbors Julia and Stan were marvelous; nobody could compare to them. Julia was there in the morning to see that I got up, and the minute I stepped into the house in the evening, she was there. Their home was open to me no matter what. Cy Goldman was extraordinary too. When I had to sell the house, I felt like my whole life was being thrown away, and Cy stayed with me every bit of that time. He was incredible. I can't tell you the people who reached out to me. Everyone was superb. They were beyond belief.

Many people feel similarly. "People sent flowers to me, people gave me hugs. They even quietly gave me money—needed and appreciated," a bereaved young mother reported. "There were people who stunned me with their thoughtfulness."

Even mourners who neither seek nor desire outside assistance find that they draw strength from it when it is offered. "At first I didn't want any help or support," said Paul Grisanti, whose son died in the hospital sixteen hours after he was born. "But a friend who brought fruit to the hospital room and made us eat was great. And a colleague returned all my client calls and actually paid a couple of bills that came to the office rather than let them become delinquent. I repaid him later but it was very good."

Kindness comes in many forms. When my friend Bunny Corbin came to see me after Cari died, she brought a book about grieving and offered it to me. But I wasn't ready for it so she read it herself to learn what I was going through. A lot of people in trying to comfort a traumatized griever fall back on their ignorance and lack of experience. "I don't know what to do for you," they say. "I can't imagine how you feel." Bunny went out of her way to find out.

I was also touched by a kindness from a stranger. On the day of the funeral, I received a letter from a woman whose son died when he was hit by an automobile while riding his bicycle. She had read about Cari's death in the newspaper and was so overwhelmed with sadness for me that she wrote me a lovely three-page letter. She even included her phone number in case I wanted to talk.

Typically, the majority of the help is offered in the beginning. Immediately after the death and for a few weeks following the funeral, friends can be exceptionally sensitive and giving. Flowers, food, phone calls, fond reminiscences, and, above all, the mere presence of other people are profoundly consoling. They convey the message that others recognize the depth of the loss, understand how difficult the adjustment is, and want to help. This is something mourners are grateful to hear.

· BAD GRIEF

Unfortunately, grief can also bring out the worst in people, and when that happens, mourners feel slighted, insulted, disappointed, and alone. Perhaps a good friend disappears from sight or makes an incomprehensibly cruel remark, like "I thought you two weren't getting along that well anyway" or "He was always a problem child, wasn't he?" or "She's in a better place now." Perhaps people don't understand the grieving process. A few weeks later, desperately trying to adjust, you're barely functional, deep in mourning for a loved one whom you miss every moment of the day, and some people around you act as if you must be neurotic because you seem sad. A recent widow was sitting in her house one afternoon when an acquaintance pulled his car into her driveway, rolled down the window, and yelled out to her, "Are you over your grief yet?" She was rendered speechless: it was five days after her husband's sudden death.

The sad truth is that you can expect some of that. There's usually more than one person who can't handle your grieving, who offers no support at all. One of the unrecognized problems of grieving is that, in addition to learning to live with the loss of your loved one, mourners have to cope with the loss of other people as well. For although death brings out the kindness in some people, others will avoid you, inadvertently say cruel things, or even blame you. They want to distance themselves from everything that reminds them of death—including you. Good grief, bad grief: every mourner knows the story. Deborah Ryan, a thirty-eight-year-old screenwriter in Los Angeles, described a friend's response after her sixteen-year-old son, David, was killed by a drunk driver:

> The most painful reaction was that of a very close friend of mine who was recently pronounced "cured" after an intense and sudden year-long bout with leukemia. He went through a lot and I was there for him through that experience to an incredible degree. I was on the phone day after day with him while he was ill. But you're either a person to whom that matters or you're not. After my son was killed, I had a patently plastic,

brief conversation with his wife, but I have heard not a word from him.

It's not that people don't feel for you; often they do. But the flood of feeling that you are obviously experiencing is more than they can bear. They don't want to be around it; they don't want to feel it; they don't want to think about it. They are terrified that what happened to you might happen to them. "Nobody wants to hear you talk about someone who's dead," said one mourner. "They don't want you even to mention it, so you learn not to bring it up." It's not your pain they fear so much as their own.

That's what happened with my sister Kathy. After Cari died, Kathy flew in to town immediately. As soon as I saw her, I ran toward her, hoping to be comforted. Instead, she pushed me away. "Don't start crying," she said. "It will just get me crying all over again." She wanted me to control myself—the last thing I needed to do at that moment! To protect her from her grief, I had to suppress my own.

Other people made comments that I am certain they thought would be comforting, though I can't imagine why. For instance, because Cari was an identical twin, people said to me many, many times, "At least you've got another one who looks just like her." Did they think that it's not so bad for a child to die if that child is a twin? Did they think that, since I had two, I wouldn't mind if one died? Let's face it: they didn't think at all!

One friend of mine who was never able to tell the girls apart came over to the house a month or so after Cari died and continued to call Serena by her sister's name. I corrected her repeatedly. I would say, "Serena," and five minutes later, she would call her "Cari." This went on all day. Finally, I said pointedly, "This is not Cari. Cari is dead. This is Serena." She said, "Oh, you know how I always got them confused." She probably thought it was an understandable mistake. It wasn't—not anymore.

Mourners have been subjected to plenty of insensitive comments. Joyce Selbo reported that after her husband died, "A neighbor said that I probably would not be missing him too much since he was away from home so often!" Theresa des Lauriers, whose beloved niece committed suicide, was astounded when someone said, "She must have been crazy to do such a thing." Ruth Kieffer was not consoled when she was told, after her baby was stillborn, "It's a good thing he died before you got him home." And in the aftermath of his father's death, Giles Slade was perplexed when "a friend who knew I was a recovering alcoholic offered me a drink. That still amazes me," he said.

But my favorite thoughtless statement—and I am not making this up—is this one: "I know just how you feel," one woman said. "My dog died two weeks ago." Now, I don't dismiss for a moment the sorrow of losing a pet. (See Chapter Ten for more on that topic.) But I believe with all my heart that this woman did not know how I felt!

People do not intend to be offensive. Although they may make inappropriate remarks, they mean to be sympathetic. But although they don't intend to hurt, they sometimes hurt nonetheless.

Certain comments are comforting to some people and infuriating to others. After her baby died, for example, a young mother found that "it was very helpful when someone said, 'You'll have another baby.' " Other bereaved parents hearing similar remarks felt as if their loss had been dismissed, as if they were being told to exchange one child, the dead one, for another—the imaginary one that they might have in the future.

The most problematical comments are the ones about God. Virtually every mourner, sooner or later, is going to be told, "It was God's will." Some people may feel consoled by hearing—or saying—that statement. Others, including myself, are not. To this day, it remains a mystery to me why anyone would take comfort in the notion that God wishes children to be hit by automobiles or to die alone in their cribs of unknown causes. I think it's a terrifying idea!

The real message behind "It was God's will," "God never gives us more than we can bear," and similar statements has little to do with theology. Although many people turn to God when they can't explain something or when they're afraid, the unacknowledged goal of remarks like these is often to get the griever to stop expressing sorrow, to make it easier for everyone around by suppressing the bereaved's emotions. They mean to say that if it's God's will, then who are you to complain? The same is true for statements such as "He's with God." This was said to Charlene Kelley Phillips after her two-year-old died. "The idea that he's better off there instead of with his mother just made me mad," she said. Mourners don't want their loss to be justified; they want their sorrow to be acknowledged.

AS TIME GOES BY

Like other mourners, I learned that after the funeral, support can fade alarmingly fast. Friends don't intend to abandon you, although that is how it feels. They believe that the tough time is over. "People told me, 'Get on with your life' and 'You should be over this by now,' " one widow said. "It's hard to believe people can be so cold—and it's hard to forgive."

In fact, people have little understanding of the depth and length of grieving. Haunted by thoughts of death and uneasy in the face of grief, they don't want to talk about your loss. They want you to get over it fast. Consequently, mourners often find themselves hiding their feelings in order to make the other person more comfortable. Deborah Ryan explains:

> This is every parent's nightmare. And every sensitive person can understand that nightmare. Yet I end up comforting others on a regular basis. One of the reasons I am reluctant to say, "My son was killed," is that I'm going to have to say, "It's all right, I'm okay." And it's not all right, and I'll never be okay. I feel like I'm betraying my son by saying that it is all right. And on the other hand, my grief is too private to display. There are people who think you're seriously damaged because you're grieving. They say, "You've been through a lot and you need help." They see themselves as facilitators. They say, "It really concerns me that you aren't in therapy." Even my boss, who has the kindest heart on earth, says, "You seem down." Well, my son was killed. I have a right.

WHO HELPS?

Those who help you are not necessarily the people you'd expect. It might be your best friend; but it might not be. My friends Dorie and Dan Thome, for instance, really came through—and I hadn't seen them since shortly after Cari was born. I hadn't spoken to my friend Cheryl Hart in a year because we had been feuding. Yet when Cari died, Cheryl knew right away what was important and what wasn't. When I opened my door that awful day, Cheryl was right there. A little later her sister Nancy Lemmon came over—to see Cari. She hadn't heard the news and was terribly upset by it. She put her arms around me and stayed. And my friend Leslie Hidley cooked for a week. I'll never forget their help.

Often, the most supportive people are those who have also suffered a major loss. My friend Shirley Curtis had lost her husband the previous year. As a result, Shirley understood the grieving process from the inside. She was there in the beginning, as most of my friends were, and she was there as time went on, as most of them were not. Shirley talked to me frequently, and she allowed me to grieve; she'd drop by on her way to the movies or to dinner and invite me to come along; she and her daughter even arrived at my house on Mother's Day the week after Cari was killed with a lemon meringue pie—my favorite. The fact that they thought of me meant so much. Shirley understood that mourning takes a long time, and she was willing to give and give.

People who disappear don't understand, I suspect, that they don't have to do a whole lot. There are no magic words they need to speak. As widower Byron Callas said, "The people who were the most helpful after my wife died were the ones who just allowed me to have their company when I needed it or wanted it; who didn't expect me to be or do anything for anybody; and who didn't say platitudes."

People who do that earn a profound kind of gratitude. Jennifer Block is a twenty-six-year-old actress whose mother died when she was eighteen years old. She told us about her reactions and the ways other people responded:

I had a lot of friends. I divide them into two categories: the ones who made it through the experience with me and the ones who didn't. Mostly the ones who didn't just couldn't handle it. They didn't know what to say to me. My personality completely changed after my mother died. I was difficult to deal with. I had always been very social, very funny, very lighthearted, the life of the party. After my mother died I was in a severe depression for two years. I was unable to do much. It was unheard-of for me to go to a party or to go out to dinner with somebody. I couldn't sustain a conversation. I had no interest in anything. I would get furious if somebody started to tell me about something positive in their life, like a boyfriend or a girlfriend or that they got an A on an exam. This was my first year in college. I would meet people and hate them on sight because they were so normal and their mother hadn't died.

My best friend would take me places. She'd call every day. I wouldn't have called me because I was nasty and I was mean. But even though I said I didn't want to talk, that wasn't really true. I wanted to talk but I didn't want her to hear me cry, I didn't want to be emotional every second of the day. I was afraid that if people looked at me, I'd start to cry, and I tried to suppress it, but at the same time, I wanted to. She would listen to me talk, she would listen to me cry. She was the only person I would cry in front of. It would take a lot but I would finally cry, and she was completely empathetic, even though I could see it pained her to listen to me talk. She was great.

GETTING THE SUPPORT YOU NEED

Bereavement is a needy time. Mourners are vulnerable in the extreme. A million tasks cry out to be done, and yet the world is crashing in on you. Everything in your life has been shattered, you're getting an hour and a half of sleep a night, and every time you open the closet and smell your loved one's clothing, you fall apart. Meanwhile, your friends are saying things like "It was God's will" and "I could never do what you've done. I wouldn't have the strength."

In the immediate aftermath of death, people visit, call, bring food, attend the funeral. But after that, there are no social dictums about what they ought to do. That's why, to get your minimal needs met, you may need to be assertive. Here are some ways to get the support you need:

• **Tell people that you need to talk about your loss.** Normal social interchanges may not be possible during the first few weeks; it's just too hard at first to maintain even a passing interest in other people's problems and triumphs. People understand that. But they don't know how to deal with it. For instance, frequently friends and family may try to "take your mind off of it." It doesn't work—not for a second.

People talk about everything else under the sun except death because they can't handle the feelings themselves and because they don't want the griever to feel bad. But the griever feels bad already. Not being allowed to discuss the loss only makes it worse. Sometimes you have to tell that to people directly.

I found that whenever I tried to talk about Cari, people would change the subject. One day when I was talking with my friend Sue LeBrun, I mentioned Cari's name, and Sue immediately tried to change the subject. I got angry. "Damn it, Sue," I said. "If I want to talk about Cari, please let me."

Her response was revealing. "I don't want to see you hurt," she said.

"I'm going to hurt whether I talk about her or not," I replied. "Talking about her actually helps, even though it is painful." From then on, Sue was willing to listen. That experience taught me how important it is to tell your friends: "I'm going to have to talk about this for a while. Please bear with me."

• **Ask for specific help.** Many people make offers that are well intentioned but vague: "Let me know what I can do," they'll say. When that happens, tell them. Ask them to help you rake the leaves. Ask them to baby-sit. Ask them to bring food. If you need to sort through your loved one's clothes or to go to the mortuary to choose a casket, ask someone to accompany you. If you need to notify dozens of relatives and friends with the sad news, and that thought is overwhelming, ask someone to make a few calls for you. This is a time when people will be glad to help.

The most important thing is to communicate your needs, whether they are physical or emotional. Do you need help decoding your insurance policy? Are you stymied by some task that was always assigned to your spouse? Do you want someone to rub your back? Do you need to be held? Ask.

• **Balance your need for company with your need for solitude.** In the beginning, when people gather together, you may desire some time alone. You may need to request that time, to tell people you want a few hours by yourself.

But as time passes after the funeral, loneliness may become a larger problem. You can expect some people to be so uncomfortable with grief that they don't want to be around you. They usually won't say it directly. They'll say they've been busy. They may even say that they thought you wouldn't want to be disturbed. Some people are simply no good during these difficult times.

For those whose spouses have died, and for widows in particular, watching old friends gradually disappear is an additional sorrow. It happens especially with other couples. They feel ill at ease inviting you to social occasions where everyone else is paired, and they certainly do not want to be reminded that all couples, inevitably, must part. Your presence is a constant reminder of death. They may resolve the dilemma of their discomfort by not seeing you at all, or by seeing you at less significant times. Invitations for Saturday night evaporate; now it's Tuesday lunch. Martha Cooper, whose husband died after many years of marriage, describes her experience—a typical one:

> There are no couples anymore in my life. There are no dinner invitations, and on weekends, you have to make your own plans. You're the odd man out. Even with friends of twenty-five, thirty years, it's all over. If you do anything at all, you do it with the wife. I don't see how they could think you were a threat, but I guess they do. Life has changed that way. It's really disappointing.

Seek out people who are willing to listen and tell them what you need. Don't wait for them to figure it out. If you hate being alone on weekends, you must make plans. Don't just hint around. "I mentioned to one friend that the weekend was the hardest time for me, and I was told, 'You'll just have to find something to do,' " one widow said. Call someone else immediately! Although it is hard to initiate social encounters, especially when you are grieving, it is important to do so. If you need time to yourself, be sure to take it. But if loneliness is a problem, it definitely helps to schedule events in advance. Make sure you're not alone for too many days in a row; make sure you have something to look forward to;

and make sure in particular that you have plans for the most difficult times.

• **Prepare for holidays and anniversaries.** This is essential. Many people become depressed during the Christmas and Hanukkah season even when they are not grieving. So the chances of your becoming depressed are high. You may feel that other people should be able to intuit this for themselves, and they should be. But don't count on it. Provide for yourself by making specific arrangements to be with friends or family.

The anniversary of the death, as well as the day or two before the actual date, can be an especially painful time. You may want to visit the cemetery or attend services at your place of worship. But you may also want to schedule dinner with a close friend. Be frank with them: it's one year since the death (or two years or ten years), you can say, and I'm feeling down. Can we get together?

• **Consider the needs of others.** Or, to put it another way, try to be a good companion. The truest of your friends will be willing to hear you out, willing to comfort; but others among your acquaintances may have a lower level of tolerance for grief. You know who they are; you can see the discomfort in their faces. Deborah Ryan was aware of that reaction. "People would look at me and think, 'I'd like to go out with her and have lunch—but she might cry. It could be embarrassing. It could be uncomfortable. I won't know what to say.' " With people like that—and they are legion—you may have to remind yourself *not* to tell the story again and again, even though nothing else is as compelling. You may wish to avoid these people for a while. But if you do want to maintain these social contacts during this rough time, make it easy for them. Among other things, that means giving your friends a chance to discuss their own problems—no matter how minor those issues may seem to you.

• **Don't rely on your family.** Family relations are always complicated, and when everyone is grieving, no one is strong. Sometimes expecting a lot of help from your family is just adding pressure to an already stressed-out system. Even talking about your feelings within the family may prove to be an impossibility—as Mrs. Cooper found out:

> He died suddenly about 3:45 in the morning, right next to me in our bed. No warning. It was awful. The rescue squad—the coroner—all the horrors. The shock devastated me. I was so depressed and the pain was so great, I considered suicide. But I couldn't put that burden of guilt on my two adult children.
> Our son and daughter do not discuss their grief with me. My

daughter has been very supportive, but I know my tears upset her. I feel I must not cry in front of my son. They do not come home as often since their father is gone, and that hurts me too. Empty house. Empty bed. There's no real reason to get up in the morning. No one else cares like he did. Nothing is the same.

That situation is far from unusual. In his book *A Grief Observed,* C. S. Lewis described the way his children reacted to his sorrow over the death of his wife: "I cannot talk to the children about her. The moment I try, there appears on their faces neither grief, nor love, nor fear, nor pity, but the most fatal of all non-conductors, embarrassment. They look as if I were committing an indecency. They are longing for me to stop. . . ."

You might try telling your children—or your parents or your spouse— how you feel, in the hopes that things will improve. But realistically, it may be wise to seek support elsewhere. Surprisingly, new people may arrive in your life. After Roseanne Lurie's thirteen-month-old baby died, she met and became friends with another young mother in her neighborhood who had also lost a child. Mrs. Cooper joined a widows' bereavement group and as a result, she said, "I have made good new friends, who were very supportive. Other people seemed not to want you to discuss your loss and grief. It makes you feel more alone than ever. That widows' group was my salvation."

HELPING THE MOURNER

What most people seek when they are in mourning is an indication that they will live through this sorrow, that other people understand and sympathize. If you have a friend in mourning and indeed you do care, there are easy ways to get that message across.

• **Acknowledge the death as soon as possible.** Call, drop by, send your condolences. You don't have to say much: "I'm so sorry" will do. And remember that most mourners are supremely touched when friends share stories about the deceased with them.

Tokens of recognition such as flowers or cards pack a lot of meaning —more than you'd guess. Marty Winthrop, speaking of the deaths of her father and mother at different times, made this comment: "I was amazed at how comforting ordinary sympathy cards were. I've always looked at them in the stores and thought, who would appreciate these horribly written cards? Well, I found out who appreciated them! People who needed them, like I did."

• **Provide practical help.** Offer to go to the dry cleaner's or wash the car. Bringing food is an old custom that still serves today. Bake a casserole, make a huge salad, or bring a roast they can nibble on for a few days. People in mourning need to be taken care of in the most primal ways, including being fed.

• **Attend the funeral or memorial service.** Attendance counts: many mourners have been incalculably moved by a large turnout. "My father died when he was forty-five years old," said a successful author. "The first thing that made me feel better after he died was that the cantor at the funeral said to a motorcycle cop, 'This is the biggest funeral I've ever seen.' " It makes a difference to know that other people share your grief. And it's nice to know that your loved one affected so many others.

• **Spend time together.** Take walks, share meals, or help the mourner clean out the garage. Your presence is what matters. Many bereaved people spend a great deal of time alone; they dwell in grief, fear, and despair. During those empty hours and days, nothing is more soothing than the presence of an understanding friend.

At the same time, keep in mind that some people may want to be alone. Or they may wish to be spared the necessity of talk. Men more than women are likely to react in this way, and it is important to note that this is not necessarily bad. It *can* mean that mourning is being repressed; it also can mean that mourning is happening in private. So don't feel rejected if your help is refused. If a friend requests some solitude, that request should be honored. Your role is to be a friend—not a psychiatrist.

• **Continue to call weeks and months after the death.** That's when many people begin to disappear into the ether, and that's often when contact is most appreciated. You might ask, "Is there something I can do?" But be prepared for the answer to be, "There's nothing anyone can do." In that case, ask "What would you like me to do?" And if that doesn't work, make specific suggestions. Do you want to talk? Would you like some company? Do you need to get out of the house? Would you like to walk around the lake? Would you like to take a drive? Would you like to see a movie? Sometimes your questions can help them clarify their needs.

• **Touch the mourner.** "Sometimes just a pat on the shoulder or back is all that is needed. Or a hug. I received a lot of hugs," reports Carolee Rake, a sixty-four-year-old widow. It means a lot, because, among other problems, a person in mourning is often touch-deprived. Widows and widowers certainly feel this deprivation, but so do people who lose children—especially if they're single. I was a divorced, single mother when Cari died, and I remember how very much I wanted to be held. Deborah Ryan reacted similarly. "Being a single mother, physical touch is so important! I would have loved to bury my head in someone's shoulder and cry, but I didn't have that. I wanted to say, 'Somebody hold me!' 'Somebody pat me on the head!' Luckily, a number of people did—just for three minutes—but right when I needed it." To have someone there to hug you, to put an arm around your shoulders or to touch your hand, is extremely comforting. Don't be shy.

• **Let the griever speak.** Less than a century ago, it was thought mannerly to leave people alone in their grief, not to intrude. Today, experts recommend the opposite course. Mourners are virtually unanimous in stating that the most important help they received came from people who were willing to spend time with them and talk.

Yet it's easier to do that in the abstract. Actually sitting in the kitchen listening to someone who is recently bereaved can be difficult. It may mean tears and lamentation, anguish, guilt, and inconsolable sorrow. It may mean the same sad story, again and again: what the blood test showed, what the doctor said, what the other doctor said, what they should have done, and so on. Keep in mind that the obsessive repetition of this litany makes the death real for the griever. When someone you love is mourning, it is a kindness to listen even if you've heard the story before. If the mourner brings up the subject of the deceased or the death, do not change the topic, even though it may churn up a lot of feelings. Attempts at distraction are pointless: no other topic—not the weather, not the elections, not the Academy Awards—is likely to take anybody's mind off a recent loss.

If you really have heard the exact same story in the exact same words three times already, you might give the mourner the opportunity to discuss the loss by looking at a different aspect of it. Ask questions: How did you meet? What kind of a baby was she? What did your mother like to do for fun? Answering these questions will be equally useful to the bereaved, who won't need to talk about this forever. But in the beginning, the need is both strong and natural. "Being there" means being with the mourner in the midst of grief—not on the opposite shore. Let the griever speak.

• **Let it be known that you are available—anytime.** Insomnia strikes many mourners, and often it is during those sleepless hours that they feel the most in need of human contact. "In a real dark night of the soul it is always three o'clock in the morning," wrote F. Scott Fitzgerald. Let the mourner know that, during those desperate moments, you won't mind getting a call. (However, if in fact it will make you crazy to hear the telephone ring in the middle of the night, don't offer.) Very few people will take you up on the offer—and if they do, it'll happen seldom. But to know that it's possible, to know that in their own dark night of the soul they can reach out to another human being, means a great deal.

• **Don't cross-examine mourners.** Don't barrage them with questions about specific aspects of the death, especially if they seem hesitant to discuss them. After his son died of cancer, Richard Haboush reported, "Some people wanted to know the exact details and specifics about his death—which I am unsure of myself even after talking with the doctor." Oliver Mann, whose daughter committed suicide, was also disturbed by constant queries. "Questions were very bothersome! If we knew the answers, our daughter would be alive."

Don't criticize the mourner's actions either. Ginger Curtis of Tulsa, Oklahoma, lost her two-month-old son, Ross, to sudden infant death syndrome (SIDS). "Just two weeks before, my husband had completed an industrial safety course that included infant CPR. But immediately upon hearing that he had tried to administer CPR to Ross, my sister-in-law said, 'That could be very dangerous. You could harm the baby.' " Maybe. Doesn't matter now, does it? So why say it? Don't add to the mourner's guilt or self-doubt.

• **Remember anniversaries.** Call. Visit. Send flowers, candy, or a note. And the same goes for holidays. Even mourners who reject social interaction much of the time probably don't want to be alone on Christmas or Thanksgiving. Extend the invitations—and not just the first year either.

• **Don't impose your ideas about how long grief ought to last.** Don't say, "Don't you think you should be over this by now?" Frequently, those remarks come from people who have not suffered the death of a loved one, and as a result may believe that grief takes considerably less time than it actually does. "It's been four months since my husband died, and as time goes on, people assume you are okay and gradually stop checking on you," said Vera Reagan. "Our society expects quick fixes and a going back to normalcy too soon." She's right. Most people are still in the thick of it four months later. Don't be impatient.

• **Don't utter clichés:** "This will make you stronger." Don't say, "They're better off this way" or "You'll get over it" or "Time heals all wounds." Most people will, indeed, feel better as time goes by, but these sorts of comments imply that they will get over the loss. They will not. Nor do they want to. They will incorporate their grief; they will manage their loss. But the loss will still matter to them, and they do not want to be told that it won't (even if that's not what you meant).

Avoid, too, the New Age nostrums, especially if you don't know how they will be received. Don't say, "She chose to leave the earth" or "He created his disease for a reason." Statements like those can create guilt and despair by suggesting that the deceased was unhappy. In short, do not impose your spiritual beliefs on other people. Stick with "I'm so sorry" and "What can I do?"

• **Do not compare.** Competitive mourning is a strange, "Queen for a Day" phenomenon whereby everyone competes for the worst story. It frequently happens in bereavement groups but it can occur anytime. One woman who lost a beloved grandmother and two close friends within a single year found herself frequently discussing the grieving process with a friend whose six-year-old nephew had died in a freak accident. To her irritation, the friend insisted on comparing griefs. "She subtly got it across to me—every time we talked—that her grief was worse than mine because her nephew was so young, and because she was there when he died. I think it's awful, what happened to her nephew, and I know she's in enormous pain about it, but I don't understand what she's getting out of this idea that her loss is somehow 'worse' than mine. It makes me feel completely discounted." If you have a story you want to share, do so. To suggest that one loss is worse than another—no matter how blatantly true that might appear to be—is to discount the nature of grief. Death is not a competition; we all lose in the end.

Similarly, do not diminish the grief a person is feeling by pointing out that things could be worse. Do not say that the bereaved should be grateful because the death was swift or the person was old. Age does not diminish grief. Do not say, "At least you only had him for a few months" or, as was said to me, "At least you had her for thirteen years." I wanted my child for the rest of my life. Do not say that other people have suffered more or that life is harder in Bangladesh. Comments like that only force mourners, at a moment when they may be suffering the worst loss of their entire lives, to agree with you that things aren't so bad. That may make you feel better. It makes them feel manipulated and unrecognized.

• **Do not make comments to the effect that the loved one can be replaced.** "You can have more children" is a comment that far too many grieving parents have had to grit their teeth through. And the same is true for "You'll marry again." Whatever happens in the future doesn't affect the loss that has occurred, which is the death of a singular, irreplaceable human being.

• **Do not say "I know just how you feel" if you have not experienced an equivalent loss.** Every relationship is unique, so no matter how deeply you may empathize with the pain, you probably do *not* know how they feel. Consider the complaint of one bereaved mother, Jennie Santos: "The majority of the people I talked to said they know how I feel. But they don't because they have not had a child murdered."

On the other hand, if you have suffered an equivalent loss, it's fine to say, "I share your pain." People respond well to that.

• **Don't disappear.** If you can't bear to be around a griever, send notes. "Thinking of you" means a lot. I remember looking out the window one day and there was my next-door neighbor Basil Schwan mowing my lawn. He never said one word about it to me, but I got the message. There are many ways to say, "I'm with you in this time of pain," and some of them are nonverbal.

Above all, remember that the reason being around a person who is recently bereaved can be so difficult is not that *they* aren't coping. It's upsetting because it stirs up our own terror of death. In summary, there's really only one rule you need to remember when a friend is in mourning: be compassionate.

CHAPTER 4 | Funerals and Mourning Customs

I wanted to dig my son's grave. They wouldn't let me. They used machines to do it. I would have had great satisfaction if I could have dug the grave.

—RAY TANGUAY

Our attitudes toward death and mourning have changed dramatically in the last two centuries. In the nineteenth century, people threw themselves into dramatic, impassioned mourning. They used parasols, handkerchiefs, stationery, and even tea sets designed exclusively for mourning; they wore mourning rings and pendants which might encase a lock of hair of the deceased. The excesses of the age can be seen most vividly in Queen Victoria, who mourned for her husband, Albert, nonstop from his death in 1861 to her own in 1901. For forty years, she put out his shaving supplies every morning and kept a picture of him propped up on his side of the bed. Nor was her extended mourning for Albert the only example of her sense of propriety about such matters. In 1859, when her great-grandmother died, Victoria was outraged to learn that one of her great-grandmother's descendants in the Prussian court was not dressed in mourning—despite the fact that the child was only five months old. Lilac and white, she suggested, were proper mourning colors for babies.

Black, of course, was the preferred color for adults, and especially for women, who unlike men were expected to be clad entirely in that color. During the first year, widow's weeds were made of dull black and accessorized with veils, hats, and "weeper cuffs." During the second year, shiny black, such as silk, was permitted. Afterward, one might gradually look toward other colors—beginning with white, also a color associated with mourning.

During this period, although there was much overt mourning, death was romanticized. Nineteenth-century novels are filled with tear-jerker scenes such as the deaths of Beth in *Little Women* and of Little Nell in Dickens' serialized novel *The Old Curiosity Shop*—an event which caused weeping crowds to gather in the port of New York avidly awaiting the next installment in the futile hope that Dickens wouldn't let her die.

In the twentieth century, there was a rebellion against the maudlin extreme of the Victorians. In its place, people embraced twentieth-century repression. In an essay originally published in 1955 and titled "The Pornography of Death," British anthropologist Geoffrey Gorer explained that, during the Victorian era, sex was unmentionable but "death was no mystery, except in the sense that death is always a mystery." By the middle of the twentieth century, it was the other way around. "Whereas copulation has become more and more 'mentionable,' particularly in the Anglo-Saxon societies, death had become more and more 'unmentionable,' " he wrote. Mourning costumes disappeared; houses were no longer draped in black; black mourning wreaths were no longer in fashion (in part because, on the day of the funeral, they provided an easy mark for burglars); death became a private affair.

Today, although a considerable movement is concerned with the process of conscious dying as a significant life experience, the prohibition against mourning remains. But turning away from mourning is ultimately as self-defeating as drowning in grief. The balanced way to travel through grief is to acknowledge its varied emotions. In many ways, that journey begins with the funeral.

The funeral is the first major event of the mourner's life without the deceased. More than an unhappy gathering, more than a formalized farewell, the funeral is the pivot between before and after. Like other rituals, it is a rite of passage that provides a framework for change. At the funeral, if at no other time, the awesome passage from life to death is seriously addressed. The funeral is a ceremony of separation that provides an opportunity to express strong feelings, to be recognized and comforted as a mourner, to say farewell with structure, solemnity, and support, and to realign ourselves with the community of mourners—the living. For all those reasons, the funeral or memorial service can help enormously in the process of grieving.

This is true even under the worst of circumstances, when death has come in an untimely and brutal fashion. Elizabeth Pearson is a Shakespearean actress whose brother Billy died in 1971 when he was in the armed forces. He was shot in the head at a military base, and the details of his death were never entirely clear:

My brother was a budding hippie, just getting into his own thoughts about the war. He should have been a conscientious objector. He was shot in the head, and they said it was suicide. But were his fingerprints on the gun? I don't even know. People I've spoken to since have said, "Your brother was fragged, shot by one of his own men. Without a doubt. Your brother got wasted." It was my mother's choice to have a military funeral and it astounded me because I felt it was the military that killed him. I was angry at the decision.

But in retrospect, I feel differently. There was protocol and that comforted me. Family and close friends sat in rows under a canopy and faced a brand-new aluminum coffin with a flag draped over it. There was a thirteen-gun salute. It was outrageously dramatic—which I think helped, first because there was no denying that this boy was dead, and second because I knew he was going to be properly laid to rest.

There's no way to know what elements of a funeral will make an emotional impact. The most reassuring aspect of a funeral may be the number of people who appear; it may be words said by the minister or rabbi or a eulogy spoken by a friend; or it may be a small, symbolic gesture that provides emotional release. That's something Lee Shelton noted after his eighty-year-old father was killed in an automobile crash:

I don't place a lot of credence in ritual. But at my father's funeral, one part of the ceremony did affect me. I went out of my way to toss the first bit of soil onto his coffin. Tossing that handful of soil onto the coffin was like the final good-bye. It brought everything into such focus at that moment but it was freeing thereafter.

At Cari's funeral, I was especially touched when her classmates filed past the casket and one by one placed a single rose on top. That gesture told me that her death would be mourned by many. Over three hundred people were there; my sorrow was shared. This is one of the great benefits of funerals: they place the death in a social context by giving us an opportunity to mourn together, and in so doing, they help us to feel less alone.

CULTURAL AND RELIGIOUS TRADITIONS

While death is universal, ways of dealing with it are as varied as the languages people speak and the ways they think. Some cultures, such as those of the Mediterranean, encourage strong emotional reactions at funerals; others favor the stiff upper lip. The Balinese, who are not known to cry at all, at least in public, actually encourage laughter at funerals by dropping the coffin into a creek—sometimes more than once. The Samoans have an extremely brief period of mourning, whereas in Greece, widows are expected to wear black for the rest of their lives. In Southeast Asia, emotional reactions are considered perfectly acceptable in public but in private grievers are expected to maintain some control. The English generally take the opposite approach. What feels natural to one group may seem deeply unnatural to another; what is meant to be comforting in one tradition may, in the context of another, appear disrespectful.

In the United States, styles of mourning vary widely. The funeral of a jazz musician in New Orleans with its syncopated parade resembles very little the subdued farewell given their loved ones by the Quakers of Pennsylvania. At the funeral and during the period of mourning that follows, a behavior considered utterly natural and important by one group, such as wearing black or visiting the grave, may strike another group as unnecessary. Among Afro-Americans, funerals are occasions for large family and community gatherings, and attendance is given enormous emphasis, even for distant relations. But after the funeral, according to research conducted in 1974 by David K. Reynolds and Richard A. Kalish comparing ethnic groups in the United States, Afro-Americans put the least emphasis on visiting the grave of a deceased spouse. Americans of Japanese and Mexican descent, on the other hand, overwhelmingly thought it was important to visit frequently.

Even within the context of a single ethnic heritage, patterns can vary markedly as families develop their own styles. Lisa Curran contrasted the ways the two sides of her family—both Irish Catholic—cope with death:

> I've heard wild stories about wakes from one side of my family. My great-grandfather owned a hotel that had a saloon and my Uncle Timmy told a story in which a dead body somehow ended up propped up in the saloon. You hear stories like that. As far as I know they never actually happened. But everyone drinks a lot and it becomes a party.
>
> On the other side of the family, the wakes are morbid, down-trodden, and depressing, filled with guilt and remorse. When my grandparents on that side of the family died, we stayed at the funeral home for several days. Since my Uncle Denny was a priest, everybody up to the bishop said the funeral mass. There were maybe fifteen people—definitely holier than thou.

The goal in every era and in every culture is the same: to provide a proper conclusion to a life and to begin the process of living without the deceased. Those tasks are generally considered to fall into the realm of religion. Whether the service takes place in a church, synagogue, or funeral home (as is increasingly the case), the solemnity of the proceedings, the religious trappings, and the presence of clergy underscore the gravity of the event.

Protestant customs vary, depending on the denomination. Generally, there is a brief service at the church or funeral home that includes a reading from the Bible, prayers, organ music, possibly the singing of hymns, and a funeral sermon or meditation. Selections of poetry or prose are sometimes read. The casket may be open or closed, depending on the denomination, and there may or may not be a eulogy. At the grave, there is a brief committal service. Afterward, as in other groups, people usually gather together for a meal.

In Catholicism, the rites ideally begin prior to death, when the dying person receives the final sacraments. (When death is sudden, the priest is permitted to give penance and extreme unction up to several hours after death.) The funeral itself is comprised of three parts: the wake, the funeral mass, and the graveside service. The wake, which occurs the night before the funeral, is conducted in the presence of the body, which is in an open casket. Held either in the funeral parlor or in the mourner's home, the wake service may include psalms, prayers, a rosary, and a short homily on the meaning of life, death, and resurrection. For many hours, friends and relatives come to offer condolences, to pray, and to view the body; indeed, the term "viewing" is sometimes used instead of "wake." The next day, there is a funeral or requiem mass. The coffin is closed and covered with a white pall upon which a cross might be placed. Holy water, incense, and candles accent the solemnity of the highly structured service, which emphasizes the concept of the new life the deceased has found with God.

After the funeral mass, the "final commendation and farewell" takes place either in church or at the grave site, which is blessed in advance. It used to be that the family would avoid watching the casket being lowered into the earth. Today, the tendency is to stay, so that the reality of the death cannot be denied.

In Judaism, burial takes place immediately—within twenty-four hours, if possible. The simple, wooden coffin is closed, and there are few flowers. At the funeral, which is a short one including prayers and a eulogy, members of the immediate family are given a black ribbon which is then cut to indicate their grief.

After the funeral, there is a brief service at the cemetery during which the casket is lowered into the ground and the mourners shovel dirt on it. "Shoveling the dirt is an incredibly healing thing to do. Although I would never require it, I encourage it very strongly because I find that the actual act of burying is the beginning of the acknowledgment that this horrible thing has happened and the world is forever different," states Rabbi Laura Geller, director of Hillel at the University of Southern California. Following the burial, friends and relatives gather for a traditional "meal of condolence."

Perhaps the most distinctive aspect of the Jewish tradition is not the funeral but the mourning period that follows, when mourners return home for seven days of "sitting shiva" (shiva means "seven"). Traditionally, they light a candle that burns for seven days, sit on wooden stools or benches, and receive visitors. All activities cease except for one: mourning.

The Islamic religion specifies five rituals concerning death: washing the body in a ceremonial manner; wrapping the entire body in clean, preferably white, cloth; prayer; the funeral itself, during which music and crying are forbidden; and burial. If possible, the body is buried directly in the ground, without a casket, and with the face turned toward Mecca. A stone, a few bricks, or some soil can be put under the head, but nothing else is permitted in the grave. Afterward, people bring food to the family.

According to Islam, there is one God, known as Allah, and many prophets, of whom Mohammed is the last. "Moslems believe Allah is all and He can decide when man has to live and when our life should be ended," states Abdal Mageed Nasouef, vice-coordinator of the Islamic Center in Los Angeles. Death is expected to be met with equanimity. Consequently, the mourning period is short. For a three-day period after the funeral, known as Azah, mourners accept condolences. After that, talking about the deceased with the mourners is not encouraged. "It is reminding him of his sadness," Nasouef explains. "So after three days, we should return to normal life." (The sole exception occurs when a husband dies, in which case the wife is expected to stay home for three months and ten days.) Mourners are not supposed to become so immersed in their grief that it distracts them from their relationship with God.

Buddhists and Hindus believe that life, death, and rebirth are part of the same continuum, waves on the ocean of existence. The body dies; consciousness remains. The traditional purpose of the funeral, which includes chanting, prayers, the reciting of sacred texts, and eulogies, is to help the deceased adjust to the after-death state and prepare for rebirth. At Buddhist funerals, the priest speaks directly to the deceased. The funeral is followed by a forty-nine-day period during which the person who died theoretically completes the journey from death to rebirth. During that time, mourners repeat prayers intended to ease the transition.

The philosophy and practices of Eastern religions have become increasingly attractive to Westerners during the last several decades. Ron Hammes, a Pennsylvania artist, spent a month at a Buddhist monastery after his wife, editor Tobi Sanders, died in a car crash. He told us about some of his experiences there:

> They offered a service for Tobi. There was an altar with a Buddha, flowers (which represent earth), water, incense (representing air), and fire. So it was quite beautiful. They also wrote a poem and gave it to me on a scroll with lovely calligraphy.
>
> One of the things I experienced at the monastery was, you can get support, but they don't soothe. If there is such a thing as the dark night of the soul, I've been through it. I could hardly speak. When I was sitting Zazen, I was in physical agony because the tendons in my legs were not used to sitting for two-hour stretches. The lesson was not to run from pain. It had an impact that carried me over. Not to be a born-again Buddhist, but it comes down to the fact that with every great religious mystic or searcher, whether it was the Buddha or whether it was Christ, at the heart of their teaching was their empathy for the suffering of mankind and their search, not for an escape from it, because there isn't an escape from it, but for a way to go beyond that. This is what sitting Zazen is all about in my life: not calm, not relaxation, but the issue of death, life, suffering. Beneath sitting is that issue. In sitting is the resolution.

BURIAL CUSTOMS

Throughout history, people have buried their dead in vastly different ways. Fifty thousand years ago, the Neanderthals rubbed the bodies of their dead with red ochre and buried them in the fetal position. The Egyptians mummified the deceased (including their dead cats) and, in the case of the pharaohs, erected the most elaborate and permanent tombs the world has ever seen. The Scandinavian Vikings put their dead on boats, set them afire, and sailed them out to sea. The Plains Indians placed the corpse on a high wooden platform or in the branches of a tree and only later buried the skeleton in a sacred burial ground. The impulse to treat the body in a special, ritualized way seems to be universal; but nothing else is. In some places in Europe where land is scarce, for instance, burial plots are not yours for eternity. They are temporary residences, and after a while, the bones are removed and the space is freed for someone else's use. If this sounds disturbing, it might be because we're not accustomed to the idea. Nikolas Stefanidis, Ph.D., a counselor at the Center for Living in West Hollywood, California, described his experience when he returned to his native Greece to pay his respects to his dead grandmother:

On the Greek island where I grew up, because of space limitations, we exhume the bones of the deceased. There's an interesting ritual that goes with it. They clean the bones with red wine and rosemary They count every bone and put them in a box with the person's name, the date of birth, and the date of death. Then they have a memorial service. And then you put the bones to rest in a communal mausoleum, a big building where all the bones are stored in boxes. Some people put pictures of the deceased on the boxes. When I went back to Greece, I went in and found my grandmother's skull, and I felt as if I had seen her again. It was a good experience.

For most people today, the choice is between burial and cremation. The chief benefit of burial, and it is an important one, is that it provides a safe place to mourn, a place that belongs to the deceased. "I visit my husband's grave every year on his birthday," said New Yorker Anna Shapiro. "I prune the shrub I planted there, and I clear away any weeds that might be growing, and I feel as if I am taking care of him. It's a connection—a physical connection." There can be great solace in that.

Cremation is the preferred mode in many cultures, including India, Japan, and England, where it has become so popular since the turn of the century that it now is the usual choice. In 1989, according to William Hocker, former president of the National Funeral Directors Association, cremation was chosen approximately 15 percent of the time in the United States—and in Southern California, one death in three results in cremation. What once seemed an exotic ritual is becoming commonplace.

Although cremation can be less expensive than burial, most people who choose cremation do so for deeply personal reasons that have little to do with cost. Some people, disturbed by the idea of the body gradually decomposing, as it does with burial, find cremation aesthetically less distressing. Cremation may also be appealing because of the many ways of dispensing the ashes. Although they may be kept in a cemetery vault known as a columbarium, they may also be scattered at sea or in a garden. The idea of the body being returned to the earth in this manner—possibly in a spot the deceased person loved—brings comfort to many people.

Cremation has drawbacks too. People sometimes hope that because cremation is so quick and final, it will shorten the grieving process. It will not. Another difficulty can arise when the remains are not kept in a special spot. When they are scattered over a large area, there is no marker, no plaque, nothing—now or ever.

For that reason, the final resting place should be chosen with care. There's nothing wrong with the ocean, but if it doesn't have personal associations for you, the situation of "no place to go" may prove disturbing. Choosing an accessible spot can alleviate that problem. Solomon

Berg buried his son's ashes among the trees and bushes in his front yard and then marked the spot with a statue tucked in among the foliage. Marcy De Jesus buried her husband's remains in the backyard, where I helped her plant an olive tree. And more people than you might expect keep the ashes inside the house, at least for a while. Sara and Paul Grisanti put the tiny box containing their baby's ashes in the large closet that their older children had excitedly transformed into a brightly colored nursery—a room the baby never saw. Joni Schaap put her son's remains on the mantel in the living room, where it is surrounded by athletic trophies and pictures of the blond teenager. The urge to create a spot devoted solely to the deceased is a deeply human one. In Japan, mourners of the Buddhist and Shinto religions typically create household altars that include the ashes and photographs of the deceased along with other objects such as rice and flowers. Cremation not only permits a wide choice of location, it also allows the mourners to create that spot in a variety of ways when they're ready. With a sudden death in particular, that can be a benefit.

Many people, including myself, like the idea of donating organs to people who require transplants. I was unable to do so with Cari because her body had been so seriously injured that it was impossible, and in any case, it didn't occur to me to ask until almost twelve hours after she died. By then, it was too late. Organs need to be harvested (yes, that's the word they use) immediately.

Finally, there is the option of donating the body to "science." That, too, is a decision that must be made quickly—and generally with the knowledge that it was what the deceased wanted. As a rule, when the body is donated to a school or research facility, mourners hold a memorial service without the body rather than a funeral. But it is also possible to have a funeral in the presence of the body if the funeral director is immediately notified the body has been donated. The undertaker can then prepare the body in the manner specified by the institution, and after the funeral, it will be sent there.

THE CASKET: OPEN OR CLOSED?

Another question that may arise is whether to have an open or a closed casket. Experts in the field of death and dying almost universally favor open casket. "There's a real catharsis involved, a kind of release," said William Hocker. "After the first time they see the body, the tension is broken and it's very therapeutic. With some people, it's not helpful. It has to do with personality differences. But overwhelmingly, I would say it's better for a person to see."

The reason to see the body is *not* that it will make you feel better. It certainly did not make me feel better to see my daughter in a casket. But it did help me to accept the finality of her death. Seeing the body will not stop mourners from yearning for their loved one or dreaming that the deceased is still alive. But with an open casket, grievers are less likely to harbor fantasies involving mistaken identity or loved ones wandering around with amnesia. Seeing the body dispels any lingering doubts, for no matter how skilled the undertaker is with makeup and wax, when you see the body, you know. A person you love is dead. That's the reality.

Some people worry that seeing the body will be a horrible experience; they want to remember the deceased as vibrant and healthy and they are afraid that the positive images will be obliterated by the final vision. But often, the way the body looks in the casket can actually be an improvement over how the person looked while ill. Nurse thanatologist Sherry Gibson of Louisville, Kentucky, described her experience when her mother died:

> When my mother died, she was forty-two years old and I was twenty-six. I took care of her through her illness. She was a very beautiful woman, a very proud woman, and when she was in the hospital, she had tubes everywhere. She lost all dignity and she lost so much weight and looked terrible. I was in the medical profession and knew all about that kind of stuff, but it was awful for that to be the last image of my mother in my mind.
>
> I couldn't believe it when I went to the funeral home. She looked so good. That was the woman I remember. No, it wasn't the same. Dead is dead and there is no way that a dead body looks like it is alive. But she certainly looked better than she looked when I left her at the hospital the night she died. And that was so comforting to me.

Seeing the body provides a final opportunity to gaze at the face of the person you love, to touch them, to say good-bye in their presence. It can also bring a great sense of relief because at last the person looks at peace. Bookseller Diane J. Williams of Venice, California, spent many nights in the hospital with her eight-year-old cousin who was dying of cancer. She describes her regret at not seeing her cousin's body after death:

> Lauren had been puffy and she had no hair and she looked awful, but as she approached death, she got her eyelashes back and then she got thin again and her hair grew back jet-black and curly—a different color, a different texture. She looked luminous, beautiful, and perfect. But she was full of rage and

you could read her pain in her face. After she died, my aunt said it was the most extraordinary thing: her whole body relaxed and there was no pain and her face was clear. I'm so sorry I didn't see her.

Seeing the body doesn't have to occur at the funeral. Indeed, many religions oppose open-casket funerals. Many people today are terrified by the thought of seeing, no less touching, a dead body. But keep in mind that throughout most of history, people died at home, and family members would have naturally seen the person after death. Seeing the body, whether it's in a casket or on the deathbed, can provide both a jolt of reality and a degree of acceptance. It won't be a wonderful moment, but in the months and years to come, it usually proves to be beneficial.

It also used to be customary for mourners to dress the body. Although this is much less common today, it does occur. When my mother died, her friend Dotty Ward, who is a nurse (and hence was not afraid of the body), wanted to dress her and brush her hair. Many parents whose infants have died have found solace in dressing their dead child for the burial. And within traditional Judaism, there is a special group called the Hevra Kadisha whose function is to prepare the body for burial. Rabbi Geller explains, "The notion of a mortuary that you just send the body to is not an essential part of Jewish tradition. You would volunteer to be a member of the Hevra Kadisha society, and your job would be to wash the body of dead people in a ritualized way. The body is covered so that only the part that's being washed is uncovered. It's very respectful of the body. I read an article in a magazine called *Lilith* by a nontraditional woman who joined the Hevra Kadisha of her nontraditional synagogue, and she talks about what an incredibly important experience and privilege it is to prepare a body to be buried."

THE CONTEMPORARY FUNERAL

The primary trend in funerals today is toward personalization. People want funerals that reflect the life of the departed. In the past, that hasn't always happened. In a survey conducted in the 1960s among 169 Protestant ministers of various denominations, only 39 percent actually referred to the deceased by name during the funeral services, according to Paul Irion, author of *Funeral: Vestige or Value?* In many funerals, the lofty questions of life and death and life after death may have been addressed, but the person lying there in the casket was barely mentioned. The funeral may have succeeded as a staged ritual, but as a ceremony meant to comfort the mourners and to put the life of the deceased into a context, it failed miserably. (The same might be said for a bizarre recent invention: the drive-in funeral. You pay your respects to the deceased without having to unbuckle your safety belt.)

Depersonalizing death makes it easier for everyone except the mourners to bear. Even the clergy—who may never have met the deceased or the family of the deceased—may find it far easier to preach about death in some grand theoretical sense than to think about an actual human being whose life is over. "The first time I dealt with a person who was grieving, I was a deacon fresh out of school and I felt unprepared," said the venerable Hartshorn Murphy, Jr., of the Episcopal Archdiocese of Los Angeles. "Many of us cope with that situation by hiding behind prayers. In one respect, it's healthy, in that it tries to put death in a larger picture. In another way, it's hiding. I would put on this aura of the priest and so was untouched by the pain."

For mourners, that pain is unavoidably present. Personalizing the funeral or being involved in its planning can offer a way to assuage some of that pain by doing something for the deceased. Being involved facilitates mourning by turning the grieving into an active rather than a passive process.

However, many mourners are far too grief-stricken at the time of the funeral to do anything at all. Getting dressed is hard; walking to the front door is hard; saying "hello" is hard. Fortunately, there are many small ways of personalizing the service. Choosing your own music has that effect. My father loved the big-band music of the forties and fifties, and that's what we played at his funeral. Reading from a favorite book can also turn a standard service into something intimate and moving. At Cari's funeral, we read from The Little Prince. Other mourners have chosen selections ranging from T. S. Eliot's Four Quartets to poetry written by the deceased.

Having a eulogy is an excellent way to make sure the deceased is reflected in the service. "It's important to talk about the person," states Archdeacon Murphy. "We didn't used to do eulogies. That's changing. People want to mark the life that has passed."

Mourners often feel incapable of giving a eulogy themselves, which is one reason why most of the time, the clergy does it. But you might ask a friend or relative, someone who had a real relationship with the deceased, to speak a few words. Those personal reminiscences are good to hear at that time. If it's possible, you might speak a few words yourself, as Diane J. Williams did at her cousin's funeral:

> On the day she died, Lauren's parents asked me to speak. It scared me—I've never spoken like that before. I talked about how Lauren and I became friends over a box of crayons and

how she liked gruesome movies, and everyone laughed. I talked about the three days Lauren and I spent together when my brother got married.

I was glad I spoke because most of the time, nobody wants to hear you talk about someone who's dead. It was a relief to say, this is why I loved her, this is why I'm going to miss her so much. Afterward, there was an awkward space and then people started coming up and introducing themselves to me and thanking me. It made me feel good.

At many funerals today, friends and family members are invited to share anecdotes about the deceased. The picture that emerges can be tremendously moving.

Another way to personalize the service is to incorporate photographs into the surroundings, possibly by placing them around the funeral chapel or at the grave site during the burial service. Or set up a memorabilia table filled with photographs and objects reminiscent of the deceased— things that can help the living find ways to talk about the dead.

Technology has also affected the funeral industry, and some may be surprised that its impact has been both positive and personal. When my friend Carol Shamhart's husband, Val Humphreys, died of cancer, she played a cassette tape in which he talked about his impending death. I hardly knew the man, but I sobbed, as did everyone else.

Video displays are another recent innovation. "A video screen is placed in front of the funeral chapel," states William Hocker. "Pictures of the person who died, beginning with their youth and continuing through their marriage and into their old age, are flashed on the screen interspersed with scenes from the person's area or his state. Nothing is said but music is played. It can be terribly touching and beautiful."

Probably the most creative funerals are those held for people whose deaths were anticipated, allowing the dying person to make special requests and the mourners to plan a personalized funeral. In some cases, the requests are very small. For instance, Harry Rosenzweig, who was chairman of the Republican Party in Arizona for over fifteen years, was surprised when he read his wife Sandy's will after she died. "She had picked out eight very close women friends to be her pallbearers," he said. "The mortician said he's never seen that."

Occasionally, people are extraordinarily inventive. Shortly before his own death, Los Angeles artist Benjamin Cole attended the funeral of a close friend in New Orleans who died of AIDS: "He was cremated. His friend Emily mixed his ashes with glitter and confetti and everyone got a small box. Then they had a parade to the Mississippi River and they threw him in." It's certainly not a traditional service; but because it reflects so much about the deceased, it must have been incredibly moving. And surely those who participated must have felt both connected to the deceased and bound to each other.

MEMORIAL SERVICES

Many cultures, recognizing how agonizing the first few weeks of mourning are, also hold another ceremony a few weeks after the funeral. Traditionally, for example, the Greek Orthodox have a forty-day ceremony, as do many Muslims. Catholicism marks the first thirty days with a "Month's Mind Mass," although those are not as prevalent as they once were. Our discomfort with death has caused us to turn away from many of the religious observances that traditionally provided a structure for grieving and a way of releasing some of those feelings.

Secular memorial services, however, often accomplish the same goal of recognizing that initial period. Weeks or even months after the funeral, these services provide additional opportunities to make personal gestures, to acknowledge the loss, and to connect with other mourners. "I went to a memorial service for Sam Peckinpah," states actress Mariette Hartley. "Jason Robards and I had never met before, and we sobbed in each other's arms. It was an extension of our lives. Memorial services are vitally important because you're surrounded by friends, and words are spoken, and you can say good-bye with witnesses."

Because memorial services are less rigidly structured than funerals, they can be created in a form the deceased might have appreciated. When twenty-nine-year-old Benjamin Cole died of AIDS, his bereaved friends held a memorial for him. One of them told us about that event:

> I attended a party for Benjamin. It was difficult because people were drunk and emotional and weeping. The best part was that a friend of his made an incredible altar, covered with mirrors and candles and, in the middle, Ben's hand-painted jeans jacket. People were asked to bring photographs and items that belonged to him and to place them on the altar. When we left, we were each invited to take something as a memento.

Memorial services can be small gatherings at which people simply share memories. "I attended a memorial service for an art teacher who had very devoted students," a Los Angeles biographer said. "A former student, a colleague, a childhood friend—an old man he grew up with —and his wife all spoke. His recent artwork had been hung on the walls, and there was a strong sense of completion and wholeness about them.

The service really was a celebration of his life." Hearing that story reminded me of the one regret we had at my father's funeral, which was that we hadn't displayed his photographs. He was a wonderful photographer. It would have been nice to see his pictures at the funeral, and I believe he would have liked the gesture.

When the deceased had a very wide network of friends and acquaintances, memorial services can provide a more public kind of mourning. A few months after his wife died, Ron Hammes received a call from the publishing house where she had worked, asking him to take part in planning a memorial service:

> I arranged for a service to be held at Barnard College, where Tobi went to school. She was very fond of Barnard. Trying to do it in the style she would have liked, I had it catered with lots of her favorite foods. I ordered champagne and caviar. I got in touch with a young woman from the Manhattan School of Music who came and played all the wonderful songs from the sixties that Tobi loved so much. There were a few speakers, including representatives from Barnard and Bantam, a friend of Tobi's who has since died of AIDS, and Tobi's writing teacher, Joy Chu, who died only a month or two later, and Tobi's sister. I made a toast to Tobi's life. Over three hundred people were there, which I felt was a wonderful tribute to Tobi. People wanted to know what to do, and I asked that contributions be made to the American Foundation for AIDS Research. That was the way she would have wanted it.

ANNIVERSARY RITUALS

The first anniversary of the death is recognized as important in many cultures. The loss is still so fresh, the grief so strong. Yet the desire to move away from grieving and into the enjoyment of life is also present. For that reason, the end of the first year is often marked by a ritual observance of some kind.

Among Western religions, Judaism is most specific in its guidelines for mourning. Each day during the first years, mourners recite the Kaddish, a prayer in praise of life. On the anniversary, known as Yahrzeit, a candle is lit and the Kaddish is said. Afterward, it is no longer spoken daily. "The folk tradition is that the soul now finds peace," Rabbi Laura Geller explains. "Another way to see it is that the soul needs you to let go of it. It's not just for the mourners that there needs to be a time when mourning is less intense, but for the dead person as well." From then on, Kaddish is spoken only on certain high holy days and on the anniversary—for the rest of your life. "As long as you're alive to say Kaddish, you're effectively saying in a ritual way that this relationship continues," Rabbi Geller states. "It's different now, but it never ends."

The first anniversary isn't the only one that hurts. "Grief returns with the revolving year," wrote the poet Percy Bysshe Shelley, and he didn't just mean the first year; it happens every year for a long, long time. That's why many cultures and religions set aside one day in the year when mourners can take special note of the losses they have suffered. In Judaism, special services accompany Yom Kippur, the Day of Atonement, the most important day in the Jewish year. In Catholicism, on All Souls' Day, November 2, the names of those who have died are read aloud and mourners light candles. Possibly the most extensive yearly ritual is a variation of All Souls' Day: the Mexican Day of the Dead. Prior to the actual day, people create altars at home featuring photographs, flowers, cakes, candles, and the favorite foods of the deceased. *Memento mori*, including little toy skeletons doing everything from playing in mariachi bands to getting married, are ubiquitous. On the Day of the Dead, people spend the night at the cemetery, dancing, eating, drinking, and offering candy skulls and coffins to their dead relatives and friends. The idea is not to dwell on death in a morbid way but to demystify it, to allow mourners to think about death in a general way, to remember the particular deaths in their own lives, to grieve, and to move on.

Those ritual acknowledgments serve the psychological purpose of recognizing the continued grief that mourners may feel. Those feelings are most likely to arise on the anniversary: the anniversary syndrome can even affect people who do not consciously remember the date. Some years are more difficult than others. One year when I was feeling particularly sad about Cari and was far from the cemetery where she is buried, my friend Michael Bissonnette and I bought a bouquet of roses, walked to the beach, and tossed them into the ocean. Symbolic gestures like that can provide powerful release and a great deal of comfort that goes beyond what you might gain from crying on your bed (although that's also something you should allow yourself to do). By acting on your sorrow, you begin to release it.

CHAPTER 5 | Sudden Death

My brother died in an automobile accident and my mother died of cancer two and a half years later. I always thought her death would be a sorrow I couldn't live with. I now know that the unexpected tragedy takes a far greater toll on the family.

—RAE ECKLUND

Nothing so determines the way we deal with grief as the suddenness of the death. Those who experience a sudden death have no time to say good-bye or I love you, no time to resolve unfinished business, to prepare for life without the loved one, or even to imagine it. The bereaved are utterly shocked. And that shock takes a long time to get over.

When death comes without warning, grieving is slow and difficult—as people who have experienced both sudden death and anticipated death have noted to us many times. Rachel Ballon's father died suddenly; her mother died eighteen years later after a lingering illness. "My father was driving in the little town where we lived in Pennsylvania. He must have felt a heart attack coming on because he pulled over in the middle of the town square and died. And that was very, very bad because there was no preparation, there were no good-byes, there was no closure. The grief was very intense and painful because it was a slow letting go. With my mother, each of us had time to say good-bye. It's easier when you know."

The pain of losing someone you love quickly is not ultimately greater than the pain of losing someone slowly. But the shock is so strong that it makes it more difficult to adapt. For instance, research indicates that mothers who have lost a baby to sudden infant death syndrome have difficulty getting pregnant afterward. And a Harvard University study comparing women under the age of forty-five whose husbands died after a prolonged illness with a similar group whose husbands died without warning found that the "sudden widows" felt more anxious, guilty, and depressed than those whose husbands died an anticipated death. They also took significantly longer to remarry. Two or three years after the death, thirteen out of the twenty anticipated widows had found a new partner. But of the twenty-two sudden widows, not one had remarried.

Davida Singer, a writer who grew up in Vermont and now lives in New York City, was a young teenager when her father died:

> The day my father died I had a cold, but I wasn't really sick. I wanted to stay out of school a day longer, but it wasn't easy to fake it because he was a doctor. So I pretended to be asleep when he came in that morning to check on me before he went to work. I kept my eyes closed, and I remember him feeling my head and kissing me good-bye and telling my mother that I was all right. And then he left.
>
> A little later, I heard my mother on the phone shrieking and saying, "I'll be there right away." It was something about my father, and from that point on, I knew something was very wrong. A little later, I turned on the radio and found out that my father, who was a prominent physician in Burlington, had been brought into the hospital in an ambulance and that he died. That's how I heard. I was home, and I was alone, and they announced it on the radio.
>
> I ran around and around like in the children's story with the tiger and the butter, *Little Black Sambo*. I ran from living room to kitchen, around and around and around and around, and the radio was on. How long I did that, I don't know. The next thing I remember was my mother, the rabbi, and the undertaker walking up the driveway, looking like the picture of death: pale white faces. That was my rational proof that it had really happened.
>
> At the funeral, I was given the black ribbon, the torn ribbon: for close to a year I wore that thing in school. Maybe it was a way to convince myself that this really happened. Someone who lost a father: this ribbon means that! I felt like I was in a play. I was going in and out of my sense of loss and grief and playacting. It would be real and then it would be clouded over. For a long time, whenever I told the story, it *sounded* like I was telling a story. It was as if it hadn't happened to me.

The sensation of watching yourself is a classic sign of shock. As the immediate shock wears off, a residue of numbness can remain. That feeling temporarily shields mourners from the avalanche of feelings, allowing them to function, even to be active. As that barrier crumbles, grievers feel battered by a tempest of powerful emotions. With sudden death, those feelings can linger for a long time. How long is a question psychologists have not answered. Erich Lindemann, in an influential article written in 1944 after the famous Cocoanut Grove nightclub fire in Florida, suggested that with psychiatric help, an ordinary grief reaction could generally be "settled" in four to six weeks. In contrast, recent research conducted by Darrin R. Lehman, Camille B. Wortman, and Allan F. Williams, indicates that, four to seven years after the death of a spouse or a child in an automobile crash, at least a third of the mourners they studied were still depressed and suffering the aftereffects of the death. Their data clearly suggested that lasting distress after the traumatic death of a spouse or child is neither unusual nor a sign of failure to cope, as many people believe.

Many people in the early stages of grief focus on things they wish they'd done differently. Regret takes over; sad scenes from the past cloud the mind. It's important to address some of the unfinished business that undoubtedly exists between you and your loved one. It's also important during that time to allow yourself to experience grief in all its permutations. Feeling sad, hopeless, moody, lonely, obsessed, irritable, discouraged, afraid, depressed, angry, and guilty is part of the package.

It helps to remember moments of love, even though those memories may bring some pain. I remember I kept thinking back to Cari's last words to me when I said I loved her: "Oh, Mother, don't be so mushy." At first, recalling those words brought both tears and a smile. Today, they only bring a smile.

But it takes time for that to happen. The best thing you can do in the meantime is to ignore anyone else's expectations about how you should grieve and how long it should take.

Being busy can provide a constructive and positive distraction from the work of grief, but when it gets out of hand, it can also be a way to avoid grieving. I emphasize this because, as noted earlier in this book, I submerged many feelings through my involvement with MADD after Cari died. Since then, I've seen many other people using activity instead of really grieving. It often happens in movements such as MADD but it can happen to anyone. Like me, people who do this generally don't recognize the process; on the contrary, they frequently think they are coping quite competently. They may even be pleased with themselves for maintaining control, for not allowing themselves to be overwhelmed. However, being overwhelmed is an appropriate reaction when someone you love dies. If you avoid those feelings, all you do is delay the mourning. After Davida Singer's father died of a heart attack, she threw herself into schoolwork and social life. She didn't think she was putting her grieving on hold; I didn't think I was either. But four years later, she was overcome by emotions:

> In high school I became a super-achiever. I ended up with every award in the book, from editor of the literary magazine and lead in the senior play to couple of the year with my boyfriend. Four years later, it all fell apart. What happened was a delayed reaction—depression—to my father's death. I felt terribly guilty about pretending to be asleep the day my father died. I felt abandoned. I began to realize I was angry at him too. He wasn't all-knowing, all-being, all-strong. He left us no insurance! He had the audacity to believe that he wasn't going to die and nothing would happen to his family; for a professional person to leave his family completely untaken care of was a foolhardy, immature thing to do. I saw my mother suffer tremendously because of it. He set her up for a difficult future. I know it wasn't malicious, but it was arrogant and inconsiderate. I don't think I could have said that years ago and still say I loved him.

Many people who have felt shattered by a sudden death cannot imagine adjusting to the loss. But people do adjust. As they grieve, they change. Many become stronger, wiser, more fully themselves, more able to cope. It's a slow process but a real one. The most important factor may be the belief that you will one day be able to live happily, despite your loss. That attitude—and the knowledge that other mourners have survived in similar situations—can help even in the harshest of circumstances, such as multiple deaths. Harlene Marshall, for instance, is a forty-three-year-old California record producer whose fifteen-year-old son, Matthew, was hit head-on by a drunk driver in 1985. It was only the first of her losses:

> Matthew died instantly. My husband and I clung to each other in shock. My daughter Rebecca screamed for five minutes after I told her and then adjusted quite well. I felt horror, disorientation, numbness, disbelief, yearning, despair. Yet along with all that, I also had a sometimes unfortunate conviction that I would survive whether I wanted to or not.
>
> Five months after Matthew died, my husband and I were playing tennis and he had ventricular fibrillations and died. My family was ripped in half.
>
> I cried every day for the first year and a half, literally. Four years later, the sadness, yearning, and depression come and go

but I'm basically quite well adjusted. My sense of humor has gotten me through everything. Even if I were crying, I'd come out of it laughing. I get angry at being left alone, at the pain I used to imagine Matthew suffered in the crash. I agonize over those things but it doesn't occur to me to be bitter. There's a lot of good in my life except for the fact that I lost my husband and son. Everything's wonderful except that they're dead. Sometimes I remember and feel terrible; sometimes I can remember with fondness and humor. I still feel myself improving, reaching new levels of feeling good. I've changed and grown and seen things, and I'm thankful for that. I've acquired a respect for myself and what I've done.

WHEN DEATH SEEMS SUDDEN . . . BUT IT ISN'T

"My father died so suddenly. He went into the hospital and three weeks later he was dead. We had no warning at all!" exclaimed a teacher in her mid-thirties. But wait a minute! What about those three weeks in the hospital? To those of us whose loved ones have died in an instant, with nary a shadow of ill health on the horizon, three weeks of warning may sound like blessed preparation, a virtual gift. But it doesn't work that way—as a woman Nancy and I spoke with realized after a friend of hers died of AIDS:

> Kevin had been in and out of the hospital repeatedly. He had lesions on his skin and was extremely skinny. I watched him change. When I met him, he was a robust bicycle rider. But those last few months, he moved liked an old man. I knew he was going to die. But when it happened, I was stunned. I guess I had imagined that he'd die that summer or that fall. I was completely unprepared for him to die in February. It was too soon!

Knowing someone is sick, even with a life-threatening illness, is not the same as thinking that person is going to die. There are remissions; there are recoveries; there is hope. So the notion of "sudden" is a slippery one.

I learned that when my mother died. My father had always been the one who was ill, and although my mother smoked a lot, we always expected him to die first. A month after my son, Travis, was run over by a car, in the spring of 1975, my mother entered the hospital for surgery for diverticulosis. Because we were so worried about Travis, she wanted to postpone the surgery, as she had been doing for a number of years. She was afraid that once she entered the hospital she would never leave. But her stomach problems became so bad she had no choice.

Her improvement after the surgery was slow. There was talk of doing a colostomy. She gave up smoking. And then she suffered a heart attack. It never occurred to me that her prediction would come true and that in fact she would not leave the hospital alive. But that is exactly what happened. Even though she had been in the hospital for a while, it felt very sudden to us; the word "terminal" had never been spoken. Everything was supposed to be routine. When she died, I was shocked.

So when I hear people whose loved ones died after weeks of hospitalization or of slow, progressive diseases talk about sudden death, I don't argue with them. In their minds, the beloved person died suddenly. They had not imagined the death and they were unprepared for it. Call it denial. Call it optimism. If a death feels shocking and sudden to you, that's all that matters.

LOOKING FOR ANSWERS

Sudden death shatters our conception of the world. Many people feel an insistent hunger for understanding. Why did this happen? By seeking explanations, whether practical or spiritual, we attempt to reduce the terror of the loss and to reach some inner resolution about it. We attempt, in short, to make sense of the world.

Many people address that need by learning everything they can about the specifics of the death. How high was the cholesterol count? Exactly where was the stop sign at that intersection? Other people can't stop worrying about the loved one: Did he suffer? Was she terrified? Repetitively going over these thoughts can be irritating to others, but it serves a purpose: eventually, it makes the tragedy real. The more shocking and unexpected the death was, the more strongly mourners may need to do that.

Many people become preoccupied with everything that happened in the last few days before the death. They look for omens, portents, small signs that foreshadowed the death. For instance, after Solomon Berg's son died in a freak fire, Solomon found himself remembering the phone call he had had with his son the night before he died. "Usually, our phone calls were short—maybe ten minutes. This was a long, rambling call, all about himself, about us. If I were superstitious, I would say that somebody was telling me, this is the last you're ever going to hear from him."

Like many other people, he unconsciously sought a way to make the death part of a pattern. Sudden death feels meaningless and frightening, whereas in a pattern, no matter how subtle, there is comfort.

"I can list a hundred reasons why I believe—mostly in retrospect—that my son knew at some level that his life would be very short," a bereaved mother said. Many people find comfort and meaning in such interpretation. It allows them to restore some order to a world turned upside down. The impulse is the same one we see in Shakespeare's tragedies, where the inevitable deaths are always followed at the last by a hopeful restoration of order. Many mourners seek to move beyond the chaotic disorder of their personal tragedies by restoring order to the world. An explanation, whether it be biological, mechanical, or spiritual, for the death accomplishes this goal.

ACCIDENTS AND CAR CRASHES

Sudden death is *always* traumatic. But learning to cope with preventable tragedies such as automobile accidents is a particularly grim challenge —one that many people are faced with every year.

In 1986 accidents were responsible for the deaths of 95,227 people— more than one and a half times the number of Americans who died during the entire war in Vietnam. Of those people, slightly over half— 47,865 to be precise—died in car crashes. Motor vehicle accidents are the fourth leading cause of death in the United States. Every one of those deaths is needless. And every one leaves a legacy of grief that can take years to resolve.

Part of that legacy is obsession with the manner of death. MADD is by no means the only culprit in this area. Many in the victims' movement are fixated on the way their loved one died. One MADD chapter has even gone so far as to place flags at the grave site depicting a drunk-driving death. Drunk driving is a horrible thing. But so is heart disease. So is cancer. As normal as it is to think about and even do research on the manner of death, mourners who focus all their attention there run the risk of getting stuck in a single aspect of the grieving process.

Fear is another part of the legacy of accidents and car crashes, particularly when that death comes about through ordinary circumstances. After all, if it is possible to be killed while walking to a church carnival, anything seems possible. It's hard to feel safe in this world. Feelings of panic, anxiety, insecurity, helplessness, or a disturbing sense of vulnerability are common.

Anger is also part of that heritage, especially when death comes about as the result of another person's actions. When Cari was killed, the hatred and blame that I felt were not directed solely toward Clarence William Busch, the drunk driver who hit my daughter. I hated everyone in his environment who permitted that man—a convicted drunk driver—to get behind the wheel of a car. And I hated the criminal justice system that had repeatedly done little or nothing to prevent him from drinking and driving again. Other people I came to know through MADD felt similarly. But no matter how normal those feelings are, it's important that they not be allowed to overwhelm the other aspects of grief.

As stated earlier, many mourners also blame themselves. It comes in the form of the "if only" syndrome: if only a single variable had been different, the death would not have occurred. People feel guilty even when it's hard to imagine *what* they could have done. But then logic has little to do with the feelings. Eva Petersen is a Pacific Northwest chef whose first husband died suddenly:

> I was twenty-five when I was widowed the first time. It was an accidental death. My husband had a new gun and he went to shoot it at a firing range and it misfired and blew apart. I felt overwhelming guilt because I wasn't there. If only I had been with him, maybe this wouldn't have happened. Maybe I could have done something.

But what? Short of convincing him not to use the gun at all, there is not a thing she could have done. The urge to control, to keep our loved ones from danger, is an understandable one; and in the aftermath of a death, many people fantasize that they could have prevented the death. By thinking that way, they decrease the feeling of total powerlessness that death brings—and they increase the feelings of guilt. Fortunately, in Eva's case, she was forewarned about guilt and other emotional reactions. "The minister told me that these feelings would overwhelm me. He alerted me to them so that when they came, I wasn't knocked down."

Unfortunately, no one can predict when those feelings may surface. I felt anger almost immediately. On the other hand, when Joan Conley's twenty-one-year-old son, Kirk, died in a drunk-driving crash in Tennessee, it wasn't until a couple of months later that Joan felt that rush of rage:

> Kirk and a friend stopped at two different bars, and on their way home, they hit a guardrail and a bridge abutment and the car overturned in the middle of the road. Kirk supposedly died instantly. The driver of the car had a small laceration on his hand.

Anger hit heavily when only a DUI [driving under the influence] charge was made against the driver. Three months to the day after the crash, the young man responsible for it called and asked me to lunch. He acted as if he didn't remember what happened three months prior. Almost a year after Kirk's death, he was charged with vehicular homicide. I still feel some resentment against the system, which did not punish the driver until we pursued the case. And I get very angry at the people who do not view this crime as a violent criminal act.

Particularly in the case of drunk driving, other people sometimes find it difficult to understand that anger. Most people intend to be sympathetic, but strangely enough, many times friends and relatives relate to the driver rather than the victim. One of my close friends came over after Cari died. I'll never forget his words. He said, "My God, that could have been me that killed your child." You don't hear that with other forms of murder. In those situations, no one would dream of making such a statement—certainly not to the mother of the victim!

The fear, rage, guilt, and sorrow that trail in the wake of a tragedy of this sort can permanently alter your inner emotional structure. Traumatic, ugly images crowd the mind. It feels like a blow from which you'll never recover.

But you will. You won't be the same. Nonetheless, you will gradually find new paths to happiness, ways to live in the world without your loved one. One way to find strength is through combating the problem. If there is a court case, monitoring it can reduce feelings of helplessness. When his wife's sister and her husband were killed in a drunk-driving crash, Robert Plunk, president of Preferred Risk Mutual Insurance Company in Des Moines, Iowa, became involved in MADD. "Stan and I were high school friends who married sisters. When they were killed, I wanted to do something. We followed the court proceedings and saw to it that the drunk driver received the maximum sentence. We kept the pressure on."

With violent death in particular, helping others has a surprisingly salutary effect. It gives purpose to life and restores a sense of personal power. "I began to feel better when I knew I could help others who had suffered the same tragedy," Joan Conley said. "I'm a more courageous, empathetic, and compassionate person than I was before. Most of all, I'm much more self-confident. Today, I feel I'm a survivor who will not allow myself to be victimized again and again. I know I can survive anything."

I feel the same way.

SUICIDE

Every year, over thirty thousand Americans that we know of kill themselves. Suicide is far more common than people realize—more common even than death due to cirrhosis of the liver, which can in turn be considered a slow form of suicide. (It is interesting to note that even apart from drinking themselves to death, alcoholics have a higher suicide rate than nonalcoholics.) In the population as a whole, suicide is the eighth leading cause of death. About half of the people who kill themselves each year are adults—primarily white males—between the ages of twenty-five and fifty-four. A third of all suicides are those fifty-five and over. The remainder are under twenty-four. It is not true, then, that most suicides are teenagers. But it is true that suicide is disturbingly common among the young. After accidents and homicide, suicide is the third leading cause of death for people between fifteen and twenty-four.

Of all varieties of mourning, coping with suicide is possibly the most complicated. The initial trauma has been compared to posttraumatic stress syndrome—the stress suffered by veterans of combat. In other words, people whose loved ones have committed suicide are shell-shocked. This is especially true if they discovered the body, as Mariette Hartley, who played the lead in my television movie *Mothers Against Drunk Driving: The Candy Lightner Story*, did after her father's suicide in 1963:

> It was such a violent unexpected death. I was living with my parents and beginning to work as an actress. I did a major film, *Ride the High Country*, which was one of Sam Peckinpah's first movies. It's become a classic. I got brilliant, Meryl Streep type reviews. At the same time, my father was going through a terrific sense of depression. He wasn't working. One morning my mom and I were having brunch and we heard a pop, like a firecracker. We knew exactly what had happened. He had shot himself in the right side of his head. I remember screaming No! Peckinpah has it that you go into slow motion. It wasn't even that. It's like a twilight of awareness. You lose your own guts. You lose everything.
>
> He died at UCLA Medical Emergency Hospital. An intern brought me a brown paper bag full of his bloody pajamas. We opened it when we got home and found a suicide note in his pocket which simply said, "My life insurance runs out tomorrow." So it was planned. Hemingway had died exactly on the same day and in the same way two years before, and if you saw a picture of my dad, you'd see that he had become very Hemingwayish.

But we were even accused of murdering him! The cops came in and said, "How'd this gun get over to the other side of the room?" And so immediately I didn't mourn. I had to defend myself. A part of my brain absolutely short-circuited.

I think the first stage of grief, which not many people talk about, is the desire to go with the person who was killed. You do whatever you can to kill yourself with him. It's a terrifying thing to say. I started drinking, I started eating, I did everything I could to blot out the pain, to anesthetize myself. I fainted on beaches. I was on the verge of a nervous breakdown.

For the first two years, I'd hear ambulance pops, I'd hear backfires. Every time I turned my head to the right I would hear gunshots. It's very hard to get that sound out of your mind. I mean you come home and you pick your father's brains up off the floor.

Even now, I'll sit with my family and suddenly I go right back into it. I'm not talking about negative or positive: I'm talking about reexperiencing it for your entire life, and that's okay. It becomes your friend.

I tell people that these things happen for horrendous reasons, and you don't know what the reason is. It's going to change your life. I don't think grief ever leaves you. Grieving is not a graceful journey. It's not a journey that's filled with particular beauty, until you go past moments of it. With suicide, the sweetness and the memory can only remain once you go through the memory of the horror. My dad's death, as much as I adored him, was always covered with that horror. But you know that you're either going to die with that person or you're going to live. My choice was to live.

To make that life-affirming choice, it's necessary to deal with other repercussions of suicide: shame, anger, and guilt.

Shame is a reaction once associated only with suicide. (Today, many people who have lost loved ones to AIDS also struggle with that feeling.) Historically, suicide has been treated as a sin and a crime. In Europe, for many centuries, the suicide victim was tried in court posthumously, and if found guilty, sentence was pronounced; the body was punished. In ancient Athens, the corpse was buried in one place outside the city, except for the hand, presumably responsible for the deed, which was buried elsewhere. In England, the corpse was buried at a crossroads with a stake through the heart and a stone over the face. In France, the body was dragged through the streets, burned, and then—in case the message wasn't clear—it was tossed on a pile of garbage.

The relatives of the survivors were punished as well. Both in England and in France, the deceased's property was confiscated by the state. The bereaved were thoroughly shunned. Suicide was considered shameful—in the extreme.

Today, shame is still part of it. "When someone commits suicide in your family, it's a way of saying, 'You can't help.' People feel discounted and ignored. That generates anger and shame," states New York psychiatrist Dr. Barry Kerner, M.D.

That shame often causes a curtain of silence to be drawn across the subject. "People are so upset they don't know how to talk to the grieving person about it. So they avoid the discussion, and the person who's grieving is afraid to bring it up because no one else is," observes Joyce Chazen, executive director of the Suicide Prevention and Crisis Call Center in Reno, Nevada, the state with the highest suicide rate in the nation.

Even within the family, it can be hard to talk. "Often people can't find support at home; other members of the family are not knowledgeable, they're too hurt themselves, and there may be blaming going on," Chazen states. "There can be a really hostile atmosphere in the family after a suicide." Sometimes a tacit agreement among family members makes the topic taboo. That silence keeps mourners from screaming at each other and it hides the anger, guilt, and blame they feel. But like all attempts at repression, it stunts the mourning process.

Still, it's easy to understand why people fall into that pattern. The mere fact of such a death feels like an accusation. The taint of trouble is suddenly on the family. Something was obviously wrong. But what? Mental illness? Drug abuse? Who can tell? In the end, it comes down to one question: Why did it happen? Even when there is a suicide note, the statements in that note are only partial reflections of a despairing mind. So the search for answers can be thankless.

Guilt

People whose loved ones commit suicide often feel guilty about their own behavior. Looking back, they can often discern the signs they failed to notice while the person was alive. They may realize that their loved ones hinted at suicide, mentioned it specifically, or even started giving things away. A man I knew did that the night before he committed suicide, when he invited a friend to dinner and gave her his favorite painting. In subtle ways, people sometimes even say good-bye. Mourners may feel racked with guilt for having ignored those classic cries for help. Yet the reality is that it's usually not easy to discern such signs—and even if you do figure out what's going on, you may not be able to help. "To help mourners with their guilt, I tell them that you cannot stop people who are hell-bent on ending their lives," states therapist Judy Tatelbaum, author of *The Courage to Grieve*. Although people may know that rationally, it's still hard to give up the idea.

Nonetheless, after a suicide many people blame themselves. Mariette Hartley, for instance, felt guilty because her career was taking off just when her father was having difficulty. She made the association "that my success means somebody else's death. It literally took me twenty years to get back in those waters of success again."

Releasing guilt takes a long time. "People feel guilt because they feel in some way it was their responsibility and in their power to keep this person alive," states Wyoming suicidologist John Sanford, Ph.D. As long as they feel guilty, the bereaved can nourish the illusion that they had some power over that person's life. To give up the guilt and forgive themselves means admitting their own powerlessness. That can be frightening because it means you have to accept that the person who committed suicide deliberately deserted you.

Anger arises because the act of suicide is so purposeful. The feelings of rejection and the hurt are infuriating. Yet feeling angry at a person who was so obviously miserable can increase feelings of guilt.

Many mourners also feel relief, a reaction which almost instantly produces even more guilt. They feel relieved because the person was so unhappy, because the loved one is no longer suffering, because the relationship was so difficult, or because nothing they did ever seemed to help. Nancy and I interviewed a man who felt all of that after his daughter shot herself. The girl had been in and out of institutions for years; nothing he did seemed to help; he felt stymied and frustrated. When she killed herself, part of him was relieved. It's not the kind of thing many would admit in public, but it's not an unnatural or uncommon reaction.

The Suicidal Legacy

Wanting to die is a common feeling in any kind of grief. But most mourners, even while they have suicidal thoughts, are not actually worried about committing the act.

Not so for the relatives of suicides. For them, the thought is ever-present. According to Christopher Lukas and Henry M. Seiden, Ph.D., authors of *Silent Grief: Living in the Wake of Suicide*, the suicide rate among survivors has been estimated to be as much as 80 to 300 percent higher than among the population as a whole. Survivors make that choice for many reasons: it can be an unconscious desire to join the deceased, to punish themselves, or to be like the deceased. Like a real estate broker I once knew who killed himself several years after his brother's suicide, many commit suicide because it's a way they have learned, in their families, of coping with problems.

Suicide is not predetermined. It is not inherited. It is, according to Dr. Sanford, "a learned behavior. If Uncle Charlie or Mom or Dad kills themselves, that appears to make it an acceptable way of responding to a crisis situation." That's why, in times of stress, survivors of suicide sometimes do find themselves considering that option. Marty Winthrop is a Maine native who was thirty-three years old when her mother committed suicide:

> My mother attempted suicide many times while I was growing up. The bathroom door would be locked and then the police or the fire department would show up and get into the bathroom. Then Mother would go away for a couple of weeks. She would always come home with interesting stories about the loony bin or the booby hatch, as she called it. She herself was a psychologist, but with the clinical awareness of a guppy fish. Finally, in 1973, she took a massive overdose and died.
>
> Seven years later, I tried to take my own life. I used to walk around the house fantasizing ways to kill myself, such as driving off a cliff. I thought, with my luck, I'll miss and be a paraplegic forever. When I finally did something, it was after I had been molested by a neighbor and jilted by someone who'd asked me to marry him. I felt violated and helpless. I swallowed whatever pills I had and then proceeded to call my daughter and say what a wonderful daughter she was. She said, "Mother, you sound like you've done something." She's a perceptive young woman. She got on the phone and alerted people so I ended up in the hospital for a couple of days. When I got out, I still felt depressed, but it was like I had freed myself of that terrible curse.

To free yourself of the suicidal legacy, it is not necessary to try it yourself. It *is* necessary to deal with the emotional implications of the suicide. "A survivor support group can be beneficial because it gives people a chance to face their own reactions, to understand what they're experiencing, and to realize that what they're experiencing is normal under the circumstances. It provides a supportive environment in which they can face themselves and face their pain," Joyce Chazen states.

Perhaps because guilt is so much a part of the grieving with suicide, many people we interviewed mentioned the importance of doing something for others. Marty Winthrop suggested that mourners do three things: "Cry. Share your grief. Try to find some way to use it for good, possibly by working for a charity, cause, or religion."

Mariette Hartley found hope and comfort initially through therapy and later on by helping others. Both activities helped replace some of the negative images with positive memories:

> When I was reaching psychic bottom, I was put in touch with the right therapist. Thank God. I remember the first day I walked into his office. I was all dressed in black. I was in mourning for my life. It's Chekhov. It's Mascha. It's classic. And not chic black—I'm talking middle-aged, midwestern black. I remember the dress.
>
> Eventually, I became involved with suicide. I was terrified. It's like gun control: how do you get involved without being sucked into this negative vortex? Well, that's not what happens at all. I speak to high schools because I came from an upper-middle-class suburb and I know what goes on behind closed doors. I know the drinking, I know the secrets, I know it inside out and backward. They need to see that someone has traveled that road and survived. I tell them my story.
>
> My father was a fabulous man! He was deeply talented, a wonderful painter. When I miss him the most is when somebody walks by with a pipe. Oh, boy, what a smell. Or I'll see one of those black-and-red-checked shirts he always wore. The fondness never leaves. The grief never leaves. Instead of this raging storm which it is in the beginning, this hurricane that you battle against, the grief gradually becomes a gentle, warm, summer rain and you just become friends with it. Now you have something to pass on to other people. You become a teacher. You become a healer. You have been blessed, in a horrible, horrible way.

MURDER

Murder is a horror so ghastly that it intensifies every aspect of the mourning process. The shock is titanic; the numbness can last for years; the fear, vulnerability, and rage are severe. There is often a strong desire for revenge. Dealing with those feelings requires extraordinary bravery. And social support may be woefully inadequate, for as kind as most people are, they may find the extent of the anger and horror alienating. Often, they simply do not want to be around it—which is why it can help to join an organization such as MADD or Parents of Murdered Children. Those people know how you feel.

They know, too, that violent death often requires survivors to take on a new role: that of plaintiff. Although dealing with lawyers, court dates, depositions, trials, and the paraphernalia of the legal system can add to feelings of frustration and helplessness, it can also provide an outlet for anger. With murder, the shock, anger, and desire for justice simply have to be addressed. And sometimes that means other emotions have to wait to find expression.

Jennie Santos, for instance, is a bookkeeper in New York City whose son was murdered. "I became determined to bring my son's killers to justice, and my perseverance is paying off. One of my son's killers was finally arrested," she said. "But after four years, no tears have been shed by me. They just don't come."

People whose loved ones died as a result of homicide—and according to the FBI, 20,675 Americans were murdered in 1988—are often quick to point out that with murder, mourners have to face the fact that there is someone out there who actually wished their loved one dead. Odile Stern, a New Yorker who still retains a charming French accent, is executive director of Parents of Murdered Children of New York State, an organization she helped form after her daughter Michelle, a college student at Emory University, was murdered on November 11, 1978. She talked about the murder of her daughter and the special problems of mourning when there's been a violent crime:

> It was a Saturday morning and I answered the telephone. It was the dean of women of Emory University. She said, "It's about Michelle."
>
> I asked, "What happened?"
>
> She replied, "Michelle has been hurt."
>
> Because of the tone of her voice, I said, "Is she badly hurt?" And she did not say anything. So I asked, "Is she dead?"
>
> And she said, "Yes." I collapsed on the floor and I screamed for Dick and he got on the phone. At that time, they knew nothing. They had just found Michelle's body.
>
> The police were finally able to put the story together. The previous evening, Michelle and a friend got lost in downtown Atlanta and stopped to ask directions from two guys. The guys asked for a lift, so the kids let them into the car, and the guys pulled out handguns and forced the young man into the trunk of the car and drove off with my daughter. As the car was moving, the young man was able to free himself using tools in the trunk. He jumped out and went to the police. By the time they found my daughter, she was dead.

The police found the car abandoned with one of the kidnappers shot in the head. The next day they found the man who was arrested. First they had robbed my daughter, then they took her to an abandoned house and raped her. When she tried to escape, they shot her in the back. Then they drove away and had a fight about what to do with the car and one guy shot his partner.

Outsiders don't understand what grief can do. There are stages which are common for all types of grief but ours is different because death has been caused by another human being. This is what hurts. If there is no arrest, people have to live with the knowledge that that person is still around and probably will commit another murder and can present a threat to other members of the family. That will follow them through their life. The second thing is, if the arrest has been made and the man goes to jail, nobody stays in jail forever. Eventually, parole will come and that person will be set free, walking around. You can never, never close your mind on grief.

More than any other form of loss, murder emphasizes how fleeting our hold on life is, how easily and needlessly it can be severed, how unsafe a place the world is. It forces people to deal with concepts of senselessness and evil. It produces a sense of vulnerability that takes a long time to diminish.

In addition, murder, like suicide, makes other people thoroughly ill at ease—as Joni Schaap, a speech therapist in Los Angeles, learned after her sixteen-year-old son was murdered:

We thought Jeremy was in bed. He left the house around eleven o'clock and went with a friend to a district where there are a lot of drugs. Apparently, he was either buying drugs or providing rides on his motorcycle. There was a quarrel, and the boys surmised they were in danger and took off. The drug dealer on the street said to an accomplice, "Get him," and they opened fire. One bullet got Jeremy in the spleen. The other kid wasn't hit.

Because they had a witness, they got a composite drawing of this guy. Everyone knew him by his drug name, his street name. And so they got him. They put him in jail and the police kept telling us, "Don't get involved. You're just going to jeopardize the case." After about three months, my husband, who is an attorney, called the district attorney's office to see what was going on with the case, and the district attorney said, "Oh, that case was dismissed." They had never let us know. They released him because they didn't feel the witness was a good one. He was kind of a drugged-out kid so the case was dismissed. He was out after three weeks.

People don't talk about murder. It's a taboo subject. If Jeremy had crashed on his motorcycle, it would have been a lot easier for me. It's acceptable to be sick, it's acceptable to get in an accident. But with murder and suicide, people are horrified. How many children do you have? I have three daughters and a son who died. Uhhhhh. How did it happen? Well, he was murdered. UHHHHHH. They don't want to talk about it at all. People want to distance themselves and they want to think of all these reasons why it couldn't happen to them. And they think it doesn't happen in nice families! I used to think that! If I read in the paper about a drug-related murder, I used to think, who cares? Look at what kind of people they were. They're not like me. Murder has that image. People don't think it can happen to normal middle-class families. So if I get through *that* he died, then I have to get through *how* he died. It took me six months to say "died." And it took me almost two years to say "murdered." I'd say he was, uh, uh, uh, he was shot. It's horrible.

Using the word "murdered" is a problem I've wrestled with too. Many drunk-driving victims will say my child—or my husband—was "murdered by a drunk driver." I've never been able to say that; murder seems so much more deliberate than drunk driving, although I don't consider drunk driving an accident. Nevertheless, I find that, like many other people, murder is a word from which I recoil.

People whose loved ones have been murdered have no choice but to adjust to the unthinkable. The process can make mourners feel anxious and afraid. It forces them to reconstruct their worldview—to incorporate within it the very worst of possibilities. Yet those who have confronted the agony of murder have found that it can also cause them to find unsuspected strength and purpose, as Odile Stern did after her daughter's death:

Sometimes it feels like it happened a long, long time ago and sometimes it feels like it happened yesterday. I live with it every day. My whole life has changed.

Before that, violence was far from our lives. We became aware overnight about handgun violence. I worked for Handgun Control and was asked to join the board of directors a year later.

And I started to get involved with victims. I met with Families of Homicide Victims and joined a support group in 1980. I discovered that not only did we share a lot of grief, we shared a lot of anger because of the way we were mistreated and ignored by the criminal justice system. We decided to translate that anger into action. From our experience, action is part of the healing process. If you keep the anger and pain in yourself, it can be self-destructive.

After Michelle was killed, I cried. I screamed. When I was alone in the house, I talked to her. I still talk to her. I am a religious person and I believe in an afterlife. I believe in a soul and I believe she is very close to our family. I pray to her. I derive a lot of strength from that. I feel that she has gained wisdom and a knowledge of things which we don't have.

Just as there is relief to be found in expressing feelings, there is benefit in turning anger into activism. People who try to effect change are less likely to succumb to helplessness and despair. Taking action can mean writing letters to the judge, the editor, or your representatives in Congress. The point is to do something. "Before my son was killed, I gave talks on hearing impairment. Afterward, I asked to speak on losing a child. Now I give that talk four times a year and I work at Compassionate Friends, helping other parents. It's good for me," Joni Schaap said. "My children are more important now. I don't take them for granted. Things that used to bother me or that seemed important before no longer have much significance. My priorities have changed."

A lot of people feel that by taking political or social action, the death will serve some purpose. Odile Stern reacted that way. "I did not want Michelle's death to be in vain. I feel that out of a tragedy a lot of good things have happened and will happen," she said. "In my case, it has been ten years. We are still alive, coping with life the best we can. We believe that there is a future for all of us and it's up to us to make it the best we can. We believe that if we work hard enough, violence can be overcome."

CHAPTER 6 | Anticipated Death

Taking care of him was getting to be almost impossible. But as the boat begins to list, you try to ride it, slowly. . . . In some ways, every day was its own good-bye.

—DAVID ST. JOHN

Every loss has its own shape, its own roughness, its own small comforts, and its own pattern of mourning. With sudden death, everything is left unsaid and undone. Adjustment is difficult. With anticipated death, there is a chance to prepare, to say good-bye, to spend time together, to rehearse for a future without the loved one—and to watch that person suffer. People whose loved ones are dying from terminal illness become well acquainted with the inexorable onslaught of disease, responsibility, and pain. "If a sudden death hits like an explosion, knocking you flat, then a slow decline arrives more like a glacier, massive and unstoppable, grinding you down," writes Edward Myers in *When Parents Die*. It's a good analogy. With sudden death, the dying may be horrible, but at least it's over fast. With anticipated death, the dying can take a long, long time.

During that period of preparation, mourning begins. The process of grieving while the loved one is still alive is known as anticipatory mourning because in certain of its emotional components it resembles mourning after death. With an anticipated death, mourning has a double curve: before the death and after. Oftentimes, when death finally arrives, both the dying person and the soon-to-be bereaved are ready for it.

Frequently, the most harrowing part occurs before the death. "My husband had Alzheimer's disease. For three years, he had been deteriorating mentally. For two years, he did not know anybody or anything.

89

It was so painful to see the process of deterioration," said retired librarian Polly Kaminski of Denver, Colorado. "I had been grieving for at least a year before he died. Afterward, I felt great relief and freedom from the long care. I felt at peace."

When an illness is long and arduous, the bereaved have time to confront the inevitable. They can grieve for many aspects of the loss—past, present, and future—and if they are fortunate, they may come to some resolution about it. They may even begin to detach from the dying person. In those cases, adjustment is eased.

As with every other kind of grieving, anticipatory mourning has no predictable pattern. Shock may not come at all; the recognition that the loved one is going to die may dawn gradually. When shock does occur, it can affect both the family members and the person who is dying, and sometimes that person's reaction can be the hardest part of the whole thing. My dad had been in and out of the hospital for two years getting radiation treatments for cancer of the prostate when he was finally told in November 1989 that he didn't have long to live. In addition to the cancer, he had a history of numerous other problems, including phlebitis and triple-bypass surgery which was not successful. So when we heard the news, I wasn't shocked. But he was. His absolute total shock and complete emotional breakdown were devastating.

When mourners feel shock, it often appears after many bouts of illness, when the doctor first speaks the word "terminal." The poet David St. John told us about the day when his father's cancer, hitherto limited to superficial skin cancers, first became ominous:

> They discovered a cancerous development in one lung and realized it was serious. He got admitted into an experimental cancer therapy program in San Francisco where they cultured antibodies from the person's tumor. He was literally on the bed waiting to be wheeled into the operating room for the first injection of those antibodies when they told him they couldn't do it because his kidneys weren't in good enough shape. Until then, his spirits had been extraordinary. But when they said they couldn't operate, he knew that was it. It was a death sentence.
>
> In some ways that day was the hardest of all. He'd had skin cancer so long, but now I realized the cancer was going to kill him. There were other days that were horrible and awful as he began to lose ground. But none were as shocking as the first day.

It should be noted that not everyone mourns in advance, and for a good reason: the loved one is still alive. Perhaps death won't come at all!

For these people, denial and hope become indistinguishable. Still others suppress their feelings of grief because they don't want to upset the person who is dying. These are understandable reactions, for watching a loved one die is a process characterized by despair and recuperation, relapse and recognition, and the possibility, however remote, of a miraculous recovery. Some people never admit to themselves what the inevitable outcome must be. Dr. Phyllis Silverman reports that information gathered from the Widow to Widow program indicates that although many women changed their lives to adapt to their partner's terminal illness, they did not necessarily grieve during that time. They adjusted to the idea of having an ill husband—not a dead one. When their husbands finally died, even after several years of serious illness, they experienced both shock and denial. That's how Californian Alyce Birkett, a retired teacher's aide, felt when her husband, Kenneth, died. "My husband had been in and out of the hospital so much. He died in the ICU where he spent the last twenty-nine days. Though he had been ill for four years, and his death should have been expected, I couldn't believe he was dead. For many days, maybe weeks, after he died, I was in a daze." No matter how clear it may be to other people that death is imminent, if it's not clear to you, the death is unexpected and there may be no anticipatory mourning.

You'd think that denial would disappear when death actually arrives, but it doesn't always work that way. Doris Slaven is a Kansas housewife whose son Michael died of AIDS. "He was very sick for about four months before he died. We knew it was going to happen—except if a miracle occurred. And even afterward, many a time I felt that he was still alive in California and it wasn't possible." That kind of denial is a very normal reaction.

During the weeks and months that precede death, it's common to ricochet wildly from one mood to the next. But emotional needs during this time may have to be pushed aside in favor of the practical tasks involved with dying. During anticipatory mourning, the focus is not inward but outward. The person who is dying commands our immediate attention. Some people detach from the dying person during this process. Others grow even closer. Caretaking often becomes the center of their lives.

CARETAKING

Taking care of a person who is dying is hard work requiring courage, equilibrium, and enormous energy. It's stressful, emotionally demanding, and financially burdensome. Many people end up sacrificing their own well-being, as Susie Fagan did when her husband was dying:

Beginning in November 1986, when my husband was hospitalized and underwent some totally unnecessary and dangerous tests which resulted in a stroke (followed by a subsequent coronary bypass), I neglected my health totally. When I brought him home, after converting our apartment into a hospital-like facility, I worked very hard. With my daughter's assistance, together with that of excellent nurses, we managed to keep Sid as comfortable as possible. He had been left totally paralyzed and needed maximum care, but had learned to use his right hand. The Braille Institute was wonderfully helpful in supplying books on cassette. Sid had been an avid reader and they soon learned what his taste was and sent books regularly.

All my time was spent running our little hospital, and when I had to work, my daughter would be there and the nurses would put in some extra time. After a while, when funds were beginning to run low, I became the night nurse, with the help of intercoms all over the place. I found rehabilitation facilities and transportation to and from and we never, ever stopped trying. I was completely stressed. I ate anything and everything that was handed to me. I gained weight, my teeth and gums were neglected, and everything that seemed to be going wrong with me was "stress-related."

Caretaking is as all-encompassing as any task you will ever do. The work is time-consuming and psychologically demanding for everyone concerned. Family members who don't participate often feel guilty, but even those who are vigilant in their attentions to the dying person can feel the pangs of guilt for not doing more. "I felt guilty about a number of things," one widow confided. "We were going to the hospital twice a day and I could have spent more time with him but I didn't. I felt so mad at myself, but I thought I was tiring him. And I thought back to some of the times when I'd gotten mad at him and I felt guilty about that too."

Many people are unreasonably harsh with themselves, expecting perfect twenty-four-hour-a-day caretaking. If they unconsciously hope they can save the person, they may feel that nothing they do can ever be enough. They may also want to avoid feeling guilty after the death. But guilt is not something you can entirely avoid. No matter how self-sacrificing and saintly you are, when death occurs, you will be alive and your loved one dead. If there are specific actions you can take now to reduce guilt later, do so. But no one is superhuman. We do the best we can.

To be a good caretaker, it's important to step away from the pressure and occasionally nourish the self. "I needed a lot of time alone while my mother was dying," one woman said. "I found it very hard to be social over small things. Going to the movies and going on walks was helpful."

"The nights were hard for me because it would have been a day of trying to hold the seawall against the impending floods. It was always difficult to let my body relax," said David St. John. There's no question that the pressure and strain of caretaking expresses itself through the body. Exercise, massage, yoga, and meditation can help to reduce that stress.

Annabel Kaufman, whose five-and-a-half-year-old son died of AIDS, benefited from a personal volunteer's assistance. She also found that a weekly dose of distraction provided some much-needed relaxation and pleasure:

> I spent five and a half years of my life doing nothing but taking care of Zack. Most of the time we were trying to make his life meaningful doing whatever he wanted to do. If he wanted to go to Disneyland, I took him. When I was really desperate for a break, we got this lovely volunteer from a family outreach program for families of chronically and terminally ill children. She became his buddy. They adored each other. She would come and play with Zack about six hours a week, and I could do other things. I could be in the other room and make phone calls or go to the market or whatever.
>
> Also, on Saturdays, a friend would come over and watch Zack in the morning and my husband, Jerry, took him in the afternoon. I would go to this jewelry-making class. My child was home dying, and all these people would be chattering about all this happy stuff. I was pretending to be normal for a day. It was very strange. In some ways it was excruciating because there was pain and I couldn't share it. But in other ways it was very good because it gave me a break.

Talking about dying takes tremendous courage. When the people involved, including the dying, are brave enough to initiate such a painful conversation, they are frequently able to reach a new level of serenity.

But it's easy to sentimentalize these possibilities. Despite what we may see in the movies, being emotionally open when people are dying is difficult—possibly more so than at any other time. Barriers to communication can come from the person who is dying, who may deny the truth of what is happening. "She would never talk about the fact that she was going to die, ever, ever," said Byron Callas, whose wife died of cancer.

But barriers are also internal. Just because you would like to discuss certain topics doesn't mean you'll feel comfortable doing so. Painful childhood memories or unresolved marital difficulties may now be harder to talk about than ever. Issues directly linked to death are especially sensitive, because when we deal with the death of a loved one, we face our own mortality as well. Rachel Ballon recalls her attempt to discuss dying with her mother:

> I wanted to put my arms around her and say, are you scared? Are you lonely? What are you feeling? And I just couldn't do it. At moments of truth, it's hard to be huggy kissy. So I tried to fix her bed jacket around her shoulders and suddenly we both burst into tears and I put my arms around her and told her I loved her. She said she loved us, and she started to cry, and that was it. That was the only time we ever discussed it.

In addition to anger, guilt, depression, discomfort, and other feelings associated with loss, those whose loved ones die slowly have to cope with the pressure of making life-or-death decisions. "I was left with the decision about pulling the plug, which I didn't want to do," said Marcy De Jesus after her husband's death from liver cancer. "They had been pressuring me all week and I couldn't let go until Sunday. It was his birthday, so I talked to him for a few minutes and I told them to go ahead and do it. He died immediately. The whole house was falling in on me."

Fortunately, the pressures of caretaking are balanced by the opportunity to break through some of our fears about death. As difficult as caretaking is, the rewards can be equal to the work involved. David St. John described his experiences:

> My father deteriorated rapidly. He wanted to die at home, and it's a decision that I'll always be grateful for. The last month, it became very difficult. He couldn't move without help, he couldn't get to the bathroom, he couldn't eat, he couldn't do anything. Emotionally, it was just debilitating.
>
> He died the third week in July. Seeing his courage and his humor and the grace with which he approached his own death is something I could never have expected to see. One of the reasons why the process of grieving was less traumatic to me is that along the way, I felt I was internalizing the values my father saw as meaningful. Being there on a daily basis gave me a chance to feel acquainted with his death in a way that otherwise would have been cut off from me. In many ways, I was fortunate.

FAMILY RELATIONS

Many families pull together when someone is dying. Petty jealousies and ancient resentments can be put on hold. But it can also go the other way. Death can exacerbate family feelings, revealing the tensions we normally hide. Family members may disagree about what ought to be done. They can differ in their abilities to deal with death and dying, as well as in their levels of denial and in their willingness to take on responsibility. Parents and children may quarrel. Adult siblings caring for a dying parent may argue about what tasks each of them ought to be doing; suddenly, the rivalries of childhood spring to life again. Some people, unable to cope with the reality of what is going on, drop out entirely; others take charge—grabbing the reins of responsibility in their own minds, becoming a tyrant in the minds of others.

Beyond that, individual philosophies can differ, so that while one person may believe in giving the dying person hope, another member of the family may be an equally strong proponent of being honest. One person may want to discuss the past; another may wish to avoid it. Differences can emerge on matters of religious faith, nutrition, medical treatment, and every other issue; and any of those differences can spark an argument. Doreen Smythe faced some of those difficulties while her mother was struggling with cancer:

> We found out that she had cancer in the summer of 1987. By December the doctors realized that the treatments were not working and they told her there was nothing they could do. I decided to leave my employment and I went north to take care of her. She was not ready to give up.
>
> My mother has five sisters in their late eighties and nineties. One of them came up with this combination of fermented honey and port wine. She said this mixture had been used in Russia and people had been cured of cancer. I was hesitant to use it and she got very agitated and said that I didn't really love my mother—that if I did, I would let her use this. I debated and debated because I recognized the value of the placebo effect but I also felt it would divert my mother's focus from "how can I heal myself?" to an outside cure: take this elixir three times a day and it will heal me. I was in real turmoil about that. Of course when Mom found out, she was determined to take it.
>
> When she began to refuse food, I checked with the doctor and he said, "At this point, food is not going to help her." Once she started consistently pushing away the food, I respected her wishes. But the family is from the tradition that if you feed

someone healthy food, they're going to get well. So there was conflict over that too.

I had asked everyone to talk to her. I said, "Tell her how you feel and let her know that it's okay with you that she leaves here." She was still hanging on. Well, my dad can't express his emotions. He could not at any time have conversation with her, except to say, "You're going to be okay, Hilda." He refused to believe that she could hear us talk. Around nine-thirty on the night she died, I decided to leave the room and let my father be alone with her. I said, "Dad, if you can, go ahead and talk to Mom." He didn't say anything, but half an hour later he came into the kitchen and said, "I think it's happened." So I went in, and she had stopped breathing. I arranged her on the bed, closed her eyes, put her false teeth back in. It was a very peaceful death.

My family had been very vocal about their feeling that I was not taking care of her appropriately but I think they came to recognize that I did what was necessary. But it didn't bring us closer together. It just diffused any antagonism there might have been.

OUTSIDE HELP

Many people besides the family are involved when someone is dying. Daily contact with doctors and nurses can make them very much a part of your life, so much so that when the death occurs, their absence may be something else that needs to be mourned.

But problems can also arise with medical personnel. Doctors, for example, can be surprisingly susceptible to denial. "The medical profession has, as part of its dogma, the triumph over death," states Pennsylvania therapist Jeffrey Kauffman. "That means that death can't be admitted into the rituals or consciousness of the profession except in a very secondhand way." Many people felt frustrated or angry at their doctors for not being emotionally supportive. Hospitals also come in for a lot of criticism over the way they treated the dying. Perhaps the reason is that they're understaffed. Or maybe it's just that, in the face of death, most of us seek someone to blame, and the medical profession is a handy target. In any case, many people interviewed for this book described frustrating hospital encounters. Rebecca Green works as a lobbyist in Washington, D.C. Her husband was a politician who died from Lou Gehrig's disease. Her dealings with one doctor were especially disturbing to her:

Being in the hospital was the most dreadful experience in my whole life. Unbelievable. The doctor was the most inhumane person I have ever met. He would not let my husband have the kind of respirator he wanted, even though we had done all the research and knew the kind he wanted would have been helpful. The doctor just didn't like his authority being challenged. Another time, after my husband's muscles had atrophied, they sent a new intern and it took him forty-five minutes of gouging around to take blood. It was hideous. So the next time my husband asked the doctor to do it and he refused. Why couldn't the doctor take the blood?

Many people find refuge in hospice. Founded in England for the express purpose of assisting the dying to live as fully, comfortably, and pain-free as possible, hospice is based on the philosophy that death is a normal process, and that both the dying and their families should be treated with care and with dignity. Hospice may provide care at home or it may offer a homelike facility where people can die in peaceful, personalized surroundings. Oregon artist Tim Eberhardt described his experience with hospice when his mother was dying:

She was diabetic, had bad circulation, and knew she was dying. She lost one of her legs, she was going blind, and she had to have people around to give her medicine. She was becoming very dependent, and it was debilitating for her. For the last four or five years, I became the sibling who spent most of the time with her.

I had to see her deteriorate and take her to the doctors and listen to all the things she had to go through. She never wanted to admit that she was going through traumatic experiences; she wanted to appear strong, and she just couldn't after a while, and it was hard.

At the end, she wanted to be in a hospice where they would take care of her. It never really came about until the last couple of days before she died. Hospitals are traumatic things. The hospice was wonderful. It was a four-bedroom house with six beds in it for patients, and a kitchen and a living room and a little chapel and people who deal with the dying. I got up there about a week before she died and all my brothers and sister showed up and got to talk with her. She said some amazing things. She sort of had a glimpse of the other side. She said that you don't stop thinking and that your mind continues.

Many people have found that hospice offers a humane alternative to either hospital or in-home care (and it does so on the basis of voluntary contributions). Medical personnel and trained volunteers are available for a wide variety of tasks, from help in locating financial and legal assistance to bereavement counseling. "We also provide transportation, companionship, light cooking sometimes. We'll write letters, read books, water plants, mail bills, feed animals," reports Robert S. Richards, co-founder of Santa Monica's Hospice in Home. "We respond to their needs."

Unless there is some recognition of the proximity of death, however, hospice may be ineffective. "Hospice was supportive but they're also about death," Doreen Smythe recalled. "I told them that the doctors had given up on my mother, but she had not given up on herself. They sat there saying, 'Oh, Hilda, that's too bad. . . .' It was as if they were attending someone's deathbed. After the visit, I walked them out and said, 'I don't think we're ready for you.' " But at the end, like many people, Doreen and her family turned to hospice once more:

> I was on a round-the-clock vigil. The most harrowing time was the last night when she was laboring so hard just to breathe, and she began to foam a little at the mouth. I called hospice at three o'clock in the morning and said, "This I can't handle. I'm so afraid Mom knows she's choking to death." They were very in touch with the levels of medication we were giving her. The nurse assured me that my mother was not aware of what was happening to her body. After she died, I called hospice and they said, "Don't do a thing. We'll call the mortuary and we'll be right out." They sat with us and the mortician came and hospice stayed for another hour or so and then they left. They were very supportive.

PREPARING FOR THE DEATH

A great deal can be done during this intense time. First of all, expect to experience every emotion you can name. Expect to have difficult encounters with the dying person, with the doctors, with relatives, with the man at the dry cleaner's. And remember that everything people normally experience after a death is something that you may feel before that loss: insomnia, shortness of breath, heart palpitations, dizziness, a feeling of constriction in your throat, changes in appetite, changes in sexual desire, digestive difficulties.

Pay attention to your relationship with the dying person. That may mean having to face the fact, possibly for the first time, that you are never going to get what you wanted from your loved one; now is the time to stop trying, and simply to accept that person.

Begin by saying "I love you." Failure to do that is one of the omissions people regret the most. Say good-bye. If there are things that you wish you hadn't done, apologize. Say "I'm sorry." If there are things you've always wanted to say, say them now—with love. Write them if you can't speak them. And be affectionate. Hug the person. Touch them. Hold hands. Read to them. Play their favorite music. Reminisce. Tell them that you'll miss them. And give them permission to die.

If it's possible, ask your loved one about funeral arrangements. Many people want the opportunity to plan their own funerals, so you may be doing them a favor by bringing up the subject. You might ask, "Have you thought about any arrangements you'd like to make in case you die?" They might be relieved that you brought it up. Or they might hate the idea of having such a conversation—in which case, you can change the subject. But if they are willing to discuss it, the discussion need not be morbid. Doreen Smythe discovered that when she and her mother went shopping at the mortuary:

> We went to the doctor's and afterward she said, "I want to stop at the mortuary." So we dropped by the mortuary and spent the next hour and a half making arrangements. We ended up laughing. At the end of the interview, the funeral director said, "Now it's time to pick out your casket." We went into this room where maybe fifteen caskets were all laid out, with different prices and everything, and we started going down the line. She'd say "What do you think about this one?" and I'd say, "Well, Mom, it's your decision . . . it's your casket." And she'd say, "I don't like that color." And we'd go on to the next. And all of a sudden we started laughing. Finally, we came to one that was sky blue, which is a beautiful color for her because she was such a lover of nature and lived on a ranch all her life. It had three birds in flight and it said "Going home." It was perfect. She paid for the casket and we went home. But I got a lot of flak from the family afterward!

The family might not have liked it, but Doreen felt that she and her mother had shared a difficult and intimate experience, and they'd done it with laughter.

The most important thing you can do is to talk to the person. Surprisingly, it can help to talk about the future. Discussing your own plans in a positive manner can help the person who is dying by relieving some of their anxieties about you. And talking about ways in which they'll be included in your life, ways in which you will remember them, ways in which they have made an important contribution to you, can be reassuring.

I thought about that when my father was dying. I knew he was concerned about me and my children. He had always been such an important part of my life. The whole time I was with MADD, my father was right there, following me around with his camera and working in the office: the true volunteer. He was always staunch in his support—emotional, moral, and financial. Toward the end, he was ravaged by cancer and could barely talk. I'd flown back and forth to see him many times. He finally told me he did not want me to see him again. He didn't want to see people; he was embarrassed by the condition of his body, which had wasted down to next to nothing, and he was also humiliated by his dependence on others. He actually told my children he was "an old man no good for anything." He had always been there for me, and now he couldn't be. Although I wanted to be there for him, he couldn't handle the role reversal.

But shortly before he died, when he was beginning to slip in and out of consciousness, I felt strongly that I wanted to have at least one more conversation with him and basically say my good-byes. I asked my sister to call me whenever he was alert so that I could speak to him, knowing full well that he probably could not communicate to me but at least he could hear and understand me. On a Sunday afternoon, when I least expected it, she called. All of a sudden I was faced with saying good-bye to my dad—on the speaker phone, because it was very hard to hold the phone up to his ear. Although I'd been thinking about what I wanted to say, for a moment everything I was planning to say flew right out the window.

I told him that the children and I loved him, and that we did not believe death was final, that he would go on in our lives forever, that in essence he would not be gone. I said we would always have a part of him with us. I told him, "You've imparted a wonderful legacy to us and that's your sense of humor. It's something we'll always remember you by." I said that he would be with Cari and my mother and I wanted him to tell them how much we loved and missed them. I thanked him for always being there when I needed him. I made it a point to let him know that Travis was doing fine, and what he was doing with his life, and I told him about Serena's plans. I told him about an up-and-coming speech I was giving and I reassured him about where I was going financially, because that was always a worry of his after I left MADD. I also discussed this book with him and how excited we were about its publication. I talked about the future with a lot of optimism. Several times while I was talking about the future, he would say, "Good."

Then he said, "This isn't the conversation I wanted to hear."

I replied, "It's the conversation I need to say."

He said, "Well, I'm still in there fighting."

At one point, I said something very loving and he thanked me. I laughed. "You don't have to thank me for loving you," I said. "You don't have to thank me for being your daughter."

And then he said something I didn't hear. My sister got on the phone and asked, "Did you hear him?" I said no and she said, "He said he loved you too." And that was it.

During the conversation, I tried to downplay my emotions, because other people were in the room and I didn't want everybody to start crying in front of him. I didn't think that was something he was prepared for. Afterward, when I hung up the phone, I sat down and cried. And then I called a friend. As wrought up as I felt at that moment, I was glad to have had that last conversation with my dad. He died three days later.

THE MOMENT OF DEATH

Even when death is anticipated, the manner and the moment of its arrival are impossible to predict. The loved one might die during sleep, or during the two minutes when you leave the room. Immediately before death, the person may slip deeper into unconsciousness, so that the moment of death might be a peaceful one. But disturbing physical symptoms can also arise, such as the choking that worried Doreen Smythe when her mother was dying. Many people who work with the dying, such as Elisabeth Kübler-Ross and Stephen Levine, author of *Who Dies? An Investigation of Conscious Living and Conscious Dying*, recommend sitting in silence or breathing in sync with the person who is dying. Many people believe that, even in unconsciousness, the dying can hear you. They recommend talking to the person and saying that it is all right to die. Both the last rites of Catholicism and the tradition in Judaism that the dying repeat to themselves the Sh'Ma, the most central prayer of the religion, affirming the unity of God, are designed in part to bring the dying to a place of peaceful acceptance.

But when the actual moment arrives, all the philosophy and preparation in the world cannot determine its shape. San Francisco resident Byron Callas, whose wife died of cancer in 1984, when he was thirty-five years old, describes their relationship and the circumstances of her death:

I met Vicki and fell in love with her. She had no interest in me whatsoever. She thought I was a nerd and a jerk—probably right too! But I was actively pursuing her and in the middle of this pursuit she found out she had breast cancer. I didn't know her that well. I didn't even know whether I ought to love her. But I was completely taken with her. I made a choice to pursue our relationship even though it was clear that it could end in her dying young. Most of our relationship was conducted in the context of her illness. We were together five years.

She died from complications resulting from a long bout with metastasized breast cancer. That day she had been tapped to remove several quarts of fluid from her abdomen and she went into a dazed state. I called the doctor and he said, "Feed her things with salt in it." I tried to get her to eat and we got into an argument. She was sitting on a couch in the living room and she started saying that she was dead.

I said, "You're not dead. You're sitting here! You're talking to me." We got into this argumentative game. I'd hold up my hand and say, "How many fingers do you see?" She would say, "Five," and I'd say, "A dead person can't do that so clearly you're still living." She said, "No, you don't get it. I'm dead. I'm not here anymore."

At some point she wanted to go to the bathroom. I picked her up. Suddenly, she went into the death rattle for what seemed like two or three minutes—it was probably ten seconds—and it was a remarkable experience. Her body stiffened and she did this back-and-forth thing that was a sound. I couldn't tell whether it was coming out of her, whether it was around her, or what. I just started looking at her eyes and going, "Vicki, come back. Vicki, come back. Vicki, come back." Her fists were clenching and then she collapsed.

I called 911 and they sent a paramedic team. As soon as they came, they shook their heads and said, "She's gone." They called the coroner and left. Then, for close to an hour, I sat on the floor with my dead wife, waiting for the coroner.

During that time, I pictured things that I had read in the *Tibetan Book of the Dead*. I said, "You're dead. It's okay. If you're trying to talk to me, I can't hear what you're saying." I remember saying, "I love you. If I've done anything wrong, I apologize. I'm sorry that we were arguing." I said I hoped I'd be forgiven. And I told her how great my life had been because of her, what a rare experience it had been.

I felt sad. I cried. I was relieved that her suffering was over and that I was free to live a more normal life that wasn't constantly about her illness. I also felt that I had been negligent and that I had killed her by picking her up too quickly. I felt guilty that her dying wasn't beautiful and peaceful. It was not like *Terms of Endearment*. It took me three or four years to see that if she hadn't died that day, she was going to die the next day or in the next two months. I thought that I should have taken her to the hospital and they would have kept her alive. I thought I had actually killed her.

Frequently, death comes as a welcome relief after months of pain. People who are present when their loved ones die often find that it can be such a peaceful and moving experience that they are grateful to have had the opportunity to be there. Rebecca Green had that experience when her husband succumbed to Lou Gehrig's disease:

One day, after he'd been ill for many months, he said, "It's time." He asked, "Do you want to be with me?" and I said, "Yes." So I pulled my chair closer to him and we took each other's hands and he sat there for about forty-five minutes and during that time I saw a physical transformation on his face. His face became illuminated. It was radiant. After forty-five minutes, he touched his skin and said, "I don't feel anything." Then he said he'd like to be outside. I helped him outside— it was the only time he ever let me assist him in walking—and his son came out and he sat down on the chaise lounge. He would start to lose consciousness and bring himself back and then he motioned that he wanted to stand up. He was so weak by then. I took one arm and his son took the other and while we were supporting him, he faded away. We put him down on the chaise lounge. He was still breathing. I put my head on his chest, and his son did the same, and we were holding his hands and we stayed with him until we heard the breathing stop. And then his son quoted a poem. And we could feel his spirit everywhere. It just hovered around. And then it left.

The serenity of that death is something many people might envy.

AFTER DEATH

No amount of planning is sufficient for the reality of death. Sorrow, depression, anger, and all the other emotions associated with grief flicker on and off. Relief is there too, and the greater the relief, the more likely you are to feel guilt. Many people feel guilty for having looked to the future while their loved ones were dying, for inheriting worldly goods, for finally wanting them to die. When California realtor David Sheridan lost his life partner to AIDS, he noticed "many conflicting feelings of relief, loss, acceptance, missing him terribly. My heart actually hurt. I was aware of an incredible range and depth of emotion I had not previously experienced."

During the first few weeks after the death, many mourners feel simply worn out by the demands of the dying. They feel exhausted and empty. Where life was incredibly busy during the dying process, they are now living in a void. If they acted as caretakers, their loved one may have become the focal point of their lives. When that person finally dies, the loss may be greater than it would have been if the death had occurred without warning, because prior to the death, the emotional bonds between them were strengthened. And now that person, whose importance may have actually increased during the last days, is gone.

After the death, there is what Emily Dickinson called "an awful leisure." Doreen Smythe felt it after the funeral, when everyone had gone home. "I walked into the living room and realized that there was nothing more for me to do. All of a sudden the loss was there. I sat down and I cried and I cried and I cried and I cried."

Sometimes, people think they have accepted the death when, in fact, they are still numb. Numbness modulates into emptiness; emptiness becomes despair. That's what California housewife Joyce Selbo experienced after her husband died of lung cancer:

> To my surprise, immediately after his death I was very matter-of-fact and accepting about his death. The first three weeks were filled with funeral arrangements and friends and relatives who came from back East to be with us. It was easy to focus on people and things happening around me, not on my husband's death. But after three weeks, the reality of my situation came to the fore. I was angry that I was now alone. I started to feel depressed and guilty over things that were or were not said between us. I felt lost as to how I would go on.

As with any death, holidays and anniversaries are particularly poignant times. It doesn't matter when the loss actually took place: the first holiday season can feel very empty. Doreen Smythe recalled:

> For about six months after my mother died, I was calm. I would visit her grave about once a week. I would sit there and talk with her and I would cry and it was fine. December came and I got hit like a ton of bricks. All of a sudden, incredible sadness.

Crying, crying. Any little thing—she was constantly with me. The loss was sitting there right on my shoulder.

I'm finally getting into a level place about it. It's almost a year. There are instances when I choke up. It's interesting. When my mother was alive, I never got homesick. I never really missed her. But we got so close and expressed so much love near the end . . . and now she is definitely gone.

Planning a meaningful funeral or memorial service is one way to provide some solace for yourself and others. "After my husband died, I had the body taken to the house, and I invited people in," Rebecca Green said. "It was not a formal occasion. We had music, and the family was there, and I fixed a lot of the food myself, which was very therapeutic."

David Sheridan taped the memorial service held for his life partner. "A friend read the Twenty-third Psalm. Then his minister spoke and a choir sang 'Bring Him Home' from *Les Misérables*. Several friends spoke. I listened to the tape over and over again. It allowed me to relive the service, reexperiencing my loss in the knowledge that it was shared with many others. It gave me great comfort."

As time goes by, remember that you can expect to feel despair, loneliness, anger, resentment, guilt: the whole nine yards. You can also expect to reach a point of accommodation, where you can look back to the past with pleasure. Grief has a varied geography. It's going to change—often on a daily basis. Feeling good again may take one year, two years, four years, or longer. Or it may also happen sooner than you expect. For mourners whose loved ones died an anticipated death, the grieving after the death may seem short. That's because the grieving began in advance—in life.

CHAPTER 7 | The Death of a Parent

I spent my life thinking I was somebody's child. But I was nobody's child.

—DVORA FREEMAN

The death of a parent is one of the most difficult experiences of a lifetime. It stirs up the primal fears of childhood. It can make us feel abandoned and vulnerable. After all, no one on earth has known us longer. No one else has known so intimately the small child we once were (and secretly still are). And in certain ways, if the relationship was a reasonably good one, no one has loved us more. Yet the idea that the death of a parent is natural, in the scheme of things, and therefore not too upsetting is deeply ingrained; there are even books about bereavement—good books, too!—which include chapters on the death of a spouse and the death of a child but only passing references to the death of a parent. "People assume you reach a point in life where you're independent and on your own and, since we expect our parent to die, it should be no big deal," states Andrew E. Scharlach, Ph.D. An associate professor at the School of Social Welfare at the University of California, Berkeley, Dr. Scharlach has studied the effects of the death of a parent during adulthood. He observes that everyone realizes that the death of a parent is a world-shattering event for children (a topic discussed in Chapter Eleven). Adults usually have an easier time, but even for people on the far side of middle age, the death of a parent can be wrenching. "I know it happens to us all," said a man whose mother died of an aneurysm at the age of ninety-five. "But it never happened to me before. It never happened to me." No matter how grown-up we are, the inevitability of a parent's death does not necessarily diminish its impact.

Unlike other deaths, the death of a parent means the loss of someone we have known our entire lives, someone whose behavior structured our earliest conception of ourselves, and someone we may have always trusted to take care of us. The death can consequently fracture our sense of security. For although we consciously realize that our parents are likely to predecease us, we may unconsciously think of them as omnipotent and immortal.

As with other deaths, the pain can last longer than is sometimes recognized. Indeed, in a study conducted by Dr. Scharlach, 25 percent of the bereaved adults indicated that one to five years after the death of a mother or father, they still got upset or cried when they thought about that parent.

The death of a parent can also affect our position in the world by shifting responsibilities onto our own shoulders. The psychological underpinnings we have relied on our entire lives are gone. Unbuffered by parental protection (even if that protection has been purely symbolic for many years), we feel the harsh winds of reality. Whatever sense of security we may have derived from our relationship with that parent— whether we called home for advice, or money, or just a friendly chat— is gone. Because the surviving parent may be coping with loneliness and despair, we may also feel a new sense of responsibility for that parent (an obligation that daughters in particular are likely to shoulder). We are forced to turn to ourselves in a way that has never before been true, regardless of our age. "My father died very suddenly of a heart attack when he was eighty years old," recalls Martha Eise of Hazelwood, Missouri. "I am trying to take care of my mother, sell some property, and handle my own family. Although I am forty-eight years old, I was instantly catapulted into adulthood at the time of his death."

When the second parent dies, we face an additional adjustment. "I was a thirty-nine-year-old orphan after my parents both died," one woman explained. "I felt like one of Dickens' little waiflike children." With the death of the second parent, our position in the world shifts. Among other changes, we lose access to our parents' memories of the past that preceded our own lifetimes. Sometimes it is only after the death that we become woefully aware of how little we know about their lives and about the lives of our grandparents before them. Nonetheless, when our parents die, we become the guardians of our family history.

More than that, we take a step up the generational ladder. Doubly bereaved, we come face-to-face with our own mortality.

DEATH OF A PARENT AND
STAGES OF ADULTHOOD

Many factors determine the way we react to the death of a parent. One of them, surprisingly, is the age of the mourner. Young adults often have a very difficult time coping with the death of a parent, even when they seem to have fully independent lives. During our twenties and thirties, roles and identities are still in flux; we may still very much look to our parents for advice, emotional support, or a sense of security. When a parent dies during these years, feelings of loss and unfairness may never entirely leave. Nancy Hathaway, coauthor of this book, was a college student when her father, Alan Berman, died in 1967:

The night before my father died, I talked to him on the telephone. He was always interested in the courses I was taking and the books I was reading. Every week, he sent me a letter full of advice, questions, household news, and an occasional quote from Dante or Plato or T. S. Eliot. This particular conversation, though, wasn't so lofty. We talked about the luggage I had recently lost on an airplane flight. We talked about insurance.

The next day my mother called, ominously early. "Daddy's gone," she said. Her voice sounded far away and I immediately got scared.

"What do you mean?" I asked. "Where did he go?"

And she said, "He died." He came home from work, went into the bedroom to do his Canadian Royal Mounted Police exercises, and had a massive heart attack. When she called him for dinner, he was dead. He was forty-nine years old.

I started to wail. The president of my very liberal, no-curfew dormitory popped out of her room and told me to keep it down. My roommate Sally ran down the steps and held me in her long arms. I couldn't stop shaking.

That night, and for months to come, sleep eluded me completely. I flew home for the funeral. My best friend, Carolyn, flew up from Maryland and took me shopping for a black dress. I wanted to drop out for the semester but my mother would have no part of that. A week later, I was back in school.

But I couldn't keep my mind on my studies, especially in my Victorian literature class (and why, I cannot say, for Victorian literature is filled with grief and mourning). My friends tried to entertain me but I could not be distracted from my grief. I was desperate for solitude. Finally, about two weeks after my father's death, I put my hand on the back of my neck and discovered that my glands had swollen to the size of golf balls. I was diagnosed with mononucleosis and sent to the infirmary, and I couldn't have been more relieved. For a week, I lay in bed, got orange juice upon request, received visitors, wrote in my journal, and cried. When I got out, I felt rejuvenated. The mononucleosis—or whatever it was—never returned.

But my grieving had barely begun. I cried constantly. I went on dates dressed entirely in black. Grief was right beneath the surface of everything I did. My grades plummeted; I got a D in Victorian literature. Having lost interest in academic matters, I simply participated in the times. I marched on Washington, D.C. I listened to rock and roll. I read *Steppenwolf.* Externally, I was busy. Internally, I was overwhelmed.

That summer I stayed home. Our dog, Teddy, died. I remember one time sitting on the crabgrass in the backyard. It was dusk and the woods were turning pink. I looked at the empty house where I had grown up and a sense of desolation swept over me.

My mother returned to City College. At her graduation, she wore a cap and gown while my brother, Paul, and I, Polaroid in hand, sat in the parents' gallery, the youngest people there. We were proud of her. But life as we had known it was utterly and eternally changed, and my sadness was persistent.

The death of a parent can be particularly difficult if it occurs at a moment of transition in the child's life, a moment when the parent's presence and advice would normally have been valued. That's what happened to Seattle resident Sigrid Solheim, a forty-six-year-old mother of three grown boys. Shortly after Sigrid's first child was born, her mother died suddenly:

Momma died of a heart attack at age forty-five two weeks after my oldest son was born. I was clear across the country and couldn't get back home because I had had a major hemorrhage. I feel guilty that I never told her how sick I was. I believe I was her favorite and she thought I was okay and so she felt she could let go and die—whereas if I'd told her about the hemorrhage, she might have rallied and hung on. She never saw my children.

When she died, I was calmer and less affected than anyone.

But the grief ended for everybody else and it went on for me. Sometimes I've felt that I've missed her every week and it's been almost twenty-four years. No one ever helped me "come to terms" with it. I don't like that phrase. Why should you come to terms with such a loss? You never see them again. That's the big thing. After a while you stop thinking of them all the time but you don't wipe away the past. You reconcile yourself to it. You carry on with your life.

During early adulthood, relationships with parents are often still in flux. But by middle adulthood, the conflicts of earlier years may have been ironed out. Perhaps illness or maturity has brought the parent and the child closer. That improved relationship doesn't ease the pain after the parent's death but it can help the mourner to move through it more rapidly. During the middle years of adulthood, when family and professional responsibilities are greatest, the death of a parent is usually less devastating.

During these years, many people watch their parents decline in health. They may unconsciously (or consciously) resent and fear their parents' increasing dependence. If, in addition, circumstances make it impossible for them to take care of their parents during this period, death can bring a heavy dose of guilt, as well as feelings of loneliness and insecurity. Else Eckert is a college registrar who lives in Bicester, England. Her mother died at age seventy-five:

> After two years of being confined to bed due to cancer, my mother died in a nursing home in Germany. I was living in another country and could only visit two or three times a year. I felt extreme guilt. It was my most powerful feeling. I also felt depressed having lost the only person who loved me totally and unconditionally. Except for visits, we were apart for most of the year. Now I miss the phone calls and the letters. There is no one who really cares. There's no one to go home to.

Those who do act as caretakers for the parent are in a different situation. According to an estimate by the American Association of Retired Persons, seven million American homes in 1987 included someone who was taking care of an elderly person. Many of those caretakers end up quitting their jobs and centering their lives entirely on the dying parent. If the parent suffers from a long and incapacitating illness, death can bring a certain relief along with a vast emptiness. But many people find that they can turn the experience of the parent's dying into a source of personal strength. Rachel Ballon is a therapist and writer whose mother died from a brain tumor when she was in her eighties:

My last child left home for college and I had the empty nest and then one month later my mother went to the hospital and it was like I lost another child. For three months, I watched my mother disintegrate before my own eyes. I never knew what to expect. One day she'd be sitting up and wearing a bed jacket and looking pretty and I'd know she was connected, and the next day she'd be in a wheelchair, asleep, with her mouth open and her head bent. I thought about taking her home. But she needed shots, she needed bedpans, she needed to be wheeled around, she needed oxygen, and we weren't equipped. Still, I had such guilt. So I got her this wonderful aide who stayed with her till she died. The social worker told me, "Give what you need to give to your mother and don't expect too much in return because when people are dying, they start detaching from you." She was right. It hurt at first. We're from the East and when I went to Washington, D.C., I collected autumn leaves from the ground and took them back to her. I got bright oranges and red reds and brilliant yellows and I said, "Mother, I brought these leaves for you!" She just looked at me and said nothing. I was so disappointed.

The dying process was worse than the death. The death was a release because she was no longer suffering so terribly and I wasn't having to face the effects of her dying any longer. A month later, I started to feel the emptiness without her.

Her death changed me. I don't think there's anything I'm afraid of anymore. You get strength from something like this. I'm a lot stronger than I thought I was and I have more courage: courage to live.

As the grown-up child begins to edge into old age, the death of an elderly parent may bring greater devastation and fear than anyone expects. There may also be a marked shortage of sympathy: the age of the parent may make the death seem not only natural but "overdue" to others. In 1980, 20 percent of people in their early sixties and 3 percent of people in their seventies still had a living parent; most of those people will have to bury their parent at a time when they themselves are getting old. To have a parent die during that difficult transition is to face your own mortality up close. Gene Brody is an educational psychologist whose mother died at the age of eighty in 1987, twelve years after the death of his father:

After my father's death, my bond with my mother grew stronger. Our relationship was a unique one. My father was the boss of the house. My mother was an immigrant who had never handled things on her own. She couldn't even write a check. I tried to teach her different things. We talked about her youth, her hardships, her coming to America and getting married and becoming a housewife. That's all she ever did. I spent hundreds and hundreds of hours with her. We'd take walks, go out for a bite to eat. I'm an emotional, sensitive person. I can see how many sons treat their mothers in a superficial way. I didn't do that.

I definitely have adjusted. But my feelings toward her remain passionate and powerful. I continue to reminisce. I make pilgrimages to the cemetery on Mother's Day and on her birthday and have unilateral talks with her. It's not totally melancholy. The cemetery's a mile from home, so when I need tranquillity I go up there. All in a row are my grandmother, grandfather, mother, and father. I just sit there and have conversations basically with myself.

When you have a strong tie to a deceased mother or father, that stays with you. I dream about her all the time and now my father is involved in the dreams too. I put this huge picture of them both in my bedroom. It's not a place to worship but it gives me a good feeling to see them.

I know that life goes on. I'm transferring the tie I feel to my sons. They sit and listen to me. And I'm about to be a grandfather again. The family name will continue well into the next century. That makes me feel good.

Single adults often feel especially alone and vulnerable when parents die. If they are closely attached to the parent, their lives may be more disrupted than are the lives of their brothers and sisters who have spouses and children of their own. They also lack the external support that their married siblings may have. For adult children who have been living with the parent, the loss of daily companionship and the habits of living with another person can make the loss similar in some ways to the death of a spouse. "For the past ten years, my mother has lived with me. My mother cooked and cleaned for me so I have to relearn those skills," said physical therapist Gloria Blankshain of Torrance, California. "Now I'm fifty-three years old and I'm living alone for the first time in my life."

THE PARENT-CHILD RELATIONSHIP

Perhaps the factor that most determines the shape of the mourning is the quality of the relationship between parent and child. Adult children who were close to the deceased parent may profoundly miss the regular contacts they had with their parent. For instance, phone calls home may have been an active part of their lives; it may even be that the older the parent got, the more frequent those calls became. Now those elements of life are gone, and the grief is strong. Fortunately, the better the relationship, the easier it generally is to move through the grieving process.

When the relationship was a good one, there is sometimes a strong tendency to idealize the deceased. To focus on the parent's most positive traits feels like an act of loyalty. But idealization can keep us mired in grief because it does not permit us to consider our relationship in a realistic manner. Instead, it turns an ordinary, flawed human being into a god.

When the relationship with the parent was an abusive or difficult one, idealization usually isn't a problem, unless the mourner is afraid to admit how hard things were. More commonly, mourners feel angry at the parent who failed them in so many ways and who has now—on top of everything else—abandoned them by dying. Marty Winthrop noticed this feeling when well-meaning friends tried to comfort her. "When people would tell me about losing their own parents, and about how loving and caring their parents had been, I'd find myself getting angry. They weren't purposely being insensitive or cruel. But goddamn it! Why couldn't my parents have been loving and nurturing and caring?"

With acrimonious, unresolved relationships, there is much to regret: miscommunications, missed opportunities, fights, cruelties, hurtful exchanges. Mourning a relationship in which you didn't get what you wanted is not easy, as Giles Slade, a thirty-five-year-old graduate student who teaches at Loyola Marymount University in Los Angeles, discovered after the death of his father:

> My father died on the morning that he and my mother were closing their farm in Canada to begin their annual winter trip south. My mother called and I could tell from her voice something rotten had happened. It was my father. After she told me, I started wailing! My wife, Sandra, held me but I was close to despair. I spent a sleepless night with pains gripping my chest.
>
> I felt abject. Things began to break and go wrong in the environment around me. Something happened to the car. I lost a contact lens and had to spend my entire stay looking out of one eye. I missed the plane home and had to wait an entire day to get another. I must have been really stressed.
>
> I still feel deep regret that I was never able to talk to my father about heart-things. We were not close. He would not allow that, although sometimes he became maudlin. While he was alive, however, I always felt that somehow there was a

chance that we would talk and find some kind of relationship. I was angry at my father for having shunned me when I was a child. It made me feel worthless and all these feelings rose to the surface with a suddenness and violence caused by his unexpected death. I needed his approval and never got it. His death removed the possibility that I ever would.

DEATH IN THE FAMILY

The death of a parent can unbalance the psychological shape of the entire family and alter relationships among surviving family members. If family members are no longer living in the same communities, it can result in a gradual drifting apart. In other instances, the extreme stress of a death in the family can cause dissent and friction. Giles Slade recalls:

> During the first few days after my father died, I experienced some extreme reactions to people, especially to those close to me. I drove my mother and sister to pick up my father's ashes at the crematorium. The directions were bad and I got lost. My sister got very bossy and I chewed her out. I also got angry at my mother. I apologized to both of them (and have again since) but I was aware that I had reacted very badly. It made me feel guilty. Also, I telephoned Sandra and accused her of fooling around on me while I was in Canada. I was looking at the world with hostility and suspicion and gradually I cut everyone off. I did not behave very well.
>
> My mother became obsessively involved in the divorce of my elder sister. She fought with both sisters and managed to drive them both away. With me, however, she was indulgent and understanding. In the months after my father's death, I would sometimes (usually late at night) get a sense of despair thinking of my mother alone with her grief in a farmhouse in the middle of a Canadian winter. At those times I would call her and I was usually right. She was sinking. Grief makes this kind of connection among survivors when they are close. Still, I wish I had not hurt my sister, my mother, and Sandra. I wish I had not driven my friends away by being so critical.

Rifts in family relationships may appear during the dying process or during the period of bereavement that follows. Within the mourner's own family, no one else may be as close to that deceased parent. The mourner's spouse may grieve the death too, but it probably won't be in the same way and it probably won't be as strong. The same can be true with the mourner's children, who may simply never have had the opportunity to become as close. Consequently, even though mourners may be surrounded by family, they may feel a lack of empathy.

The mourner's siblings may clash as ancient rivalries bob to the surface, especially if each sibling took a different role while the parent was dying. Often, the sibling who became the caretaker feels underappreciated, overworked, and resentful, while the one who dealt with the death from afar feels guilty. "I only saw my mother once a year but I sent her pretty clothes and talked with her frequently. My sister was the caretaker. She dealt with Mother's irrational thinking. I was the silent sister who got reports and didn't deal with it," said Maureen Dubin of Houston, Texas. "Now she really resents me because I was not there to share the agony."

On the other hand, the sibling who was not immediately involved in the caretaking may feel left out and underinformed. During the four years prior to my father's death, my sister and her family were living in England and I was solely responsible for him. But my sister returned to Nevada, and during the last five weeks of his life, my father moved there. So she became the caretaker. Although I was not directly responsible for his physical care, I made it clear that I wanted very much to be involved in any decisions involving his care and our future; there were health issues, questions about hospice, concerns about finances. But I wasn't right there, and decisions were made without me, some of which were only revealed after his death. I was hurt. Many siblings in the same position feel similarly; when a parent is dying, and in the process spends more time with one child than with another, it is almost inevitable that problems will arise. Death can definitely stir up the mud.

But if relationships have been good before, they may become even stronger now. Previously, the parent may have been the center of family life. Now the siblings may realize that the continued existence of the family in any real sense of the word depends on them. "In families that have been close, typically somebody takes over the role of keeping people together and in touch," states Dr. Scharlach.

THE INNER PARENT

A forty-five-year-old friend of Nancy's whose parents are both alive was terrified by the very notion of her parents dying. She confided to her father just how much she dreaded the thought of life without him. Who would she go to for advice? she asked him. How would she cope? "You'll miss me," her father said. "But you won't need me anymore because you'll carry me within you." He is a wise man. One way in which we cope with the loss of a parent is by incorporating something of that parent's outlook or behavior into our own lives. We look at things their way. We try to imagine how they would have responded. Often after the death, people begin to notice more consciously the ways in which they resemble their parent. It's a way of feeling connected.

When a parent dies, we also learn valuable lessons about what really matters. One of those values is basic human empathy. "Now when people share their experiences of grief, I *hear* them," a forty-two-year-old man said after the death of both his parents. "What tutors the heart is the experience."

Feelings of grief may occasionally arise for the rest of your life. Anniversaries and holidays can reactivate those feelings, and so can certain activities you might associate with your parent. For instance, ever since my mother died in 1975, I have been especially aware of her absence whenever I go shopping. Sometimes it looks as if every woman in the entire department store is shopping with her mother. At those moments, I miss her very much.

The death of a parent, even though it may deprive mourners of a source of comfort, can also act as a catalyst that influences people to improve their lives. Rachel Ballon discusses the impact of her mother's death:

> What did I learn from my mother's dying? I learned that you can go to a doctor and be told you're fine and the next day cancer cells can be growing or you can drop dead of a heart attack. I have no control over my destiny. What I do have control over is how I live my life. Her death was an opportunity to see that we're finite.
>
> As a result of her death, I recommitted myself to writing. Until I saw my mother's writings in her desk drawers, I never realized how prolific she was. It made me determined not to let my writing languish in drawers. I want to get that play out there, I want to get that movie out there, even if it's not sold.
>
> Otherwise, I don't have burning desires. But I want to have more fun. When I told that to my sister, she suggested that we start by having a birthday party for my husband, Bill.
>
> I said, "I *had* a party for him."
>
> And she said, "Rachel, that was twenty-four years ago! That was the last time you threw a birthday party." And she was right!
>
> I don't go to enough concerts, I don't go to enough plays, and I want to do that. Fun can be driving up to Ojai for the day. Fun can be visiting a friend and walking on the beach. I

want more fun in my day-to-day life and I want *to do* instead of thinking about doing. I've wasted a lot of my time and from now on I don't want to. That's something I learned.

It is a sad yet reassuring fact that the death of a parent can be an opportunity to do what we want without parental interference or disapproval. It can open the door to our own individuality by offering a form of freedom that, according to Dr. Scharlach, "can cut two ways. One way people think is, I'm on my own. What do I do now? The other side is, at last, nobody is looking over my shoulder. I don't have to worry about living up to somebody's expectations—even though realistically you could have ignored your parent for the past thirty years, and maybe you have." People who have tried to fulfill parental expectations can turn toward more personal ambitions; people who have made a point of rebelling against their parents no longer need to do so. One can feel liberated. I remember a woman in her early sixties whose mother had recently died. She was distraught. With tears flowing down her cheeks, she said that shortly after her mother died, she hit upon the idea of visiting the zoo. She ended up staring at a flock of exotic birds preening in the tropical foliage. Gazing at this scene, she was surprised to feel not only sorrow but elation. She felt "free as a flamingo." That feeling after a parent's death is not uncommon. (Interestingly, Dr. Scharlach's research suggests that "the sense of freedom and independence is more predominant when a father dies than when a mother dies.")

I never could seem to please my mother. She was so highly critical that when she died, I felt completely free to do whatever I wanted without harsh judgment. Her death allowed me the freedom to grow in self-confidence, which made it easier for me to start MADD. I often believe that I could not have started MADD if she had been alive.

Above all, death changes us, the living. In the presence of death, we become more aware of life. The value of the relationship is something we carry inside. The value of the death is that it can inspire us to decide what really matters in life—and then to seek it. Nancy talks about the effect her father's death has had upon her life:

> I was depressed and scared that my father died so young, before he could achieve all his dreams. I wished he had been able to work as a professor of philosophy or a writer. I became dogged in my determination to be a writer. I knew it was possible to die at any moment and I didn't want that to happen without writing some books. When my first book was published, I remember thinking very consciously, now I have written a book. I can die.

I have learned that grief does diminish but it never disappears. Most of the time my father's death over half my life ago is a distant spot on the horizon. But sometimes, as on the anniversary of that day, or now, while I am writing this book, it looms large. Maybe that's why, from time to time on this project, I have found myself doing something I haven't done since I was a teenager. In high school, I often borrowed an oversized black cardigan sweater that belonged to my father. When he died, I kept it. But I never wanted to wear it again —until recently. Working on this book, I have worn that sweater. Does it mean I don't want to give my father up? Does it mean I still miss him? It does.

Many times, I have thought about how fortunate I am to sit in front of my computer—I am certain my father would have *loved* computers!—and write. I have the career I dreamed about in second grade when my father gave me my first real book. I work part-time in a bookstore he would have liked. And I have an extensive collection of notebooks and classical music cassettes. For those pleasures—for the way I live in the world— I have him to thank.

CHAPTER 8 | The Death of a Partner

We were boon companions. All those wonderful things that were a part of my life, the hugs, all the large and little things: to say that I miss them desperately falls far short of the description. It's a tremendous deprivation.

—RON HAMMES

For many people, marriage is more than a relationship. It is the foundation upon which their lives are built. It structures their daily activities, their weekly schedule, their year-to-year planning. It provides a companion, a friend, a lover, a helpmate, someone with whom to share the burdens, pleasures, tasks, decisions, and details of daily life. It determines the way they interact in the world, providing certain social roles, affecting social status, and shaping identity—often far more than people imagine. Marriage encourages interdependency; that's the whole idea.

Death destroys all of that. It sets the mourner adrift in an empty sea. Often for the first time in their lives, the widowed feel—and are—alone. The chief source of support in their lives—emotionally, socially, physically, even economically—is gone. They may face a variety of financial and practical problems. Their position in society is altered. And their identity is shaken, because often their sense of themselves is largely linked to the spouse and to the role of husband or (more frequently) wife. They may feel incomplete. Many people compare the loss of a mate to the loss of a limb. Their lives are so enmeshed that they literally feel they have lost part of themselves.

For all those reasons, the death of a partner can be the most devastating event of a lifetime, all-encompassing in its implications and awesome in its requirements. Indeed, some experts believe that the changes involved in becoming widowed are more far-ranging and disruptive than those involved in any other kind of death. The losses and the loneliness are vast. When the widowed grieve, they grieve for an entire way of life.

That grief can have serious physiological consequences. In the first year or so after the death, the bereaved may smoke more, drink more, and suffer from increased rates of depression, suicide, cancer, tuberculosis, infections of many kinds, cirrhosis of the liver, and cardiovascular disease. "The age-old belief that grief can have lethal consequences is more than a myth," write Dr. Wolfgang Stroebe and Margaret S. Stroebe in *Bereavement and Health*. "As the poets always knew, the experience of losing one's spouse can be heartbreaking." That's how Ron Hammes, an artist who lives in rural Pennsylvania, felt when his thirty-nine-year-old wife, editor Tobi Sanders, died on May 27, 1987:

> She went to the dentist. She never came back.
>
> I was worried. She was overdue. Then the policeman came to the door and the minute I saw him, I knew. She was killed about a mile from where we live in an automobile accident on the curb. Nobody knows what happened. The car swung around and she hit a concrete abutment and her neck was broken. They said she died immediately.
>
> I was by myself from a little after two o'clock in the afternoon, when it happened, until seven or seven-thirty that night when my neighbor came home. During that time, everything looked familiar, everything had totally changed. I walked in our wildflower garden. I walked over by the peach tree we had planted. It's a third of a mile to any main road. I walked that road and I walked back. I felt an unbelievable gut-wrenching vastness of emptiness and loss.
>
> Finally, my neighbor came home. The policeman had left a card with the name of the hospital where they had taken Tobi. I had no transportation so my neighbor drove me to the hospital. At the hospital, they warned me she was pretty badly broken. I felt there was almost a suggestion on their part *not* to go in to see her, the implication being that maybe I'd rather remember her as she was in life, rather than as she is now. It was an act of love that propelled me to go in to see her body. I was tearful. I was crying. I had brought a nightshirt which she had given to me and worn. I draped her in that nightshirt because I wanted her to have something of us with her in that sterile white room. I kissed her hands and feet. I held her hand for a long, long time. After a while, I began to speak some of my favorite pieces of her writing, some poems that were very dear

to us, and certain passages which were broken and paraphrased. Little things we shared just seemed to come out of me.

Tobi's parents wanted her to be buried. Tobi wished to be cremated. Her family would have much preferred otherwise, and it was a difficult decision. After all, she was their daughter, their youngest daughter. But she was cremated according to her wishes. Afterward, I brought the ashes back here. You probably know ashes are a bit of a misnomer. It's really pulverized bone. But they're still ashes. I brought them back here and I waited until the following day. It was a beautiful day, and I spread her ashes in the wildflower garden she had planted and under the peach tree, in her herb garden, and along the side of the road where we used to walk. I spread her ashes in her favorite places, in the spot where the day lilies used to grow and in the spot where we used to love to stand and watch the fireflies.

My mind was scattered in a million different directions, emotionally, physically, mentally. The pain was so severe. But I've come to realize that you cannot run from it. It's forced me to take one simple step at a time. I didn't do that for a long, long time. Now I'm trying as best I can, one step at a time.

As with any death, the early days are colored by shock, numbness, and denial. That feeling of disbelief doesn't disappear right away either: two months after the death, according to data collected in the San Diego Widowhood Project, 64 percent of widowed people feel significant amounts of disbelief. More than one widowed person has unconsciously set a place at the table for a deceased partner. It takes time for the truth to sink in.

When it does, the pain is immense. Connie Schuman Grorud, a retired teacher, had a multitude of feelings after her husband died of cancer in 1988:

The first week was complete shock. I had no feeling. I was in a dreamlike state, very confused. I even smiled at friends and family during the funeral service.

I woke up from that numbness a week later. The awakening was devastating. Sorrow, unbelief, pain, guilt, sadness, and an almost uncontrollable anxiety overcame me. I felt depressed and hopeless, overcome by a feeling of being left alone and desolated. I felt crushed, abandoned, amputated.

During the first few weeks after the death, many mourners feel as if they're watching a play through a gauze curtain. Then the curtain rises, and the play becomes reality. The pain seems to worsen. The darkness feels unrelenting. Many people question whether they will ever be able to live a normal life again. The wonder of human nature is that they will.

LONELINESS

Possibly the most difficult feeling that accompanies the death of a spouse is loneliness. If in marriage, two become one, in widowhood many people feel reduced not to one, but to half. "He was my husband and my best friend," said Marcy De Jesus after the death of her husband of twenty-four years. "We were basically one person with two separate lives." The loss of that person's presence is keenly felt; the most ordinary activities, such as eating, become exercises in absence and isolation. The continuity of daily living is disrupted. Sleeping alone in the bed is so heartbreaking that many people move to the living room couch instead. And for the elderly, loneliness is especially severe.

Carolee Rake is a sixty-eight-year-old housewife in Grand Terrace, California, whose husband died of a massive heart attack on Easter Sunday, 1988. She expressed the loneliness many widowed people feel:

> I walked around the house like a zombie, going to someone's house and then wanting to leave shortly after I got there, but for what? You come home to an empty house again. It's awful, terrible, the worst thing I have ever experienced.
>
> Evenings are sometimes the worst. We had retired approximately three years before his death so we were together all the time and enjoyed one another's company. I sometimes don't know what to do with myself. I am very lonely.

That feeling of loneliness is powerful when mourners are involved in ordinary activities in which the spouse would formerly have been included, but it can also be strong when something new and wonderful has happened. Los Angeles resident David Sheridan experienced that feeling after his life partner, Ace, died of AIDS in 1989:

> You remember the person every day but especially when you're experiencing something terrific. You miss them because you can't say, "Isn't this great?" I'm a builder and in real estate and it'd be neat to have him see the results of my efforts. The last year he was alive I was building a big house in Montana. He saw it in renderings. When you finish things like that, you'd like the people who were important to be there with you and

obviously they can't be. You don't have someone to share your life with.

For many widowed people, loneliness is emphasized by the fact that they now live alone. They may be afraid of not being able to take care of themselves, of breaking down emotionally, of being alone at night, of dying themselves. Some mourners gradually start to leave the television or radio on almost all the time. The voices and the flickering images of familiar people provide a certain solace: the illusion of human interaction.

In social situations, loneliness is magnified by the isolation that comes from not being part of a pair. "The greatest change in my life is not to be a couple: sitting in church alone, being a third or fifth wheel, and sleeping alone in a big house with no one to share my loneliness and sorrow," said Mrs. Grorud. For many widowed people, the state of being married is something they profoundly miss. Harlene Marshall, whose husband died of a heart attack on the tennis court five months after her son was killed by a drunk driver, was very conscious of that feeling:

> I have platonic male friends, and it's amazing—it's almost orgasmic to be sitting in the car with the man driving and my daughter in the back and to be a little family unit. That feeling is so strong. I don't feel the bitterness I sense in other people who are divorced or widowed. I've gotten used to making my own decisions. But I would like nothing better than to have a body to lie down next to at night. I miss being married.

There's another form of loneliness too, and it has to do with the living. Other family members, as much as they care, may feel powerless in the face of your sorrow. No matter how attentive they are, they cannot fill the emptiness in your life. In addition, they're grieving themselves. And so sometimes they can't bear to talk about the death, perhaps because it increases their own grief, perhaps because they're afraid of reminding you of yours. "We cried together in the beginning," said one widow. "But there was discomfort on the part of my adult children when I wanted to talk about it."

Feelings of isolation can be exacerbated when there are children from a previous marriage. A widow who married a man with two sons from a previous marriage said, "One stepson was close to his father. And one stepson was impossible—he was so cruel to me. The family didn't appreciate George getting married again, especially to me."

It helps to have a close friend. Research conducted by Robert C. DiGiulio, Ph.D., author of *Beyond Widowhood: From Bereavement to Emergence and Hope*, revealed that women who did have a close friend adapted to the death and to the changes it brought about in their lives more easily than did those who lacked such a support. But as important as it is to have a close friend, one may not be enough. "One good spouse takes care of a multitude of needs, but you need many, many friends to take care of one need: loneliness," states one widow. Many mourners find that their friends are supportive, inviting them to dinner, calling at important times, remembering holidays and anniversaries.

But as time passes, that support often drifts away. Many people simply stop calling. They may feel intrusive. They may think you're "over it." Or they may find your presence too disturbing to bear—a reminder of the inevitability of death. Some mourners have realized only after the death that their social life was built around the spouse, and once that person is gone, their social life evaporates. "A lot of the socializing we did had to do with my husband's business," said one woman. "They wanted to help, but it wasn't a friendship—it was a business relationship."

Men in particular are likely to feel isolated, especially in the beginning, not only because they tend to have fewer close friends than do women but also because even their mutual friendships may have been primarily maintained by the wife. Martin Hearn is a social worker from a small town in North Dakota whose wife, Alison, died of cancer when he was forty years old:

> I think my relationships with everybody changed when my wife died. That was the biggest adjustment I had to make. She was more sociable, warmer, more outgoing, more nurturing. I was more of a doer, more solo, more individualistic. In relationships with mutual friends, she'd take care of certain parts and I'd take care of other parts. I'd be out working and she'd be spending time with the relationship—through which I would benefit. When she was no longer there to do that, it put more demands on me to take care of my own social relationships. I worked hard at it, but not being as good at it as she was, things didn't turn out as well.

Many widowed people are disappointed and surprised when their social circle gradually alters its composition, revealing itself to be "for couples only." "Couples we knew just gradually faded away because their lives were going in one direction and my life in another. We no longer had that much in common," said one widow. The loss of friends and acquaintances adds to the loneliness, as well as the insecurity, because it can feel like a personal slight. "As time passed, some people did drop out of my life," Zoe Schiff reported. "Our college friends: that was a big revelation to me. I was not their friend, they were not interested in me: it was my husband." In addition to the loss of their spouse, the widowed may also suffer what feels like a drop in popularity. But even when friends are loyal and thoughtful, the void is still there.

ANGER, GUILT, RELIEF, AND IDEALIZATION

Any death creates a web of complicated feelings. Anger is among them, whether it's anger over something that happened while the person was dying, over events that occurred during the course of the relationship, or simply over the fact that the living feel abandoned by the dead. Guilt is there too, for all the usual reasons. But another feeling that can also be present is relief. According to research conducted by Dr. DiGiulio, 43 percent of widowed women feel a sense of relief—a feeling which often increases guilt. Many of those women are relieved because death brought a release from suffering and from the burden of caring for an invalid.

But many were relieved because the relationship was difficult. One widow, asked if she missed her husband, responded this way: "He killed our love. He never nourished it. He was well liked but he was an alcoholic. My opinions were nothing, my political beliefs were ridiculed. I never got a pat on the back. I never got encouragement. That's the kind of guy I married." Although many people will not say these things, many people feel them. In Dr. DiGuilio's research, widows reported feelings of relief far more often than did widowers; evidently, men were happier with their relationships than women were.

A Harvard University study suggests that mourning may be more difficult when the relationship was a contentious one—although not in the beginning. The study showed that widows and widowers who reported several areas of conflict in their marriages seemed to cope exceedingly well during the first few weeks. But as time went on, their situation worsened. Two to four years later, 82 percent of them reported feeling anxious (as opposed to 40 percent of widowed people as a whole), 45 percent were depressed, and 61 percent were handling their roles and responsibilities with difficulty. The frustration, bitterness, resentment, and ambivalence that accompany discordant marriages are not easy to face.

Many people avoid painful memories and feelings by idealizing the deceased. In the beginning, idealization is normal; mourners miss the spouse so much that it's easy to forget how critical he was or how short-tempered she could be. "When somebody dies, you don't think about their weaknesses," said one widower. "You think about how much you loved them." That's true: mourners often suppress or deny angry or negative thoughts about the deceased. The tendency to do that is so strong that the dead sometimes sound like creatures far superior to the living. Nor is this solely a defense mechanism mourners use to protect themselves from painful memories; it's also something that is encouraged by society.

After my mother died, I watched my father idealize her. My parents did not have a particularly intimate relationship. They discussed divorce several times and they separated once. Because he worked in the military, my father was away a lot, which probably salvaged their marriage. Yet when Mom died, he preserved her things for a number of years and he talked about her so fondly, you would have thought it was a marriage made in heaven.

In most cases, idealization is strong at first but then tapers off. "People overidealize because it's unacceptable to them to feel ambivalent or negative feelings. But over time, memories tend to become less selective," New York psychiatrist Dr. Barry Kerner, M.D., observes. "They remember good and bad times. They can integrate the negative and the positive in the person who died, and also in themselves. It doesn't affect their feelings of love toward that person."

But when idealization continues, it's a problem. "Idealization creates a totally unrealistic image, a fantasy, that prevents people from going on," Dr. Kerner states. "They get stuck, immobilized by the fantasy and by guilt about their anger. They get depressed and don't function well. They also have difficulty connecting with other people, because the more someone is idealized, the more everyone else is measured against them." And no one can compete with a fantasy. "I don't idealize my wife," Martin Hearn asserts. "But my new girlfriend worries that I do. She thinks it's pretty hard to compete with Alison." It probably is.

WIDOWS AND WIDOWERS:
TWO DIFFERENT EXPERIENCES

In the United States, there are over thirteen million widowed people. Eleven million of them are women. Two million are men. The experiences they have differ markedly.

Men who lose a wife have a far harder time than women do—at first. According to studies published in the *Journal of the American Geriatric Society*, the *American Journal of Public Health*, and many other places, widowers commit suicide four times as frequently as women do. They also get sick and die at astoundingly high rates. Dr. DiGiulio reports that, compared to married men, widowed men are ten times more likely to die from strokes and six times more likely to die as a result of a heart attack: during the first four months after the death of a wife, the death rate for men jumps by about 40 percent. They also smoke more, drink more, and use more tranquilizers than do other men.

The reasons for this are varied. When a man loses his wife, he often loses his only close human connection, the one person in whom he could confide. He may literally not know how to take care of himself. He may have no intimate friends. It may be difficult for him to cry, and as a result he may hold back from active, appropriate grieving. Because women are more adept at emotional expression and better equipped with close friends, they find it easier to grieve. Men typically deal with their emotions less directly. Instead, during the first year or so, they suffer in other ways. "After my wife died, I developed a hiatal hernia, and then I ended up with a spastic colon, and then I came down with lactose intolerance. I think stress had something to do with it," Martin Hearn said. "I'm pretty good at sublimating emotions; it all goes into my gastrointestinal tract."

But after that first awful year, things change. Men remarry: over half of them in the first eighteen months. The remainder, for the most part, have little difficulty in finding new relationships. "Widows are invited out far less often than widowers are," states therapist Judy Tatelbaum, author of The Courage to Grieve. "No one wants an extra woman. Everyone wants an extra man." It doesn't seem to matter how old they are. "I was lonesome when my wife died," reported an eighty-two-year-old widower. "Six or eight months later, I ran into a friend of mine and asked if she would like to go to a party I'd been invited to. She's about sixty now. We went to this party and had a good time. Later we went to Mexico for ten days. She's never pushed me to get married but we've talked about it." Clearly, marriage is a possibility for him, as it is for most men. In her book Widow to Widow, Dr. Phyllis Silverman reports that 71 percent of older men are married, as opposed to a mere 10 percent of older women. Fewer than one widow out of twenty over the age of fifty-five ever remarries. On average, women live for another fifteen years after becoming widowed.

So for women far more than for men, adjusting to the death of a partner means learning to find happiness as a single person.

DATING AND SEXUALITY

Beginning to date can be a strange experience for the widowed, and the longer they were married, the more uncomfortable it is. It's more than being out of practice; times have changed. Many don't know what is appropriate or expected today. It's a challenge to meet people. And it's not easy, after many years of marriage, to think of oneself as a person who goes out on dates. No matter how old you are, it can feel like being a teenager again. "I remember my second date," Harlene Marshall said. "He was a business friend, and I was nervous, and I hated it. Here I was, running a business and wondering, will he like me? It was a strange schizophrenic feeling."

When widowed people do find companions, that new person can enliven thoughts of the deceased. So while dating is a sign of progress, it can also stir up a lot of sadness. Comparisons inevitably arise, which can be a problem not only for the widowed but for the person they are dating. Widowed people can feel that they are betraying the deceased spouse. If they have overidealized the spouse, they may feel that no one can ever compare to that person, in which case every date they have is likely to be disappointing.

Not everyone, however, is interested in dating or in remarriage. If the death was especially traumatic, or the adjustment especially difficult, the widowed may be afraid that finding a new relationship means having to face widowhood all over again. "If I can't have my husband, I don't want anybody," said Grace Patterson, a sixty-six-year-old widow from Albuquerque, New Mexico. "I have two men friends and we play Scrabble during the week and I have male companionship that way. I'm not interested, not at all. It's very true that in our age group if you meet somebody, you're going to be a caretaker again. Who wants to go through that all over again unless you really care about the person? Being alone is not the worst thing in the world."

Many people miss not only the companionship of the opposite sex but the pleasures of sexuality and physical affection. Sexuality is a serious and often unacknowledged loss. "For all of my life I had been a very sexual person and that part of my life with my husband was sensational," said one widow. "From the moment he got sick until today I have had absolutely no desire—none. That part of me died when he did."

But for many other people, sexual feelings do not die when the spouse does. When sexuality reenters the mourner's life, thoughts of the deceased inevitably accompany it. "I had sexual encounters. Sometimes it felt like Stanley was over my shoulder and I wanted to share it with him," Harlene Marshall recalled.

Sexuality can be a welcome balm. But appropriate opportunities do not necessarily appear at the desired times. If it doesn't reenter your life when you would like it to, consider the advantages of self-stimulation. And be sure to exercise. It may be a poor substitute for human intimacy, but the fact is that exercise, like laughter, produces endorphins. And endorphins make you feel better.

Those who don't date, or for whom a new relationship does not click into place, can feel a great deal of yearning, not just for the deceased as an individual but for the state of being in a relationship. What can you do if you want to meet people? You have to take action—when you're ready. Ask friends to introduce you. Take a job or volunteer at a place where people congregate—and where you'll have a good time even if you never meet a soul. I know several widows who placed personal ads in the newspaper and met attractive, intelligent men. One widow in her forties joined a video dating service. She hasn't met the man of her dreams, but she has had lots of dates—lots. It's not a method that anyone would have seriously considered during earlier decades. In the 1990s, it is absolutely acceptable.

MONEY AND OTHER PRACTICAL MATTERS

It will probably surprise no one to learn that the more money widowed people have, the better they seem to do. Some researchers have actually concluded that it's the primary factor affecting how people cope with widowhood (although other research has not confirmed that). Yet it is a sad fact that the old-fashioned image of the poor widow still has a contemporary reality. A 1977 study found that widows, taken as a group, had a lower level of income than any other group in the United States. Despite what many people think, they do not, by and large, come into financial windfalls. Dr. DiGiulio points out that the average life insurance policy in 1984 was worth a measly $14,270—not much even then. For older widows whose husbands have already retired, the financial fall may be cushioned by savings, pensions, and Social Security. They may not have to work. But they may have little financial savvy and no financial experience. Even today many women are not well acquainted with their own finances. When their husband dies, they suddenly have to negotiate in a land where they don't know the language.

For younger widows, there are additional problems—and younger widows are far more numerous than we thought. The average age of widows is fifty-six. For them, the death of a partner can cause real financial distress, especially if their husbands earned more money than they do— and as everyone must know by now, women on the average only earn fifty-nine cents for every dollar a man earns. Most of the time, widows take several steps down on the economic ladder, as Darcy Hall did. She is a Los Angeles artist whose husband, also an artist, died accidentally in 1984, when she was thirty-three years old.

It was the evening and we were coming home from dinner with another couple. We lived in the Hollywood Hills on a hairpin curve. My husband got out of the car and tripped on an embankment and fell eight feet off the hairpin curve onto the street below. He fell onto his head. It took him three weeks to die. I was encouraged by relatives to pull the plug, which I did not do. I kept waiting for a miracle.

My husband and I worked together as art directors and scenic painters in the film industry. We were on the set eighteen hours a day with each other. It was a working relationship that was unique. We were making two to three hundred thousand dollars a year and growing all the time. I had a house so big it had an elevator. I wore thousand-dollar dresses.

When he died, it was like losing my right arm. I couldn't function without him. I couldn't paint. I couldn't do anything. I lost my property, my money, everything. It's been a hard five years. I'm struggling financially. I'm living in a $425-a-month apartment, I have no savings account, I'm driving a used car.

Now I'm doing art again but in an entirely different context. My values have changed. Money is not the important thing to me. I want to do something that is beneficial to society.

Finances are often a problem for women even when there's plenty of money in the bank, because they may feel naive and extremely anxious around the entire topic. That anxiety can cause them to make financial decisions (such as selling the house immediately) that are not ultimately beneficial. Even when they seek advice from experts, they may not know how to assess those recommendations. One widow described her experiences:

With financial affairs, you either had the people who said "Make up your own mind" but never gave you the facts, or you had the people who made the decision for you. I was told to talk to my financial advisors, but who can afford a financial advisor? I've only seen dumb insurance men! My insurance man convinced me to do something I didn't really want to do. I said okay. Never again! I had terrible advice! Now I don't take advice from anyone except the top manager in the business. I'm learning to make my own decisions.

That's why it's so important to learn about money and how to handle it. Taking courses in financial management, consulting with financial advisors (it may be that you can't afford *not* to), or asking assistance from professionals or knowledgeable friends is essential. It's the only way to demystify money and the only way to protect yourself. Fortunately, as many widows have discovered, learning to deal with finances successfully has an unexpected payoff: it increases self-esteem.

The same thing is true for other areas in which widowed people lack experience, including household tasks they simply don't know how to do. Often—not always—those tasks are related to traditional sex roles. Retired army officer Alfred Shehab of Maryland became a widower in 1983 when his wife, Betty, died of cancer. "Since I decided to continue on in the same house, I was faced with the necessity of engaging in labor such as shopping, occasionally cooking, sewing on a button." Another widower, in the midst of being interviewed for this book, asked for advice about steaming broccoli. A widow faced different challenges:

> I have a car to sell and I'm having trouble dealing with it because I've never dealt with cars before and to sell something, to dicker with someone, this is not a thing I'm comfortable with! So I still have the car. And I had termites in my house that I had to have taken care of. I've dealt with a lot of things, but a lot of things are still waiting.

Sometimes practical problems like that seem to pile up extraordinarily fast after a death. One widow summed it up: "Houses rebel when they know you're alone. I joined a bereavement group, and we all needed plumbers." Learning to deal with these problems increases feelings of competency, reduces anxiety, and ultimately saves you money.

YOUNG WIDOWS AND WIDOWERS

People who become widowed in their twenties or thirties have a far more difficult time coping with widowhood than do the elderly. Perhaps the reason young adults have difficulty adjusting to widowhood (and also to the death of a parent) is just that, the older we get, the more we accept the inevitability of death and the more experience our friends and relatives have with it as well. When death strikes while we're young, most of us are entirely unprepared.

When young people are widowed, they have more digestive distress than do the elderly, and their sleep patterns are more disrupted. They also have more financial problems; after all, they may lose their entire family income without benefit of Social Security or pensions. And unlike older people who are widowed, they find no community of support. "I was twenty-five years old when I was widowed," one woman said. "I had two children and this was my first contact with death. I had no skills, no education, I was happy with my husband, and he was gone. I was overwhelmed. I was very alone." People in that situation may literally know no other widows or widowers of their generation. "You meet more people who are divorced than are widowed at my age, so it's difficult to share the longing," a thirty-nine-year-old widow said. And a widower in his forties made a statement few older people would be able to make: "I don't think I've ever talked to anybody else who's lost a husband or a wife."

In addition, young widowed people often face another challenge: being a single parent. They want to maintain some stability for their children, and yet their world has been turned upside down. "I was afraid," said Marcy De Jesus after her husband died of liver cancer. "It was the thought of raising my son by myself and being there for my older son, and the fear of things not changing too drastically for my younger son until I got him through high school. My focus was on keeping my job, earning a living wage, paying my mortgage." For single parents, grieving may have to be balanced with immediate practical concerns; their focus may have to be outside themselves. Yet as difficult as it is, it is important to note that widowed people with children do adapt. They learn to manage their household by themselves; they learn to cope with parenthood; they even find new relationships.

CREATING A FUTURE

You'll never, ever forget the past. But it is still possible to be happy. "I am in the process of forming a new life without Ace, whom I will always miss," said David Sheridan. "That life will hold promise for love, contentment, and happiness—but in a new context due to this experience."

In the beginning, most people want to hold on to the beloved partner. They may do so both psychologically and physically, becoming extremely attached to the loved one's possessions. "In my case there was a lot of external clinging to objects," Ron Hammes said. "Every time I let go of something—a little object, some books—it was extremely painful."

But primarily, they hold on through memory. "What I never knew about was the terrible need to reminisce with people who knew him well, because that is the process of holding on to the person, of keeping them alive," Dvora Freeman said. We hold on to our loved ones by talking about them, telling their jokes, imagining their reactions, looking at photographs, and making them a part of ourselves—a part we can never lose. Sometimes that can happen literally when the bereaved unconsciously imitates the loved one, as Darcy Hall did after her husband's death. He was an Englishman; she is a native Southern Californian. Nonetheless, she began speaking with an English accent and seeking out foods he loved. In the beginning, it is a natural reaction to cling to whatever bits of that person we still have.

Progress takes time. Friends may grow impatient. Mourners themselves may grow impatient, especially because from time to time they are bound to encounter worrisome setbacks. But sooner or later, moments of contentment, fulfillment, and pleasure sneak in. Eventually, it is possible to create a new life.

In order to do so, we have to leave the past behind in some way. That can feel like a betrayal. "People are afraid to say good-bye because they think it means to let go of the love you had," comments bereavement specialist Sandra L. Graves, Ph.D., of the University of Louisville. "But you don't let go of the love. The love is with you always. The past is with you always." Letting go means having the fortitude to move forward toward the unknown future. It's a gradual process, as grief counselor Sue Holtcamp learned after her husband and teenage daughter were killed when the plane they were in crashed into the Tennessee River. Two weeks after the accident, Sue went back to school. She talked about her experiences:

> I don't think that there is a clear-cut good-bye. You do it over and over and gradually it becomes less prominent. You may say good-bye to your husband at his coffin. You may say good-bye at breakfast when you sit there by yourself and weep over the empty chair. But you say good-bye on a very different level when you go out on your first date. It's all involved in accepting reality.
>
> Glen and Katie are both buried in the same grave, so there is just one tombstone with writing on the back and front. I remember going there when I was in graduate school, about a year and a half or two years after the loss. I had one arm draped over this tombstone. The pain was as bad as ever. I felt miserable thinking that this was never going to be over. And after a little while I began watching the trees blowing in the wind and I lost track of my grief for a moment. Before I knew it, I was outlining a term paper for one of my classes. That was the first clue, there at the grave, even while I was exhausted and in tears, that I was not back at square one. I was focusing on the future and preparing for the future, even as I sat there with my arm draped over the tombstone.
>
> In a sense Glen and Katie are with me always. My life will always be colored by the fact that these people lived in my life, that they mattered to me. In a sense I have let go of them in reality because they are internalized. They are part and parcel of who I am now.

Moving forward means incorporating some aspects of the deceased into ourselves. Mourners may find inspiration in the example of the deceased. "As the exterior objects begin to fade, the really valued things begin to exist inside," said Ron Hammes. "Tobi's spirit and quest, her drive and energy that functioned in so many different ways and with such decency, have led me constantly to try and do something with my time."

Mourners may also come to a new respect for traits they hadn't formerly appreciated. "My husband was a procrastinator to the extreme and I was an activist to the extreme. We made a good pair but we'd drive each other crazy," Harlene Marshall said. "Now I've learned the value of a certain amount of procrastination, or waiting, or pondering."

Moving ahead also involves letting go of some aspects of our identity that were linked to the deceased. In many cases, this involves a change in role; Phyllis Silverman notes that for women, the transition is from "wife" to "widow" to "woman." Making that transition successfully means learning our own strengths and becoming our own person in a fuller way. For many widowed people, that can include learning to appreciate the pleasures and freedoms of living alone. Maggie Webster, a retired secretary who grew up in Idaho, described her initial reactions and her adjustment:

My husband died when he was seventy-five years, four months, and sixteen days old. I felt like I was caught in a violent storm of emotions. Thoughts whirled in my mind. My most powerful feeling was fear of being alone with all the decisions and all the coping.

But after a year you no longer are saying, last year we did this or last year was like this. When you live alone, you can plan your own schedule—you don't have to consider anyone else. This gives me more time to do the things I like. I garden. I used to be the chief gardener. But for five or six years after he retired, my husband really took care of that. Then he was not well at all and spent less and less time in the yard. Well, I'm back to being the chief gardener. I read, I crochet, I make afghans for all the nieces and nephews and young people who get married. I am into genealogy and I started, ten or twelve years ago, writing the story of my life. It's a fun thing to do. I have made a time line of the things in our marriage and I have also started writing down just thoughts that I have had about my loss. I think it's very helpful—putting words to grief helps me, too. You take the pain out and look at it to see what it means. I have dealt with death before and I don't think it's a thing you ever get over. You just learn to live with it. I'm learning to live with it.

Creating a new future means coming to a fuller sense of ourselves and our own individuality. That doesn't occur in leaps and bounds; we inch forward. It happens, for instance, when mourners do something that they know the deceased would not have liked—such as purchasing a hard cover book rather than a paperback even though the deceased would have thoroughly disapproved.

It happens when mourners go somewhere new, regardless of whether that place is a restaurant or a foreign country.

It happens when widows and widowers rearrange the furniture or move to a new apartment or cut their hair short—something they haven't been able to do for thirty years because the deceased spouse insisted it be long.

It happens when they make new friends. "I've made new friends because people don't have to pass through my wife's scrutiny," Martin Hearn commented. "I have been able to develop relationships with people she wouldn't normally encourage."

And it happens when people find new interests. One widow stressed the importance of finding activities that you did not share with your partner and hence can enjoy without being inundated with reminders. "Dig in and do something entirely different," she said. "I took a reserved seat at our new baseball team in town and I went there for weeks and weeks. He didn't do that with me." Doing these things does not dishonor the memory of the deceased; it propels mourners forward into the rest of their lives.

If death can be said to have one single advantage, it might be this: it makes us appreciate life more. Many people, having lost a loved one, savor their other relationships more. One newly bereaved widow, for instance, decided to patch things up with her daughters-in-law. Death put the conflicts they had had into perspective, and she took steps to improve the communications between them. Feuding no longer seemed worthwhile.

Another woman commented that "I'm a nicer person, more sensitive to other people's feelings, more compassionate and much more altruistic. Before my husband died, I was self-centered and very me-oriented. I cherish my relationships a lot more now than I ever did before. I mind my behavior because who knows how long any of us is going to be around."

Death forces changes on the living, and some of those changes are positive. Spurred on by death, many mourners grab opportunities in a way they might not have done before. They go back to school and discover new interests. They change careers. They meet new people. They overcome fears and take courageous steps—and they exult in those changes.

Slowly, they discover that the great sorrow of losing a partner opens them up to new versions of themselves—better, stronger, and more creative. Somehow, they grab hold of that. They create new lives. Dr. Graves recommends making a five-year plan for yourself. It's a good idea: it's a way to imagine a future and turn it into reality. Dvora Freeman recounted her experience:

> I married my boss. I had never seen anyone so kind and patient and gentle. I really fell for him. After he died, I had to make a new life, new friends, singles, and I just didn't like anybody. I was always getting irritated and angry. And I was depressed. I saw a therapist for months. I took that one hour a week and just sat there the whole hour and sobbed. I didn't give a damn about anything. I wasn't motivated. I was always so sad. I couldn't shape up. . . .
>
> All of a sudden—I wish I knew what, how, or where—it felt good to be alive. This was about three years after Lee died. I can't imagine what specific experience moved me from chronic depression to feeling happy. A lot of things were happening at one time, but I think I was already feeling good. I was studying Kabala, the ancient mystical Jewish teachings, and I was taking classes in meditation and reincarnation, and right after I started the Kabala courses I decided for the hundredth time to go back into Overeaters Anonymous, and this time I got a sponsor. We both feel it's a gift God gave us. I believe I have adjusted well.
>
> I was always used to having my husband around, and after he died, a replacement. It could be any friend at all—just somebody I could turn to and say, Where do we go now? How do we get a cab? I finally let go of that business. It has to do with gaining confidence about functioning in the world.
>
> I never pass a day that I don't remember my husband is dead. I feel his presence from time to time, and my thinking seems to be, in many cases, a reflection of *his* thinking. I'm a great deal more independent than I was. I spend money on myself that I would not have done when he was around. My spirituality is greatly expanded. I investigate many more areas of interest. I'm more selective with friendships and how I give my time. I'm no longer depressed. I'm no longer needing to die. I feel good to be alive.

CHAPTER 9 | The Death of a Child

Sometimes I get lonely even in a crowd. Sometimes my heart hurts until I just cry. I know this: death cannot break love. But your children are a part of you. And when they die, part of you dies too.
— WAYNE MONTGOMERY

Never, never, never, never, never!
— SHAKESPEARE, *King Lear*

The death of a child is an ordeal so traumatic that for many people it is the most profoundly painful experience of a lifetime. It is the death for which we are least prepared: a loss so unimaginable and so terrible that in certain significant ways, we cannot even talk about it. "There are words in our language for someone who loses a husband or a wife or for someone who loses parents," observes Rabbi Laura Geller of Los Angeles. "But there is no word in English for a parent who has lost a child. Translated into the vernacular, it means that loss is literally unspeakable."

No matter what their age, our children are the people for whom we feel most responsible and with whom we feel the most visceral connection. As parents, we feel entrusted with their well-being; their death shakes both our faith in the world and our confidence in ourselves. Bereaved parents yearn for the touch of the child's skin, the sound of her laughter, the smell of the top of his head. Their grief is massive and all-encompassing. According to Stephen Levine, author of *Who Dies? An Investigation of Conscious Living and Conscious Dying*, "The death of a child is a fire in the mind." That fire burns for a long time, for no other loss is so difficult to accept; no other loss feels so utterly unnatural. We expect our parents to die before we do, and we know

137

that at least some of our contemporaries will predecease us. But our children? Never.

Yet the unnatural quality that surrounds the death of a child is a relatively new phenomenon in human history. Even in the beginning decades of this century, children died early and often. In the days before birth control, it was common for women to become pregnant and give birth many times. If they were lucky, a few of their offspring might grow to adulthood.

Today, we expect *all* our children to outlive us. Yet in 1986, according to figures published by the U.S. Department of Health and Human Services, 71,383 children under the age of nineteen died in the United States. Unlike children in the past, who succumbed to epidemics and childhood diseases, children today do not for the most part die of natural causes. They die unexpectedly and violently. One third of those who died between the ages of one and twenty-four were killed in automobile accidents (of which approximately half were alcohol-related); it's the most common cause of death for young people. Fifteen percent died in other accidents. Eleven percent were murdered. Almost 10 percent committed suicide. *Most* of the time, the death of a child today is a sudden, unnatural, utterly horrifying event. Those deaths are hard no matter who the deceased is. But when the victim is a child, the pain has a unique shape because parents feel they should have been able to protect that child; they are responsible for the child's well-being, and in some way, they feel they have failed in that duty. The emotional shock waves reverberate for a long time. Bennett Sloan is an engineer whose son, Justin, was a college student in Indiana when he committed suicide. He talked about his reaction:

> It was two o'clock in the morning and someone was pounding, pounding, pounding on my front door. I saw my friend Don there and I thought, something's happened to him. I thought, he's in trouble. I let him in but before he came through the door, he said, "Ben, something terrible has happened. And I'm sorry I have to bring the news to you."
>
> I said, "What?" But even as I said it, I knew that it had something to do with Justin. He said that Justin had shot himself. I let him in and he climbed the stairs, thinking I would follow him. But my legs wouldn't work! I asked him where he shot himself, and when I learned he had shot himself in the head, I knew it was over. He was still alive. But I knew. I knew. And still I couldn't get my legs to work. I don't know how long it took. It seemed like it took forever for me to get up the stairs.
>
> For weeks and months after he died, I was in a kind of shock.

I would wake in the middle of the night not remembering what had occurred and then be jolted back to reality. Was it also a way of punishing myself for not having done more for him? I don't know. I was stunned and shocked over and over again. My sister and father died several years before that, and I grieved when they died, but it didn't equal in any way what I went through following the death of my son.

Parents whose children die from natural causes such as spinal meningitis or sudden infant death syndrome may also have no warning. Parents whose children suffer lingering diseases such as leukemia watch their children slowly die. They know death is coming; they may even greet it with a sense of relief, because by then the child has been in pain for such a long time. Yet even then, it is virtually impossible to be fully prepared for the death of a child. Annabel Kaufman, forty, is a designer. She and her husband, Jerry, sixty-one, a composer, live in the Hollywood Hills in a house surrounded by trees. Their son, Zack, died when he was five and a half:

The night Zack was born, he had major surgery and many transfusions, which we later found out caused AIDS. In his first year he had a tracheotomy, a gastrostomy tube, a diaphragmatic hernia repair—it was a congenital defect—and other symptoms too. But he thrived. He overcame all of the trauma, which was a lot, let me tell you. He was a joyous, sunny, loving, bright, very gifted child.

When he was four, we thought he was a triumph of modern medicine. The only thing was, he wasn't growing and the t-cell count was abnormal. The doctor said they had to test him for AIDS. I said, "No problem. He doesn't have it." It was the farthest thing from my mind.

Two days later, I woke up in the middle of the night and started putting all these symptoms together—thrush, multiple infections, chronic diarrhea, failure to grow—and it dawned on me. I woke up Jerry and said, "He's got AIDS." It was a huge surprise. When our pediatrician finally called me, I already knew. I had realized it at three o'clock in the morning.

My husband felt strongly that he didn't want him to know that he had AIDS. For one thing, he was still in school. When Zack asked me why he was sick, I told him that he'd gotten a transfusion. I told him exactly what happened. I just didn't call it AIDS.

Jerry and I had very different approaches and philosophies.

He didn't want me to talk to Zack about death or dying because he didn't want him to lose hope. He didn't think Zack knew that he was dying. I'm sure that he did. I had to be very careful because I didn't want to say anything that Jerry didn't approve of since Zack was his child too. So it only came up when Zack asked me questions. He was frightened. He didn't know what death meant or how it would come and he was afraid for me to leave him even to go put money in the parking meter. I realized he thought he might die if I was gone. So I told him it was not something that would happen without his permission, and that was very reassuring. He asked, "Am I going to die?" I didn't want to say anything that Jerry wouldn't feel comfortable with, so I said, "I don't know, but if you are going to, you will know, and you will let me know."

He died at home. He had an opportunistic infection for which there's still no treatment. His body was swollen and he was in a lot of pain and it was horrible. I knew on Friday that he was dying, and he died Monday night. He didn't want to be held because he was in such discomfort, but I was lying next to him on the bed. Jerry was asleep and I called him. I sang Zackie's favorite lullaby when he died. I didn't want him to be afraid and he was not afraid at all. He did fine. I don't think it's hard for the person who's dying. I think it's hard for those who are left behind.

LOSING THE FUTURE

With the death of a child, a door to the future is slammed forever shut. Bereaved parents mourn for the moments they shared as well as for those that were snatched from them. They grieve for those stages and ages and events in the child's life that never came to be; they lose the past and they lose the potential. And although with time the pain will fade, the sense of loss occasionally flares up anew, stirred by the thought of what might have been.

I was very aware of this process after Cari's death. Because she and Serena were identical twins, I had a rough time on many occasions. Birthdays were especially emotional, for whenever I wished Serena a happy birthday, I was overcome with thoughts of Cari. But birthdays are annual events, and after a few years I learned to handle that particular date. I learned to greet my daughters' birthday every September with a pang of poignancy for Cari mingled with a sense of joy in Serena's own growth.

When Serena graduated from high school, I watched her graduation with such pride. But as they called the kids' names, I realized that I was actually waiting for them to call Cari. She would have been before Serena. When they called Serena, I was still waiting to hear Cari's name. This was five years after Cari died. The loss hit me all over again. It is my expectation that, from time to time for the rest of my life, that feeling will come flooding back.

The future that we lose when a child dies is not limited to graduation ceremonies and weddings and shopping expeditions that never take place. With the death of a child, we lose a claim to the future that extends beyond our own lives. This is one way in which the death of a child differs from other losses. The death of a child means the loss of a fragment of immortality—possibly the only fragment we ever hoped to have. When a child dies, we lose a significant part of ourselves—often the part we cherished most.

HOLDING ON TO PAIN

With any death, grief gradually diminishes. Many bereaved parents, however, are uncomfortable when they start feeling good again. They fear that if they laugh and have good days, they're not being good parents. To allow the grief to abate feels disloyal. One man, whose wife and toddler were killed by a drunk driver, refused to give any of their clothes away after their deaths. They hung in the closet for years. He just couldn't give them up. Other parents turn the child's room into a shrine. A decade after the death, the child's room is untouched, while the parents, needless to say, are depressed and miserable. Grief becomes the connection they have with their child, and they don't want to give it up.

That tenacious holding on isn't a subtle, subconscious pattern either: it's something many parents do consciously. "I wanted the pain to stay," said Charlene Kelley Phillips, a registered nurse in Tennessee whose two-year-old son, Jeremy, died in the doctor's office during an examination after open-heart surgery. "That way, I could be nearer to my son. I was scared the hurt would go away—and with it, my son would be farther from me."

EMOTIONAL CHAOS: DENIAL, FEAR, GUILT, AND ANGER

When a child dies, certain feelings are particularly strong. Denial is one of them, because the death of a child is a possibility so remote and horrendous that the mind simply refuses to entertain the notion. In a deep way, the death of a child does not compute. How can a child die? How can this be?

Years after the death, many parents still fantasize the child's return; according to one study, four to seven years after the death of a child in an automobile crash, 41 percent of the bereaved parents still occasionally imagine their child returning to them. Intellectually, they know how impossible that is. Emotionally, it's another matter.

Losing a child also unleashes fear, because there is nothing that demonstrates more clearly how little control we have in this world than the death of a child. One fear that frequently arises is the dread that this could happen again, to another child. A mother whose baby was stillborn said, "A year later, I was again expecting and as a result of the earlier loss was scared senseless."

I, too, worried that something might happen to my other children. I became extremely overprotective, as my daughter Serena will attest. She finally ran away from home. My overprotectiveness—I thought of it as simple caution—was driving her wild. But I couldn't get past the fear that something would happen to her.

Many parents fear that they will never be able to function normally, especially since, as the shock and numbness wear off, the pain seems to grow. They may become preoccupied with the death, and particularly with the final images. "I keep thinking of my baby taking his last breath, alone in a strange crib in a strange room," Roseanne Lurie told us. Although happier memories will eventually replace those terrifying, sad pictures of death, it won't happen right away. In the meantime, parents may fear that they are going crazy. "People often think they'll go berserk," observes Los Angeles therapist Susan Faber-Brook. "They have images where the pressure will blow them apart from the inside and they'll explode into millions of pieces. They may picture themselves rocking and wailing on the floor. Or they may feel like they're going to turn into stone." It's very frightening. It's also normal.

Bereaved parents often feel guilty because they feel like complete failures as parents: incompetent, inadequate as protectors, unable to control their environment, and powerless. This is true even when the death clearly had nothing to do with anything a parent might have done. "I always try to blame myself for the loss of my son. I feel I must have caused his death somehow," Roseanne Lurie reported after her baby died of febrile seizures. "I'll never understand why I would have to lose a little baby I loved so much. I feel like I have been given the ultimate punishment." Many parents feel similarly. They have no trouble at all coming up with ways to blame themselves. Perhaps they allowed their child to drive a motorcycle; perhaps they lost sight of their child for a few minutes, and during that time he drowned; perhaps they weren't strict enough; or maybe they were too strict and as a result, the child rebelled; or they had the wrong genes, and so the child got a disease and died. There's always something.

Many parents succumb to the "if only" syndrome. I certainly did. If only I had driven my daughter to the school carnival. If only I had picked her up . . . if only I hadn't gone shopping . . . if only. . . . It's a litany that played through my mind for a long time. Research conducted by Darrin R. Lehman of the University of California, Camille B. Wortman of the University of Michigan, and others indicates that 62 percent of the parents they studied (all of whom had lost a child in an automobile accident) fell into this pattern. Four to seven years later, 28 percent of the parents were still running through the ways they could have saved their child—if only they had acted differently.

Giving up that guilt means giving up the illusion that control is possible. "Raising children is not a science, and no parent is ever trained to do the right thing," observes television producer Richard Haboush, whose thirty-one-year-old son died of cancer. "One has to stop feeling that control and destiny are in the parent's hands. They are not." He's right. Nonetheless, the feeling can be persistent.

Bereaved parents also feel a unique form of survivor's syndrome. Parents who outlive their children are burdened by the thought that "it should have been me." They feel guilty because they are alive while their child is dead. "I thought I would not be able to go on," said Californian Jean Tanguay after her son was killed in a motorcycle crash. "I wanted to die. I felt I should have died instead of my son. He had just completed a college program at the top of his class."

Guilt is especially powerful when death came through accident, suicide, or murder rather than disease. Getting a disease, after all, is outside the parents' sphere of influence. But accidents and violence are preventable. When children die from those causes, parents are likely to blame themselves, as Joni Schaap did. She is a speech therapist in Los Angeles whose sixteen-year-old son, Jeremy, was murdered by a drug dealer:

> It took me the longest time to get over the sense that it was my fault. I thought, if I had been a better mother, he wouldn't have died. I had guilt going back to when he was one year old and I left him at a day-care center and he wasn't happy and he cried the whole weekend. If I'd been a better mother and closer to him, he wouldn't have been in that situation. It still seems partly true. Why was he out at night with this creepy kid buying drugs? Why was he into drugs? He was always rebellious. He

always walked on the wild side. He used to say, if it's not dangerous, it's not fun. He was always just this side of trouble. How do you raise a child to be responsible? I don't know. It's scary.

My therapist was training a group of therapists all of whom had experienced loss. They all felt guilty, no matter what the death was. When I think about them, I can see that they have no reason to feel guilty. But in my case, I know it was my fault. If I had been a better mother, he might have been a different kid.

It's also possible that he might *not* have been a different kid; it's probable that the choices she made seemed right at the time. In other words, the chances are she was, to use Bruno Bettelheim's phrase, a "good enough" parent. Many mothers and fathers need to hear this. They need to be reassured that it was not their fault. They need to accept the fact that as parents they were not godlike, but human.

When something so terrible happens to our child, we blame ourselves—often regardless of the facts. In the beginning, friends and family can offer some logical ballast and a little much-needed perspective. But if months go by and the guilt doesn't diminish, a good therapist can help you to assess your guilt realistically and to learn to cope with your conflicting feelings of responsibility and powerlessness. It's so hard to do this. Learning to forgive ourselves is a struggle almost every parent has.

Finally, anger is a large component of mourning a child, for the death of a child is always untimely, always unfair. "I was angry that this had to happen and I was angry at people who told me I had to accept it," said one bereaved mother. Some people, stunned by the loss, may direct their anger inward, blaming themselves. Depression can be a primary reaction for these people.

Other people get angry right away. This is especially true when death comes violently. When Cari died, it was very hard to think about her without feeling rage. It was hard even to feel love for her, because every time I did I would get angry all over at how unnecessary her death was.

It's surprising how many different targets people find for their anger. An elderly woman whose middle-aged son died was furious at the police and at the funeral director. "From the police we never got a written report of what had happened. I'm so angry. They've been so discourteous! And at the mortuary, all they could say was what a head of hair he had. He was extremely handsome," she sighed. "It's so heavy on my heart."

Anger is such a complex emotion that even when a child is killed by another person, mourners don't necessarily direct their anger toward the killer. After Cari was killed, I hated the system for allowing a repeated drunk driver back out on the road. I never really hated Clarence William Busch as an individual. Harlene Marshall, whose teenage son was also killed by a drunk driver, reacted similarly. "At first I could find no energy whatsoever to put toward being angry at the driver," she said. "I was angry as hell about not having Matthew."

People express their anger in many ways. Some people lash out at everyone around them. Some people express their feelings physically. Elisa Glatz, a nurse from Lansing, Michigan, was angry when she lost not one but two babies in late miscarriages. "I would be doing laundry and I'd start to cry and yell from my toes. I broke dishes, yelled at my kids, and would escape to the basement where I wanted to beat my head into the wall to stop the pain. I never hurt myself in any way. I did think about it, however."

There are ways to cope effectively. Groups like MADD that have a political agenda or are formed to combat the problem that led to the child's death have provided a practical direction for the rage many parents feel. And I'm far from the only parent to have formed such an organization. When Clementine Barfield's teenage son died as a result of inner-city violence in Detroit, she formed a grass-roots organization to combat that problem called SOSAD: Save Our Sons and Daughters. Donna Gaetano formed the South Carolina Bus Safety Action Committee after her six-year-old daughter was struck and killed by a school bus driven by a seventeen-year-old driver. And Pete Shields, whose twenty-three-year-old son was shot to death in 1974, became the chairman of Handgun Control, Inc. Galvanized by their loss, these parents were able to turn their grief and anger into something positive. You might not think that buttonholing one representative after another or stuffing thousands of envelopes would have even the slightest impact on the feelings of grief you have for your dead child. It won't bring your child back; that's true. It won't eliminate sorrow. But I can tell you from personal experience that activism truly helps with anger. For just as it is necessary to cry, to mourn, to go to the heart of darkness within, it is also helpful to step outside of yourself. The knowledge that you have tried to save other children from such a fate and other parents from ever experiencing such a tragedy can lend meaning to your child's death and purpose to your own life. I can assure you, it makes a very real difference.

There is one additional situation that can lead to a lot of anger, and that is the death of a child to whom you are not directly related by blood. When an adopted or foster child dies, there is a tendency on the part of other people to diminish the impact of the death. Amy Evans, a graduate student in Sacramento, lives with her husband, two adopted children, and a group of Vietnamese young people who were orphaned by the war. She told us about the deaths of two of her children:

Sean and Scott were biological brothers we foster-cared in our home. They both had a metabolic illness that was a result of prenatal drug and alcohol exposure by the birth mother. We applied to adopt both boys. Sean died after adoption and Scott died before adoption was completed. My immediate family was great. But other people said, "The pain should be less because he's adopted" or "He was only a foster child." I was also told that "he was a bad seed. If you had given birth to them yourself, they would have been healthier." My extended family—aunt, uncles, parents, grandparents—totally abandoned us. I was angry at them for fleeing when I most needed them.

Talking helps release some of that pain, but it's not easy to find people who are comfortable with feelings this intense. Many people cannot bear to think about what you've been through. They're sympathetic; but they do not know what to say and often avoid you for that reason. The bereaved mother or father in a sea of parents, like the widow or widower in a room full of couples, is like the angel of death. No one wants to hang around with you. To connect with a grieving parent is to face the possibility that one's own children might die. It's too awful to consider.

The main way you can help yourself is to understand that the emotional storm will subside. The process is slow. "If you're in the middle of a tempest, sometimes it's enough just to lie on the shore while you're exhausted and then you crawl before you walk," said a bereaved father. "It's enough just to survive."

DEATH OF A GROWN-UP CHILD

At a bereavement group meeting once, Nancy and I spoke with a woman whose daughter had gone in for a standard medical test and died, right there in the hospital. The mother was in her seventies; the daughter was in her forties. It was clear in talking to her that she had lost not only her child but also the adult friend her child had become. Her daughter called her every day; they ate lunch every week. After three years, she missed her as much as ever.

The death of an adult child has its own unique pain. Like the death of an infant, but for different reasons, the mourning may be underestimated by well-meaning nincompoops. The thought seems to be that if the child has been out of the house for some time, you'll get over it.

The truth is, you might never get over it. "When I think of my son being gone, it's gut-wrenching," said Dorothy Loring of Pasadena, California, whose twenty-eight-year-old son was killed in 1979 by a drunk driver. "When one of your children dies, the sunshine goes out of your life. Your life is never the same again, never. That piece of your heart is gone."

Nevertheless, people do learn to live with it. As one man said, six and a half years after the death of his son, "Your life won't be the same but you can do things and you can laugh and you can be happy."

And while you'll never forget, the pain will diminish with time. Solomon Berg is a retired dentist who lives with his wife in a suburb of New York. His thirty-two-year-old son, Mark, died in an apartment fire in 1982:

> It was a Thursday in May and there was a driving windstorm. Mark put something on the stove, and it must have caught fire. The wind blew the flame and ignited the newspapers that he had around the place. He couldn't get out. The fire department broke the door down and found him dead in the bathroom fully clothed. He had evidently tried to escape from the flames. He died of smoke inhalation. At least that's what the death certificate says.
>
> Afterward, I went to the crematorium, picked up the ashes in a little box, and left them in the car until it was something I could face. Then I buried his ashes in the garden. They're right by the house. There's a stone there. My wife was doing the dishes. Afterward I said, "You know what I was doing?" She said yes. I wanted to do it myself. It's no pleasure, it had to be done.
>
> The night Mark died, I played the piano and the cello. Afterward, I couldn't go near the cello. I didn't take it seriously as a cause-and-effect relationship, but I had that association. Three or four months later, my friend Stanley said, "Let's start playing duets again." I said, "Ask me in a couple of weeks," and he did. We've been playing steadily for the last six years.
>
> The piano, I didn't touch. After three or four years, I tried it again, and nothing happened—I didn't get stung, nobody bit me, my hair didn't become electrified. So I played a little more and a little more and that did it.
>
> My mother died less than a year before my son. I think about her from time to time. But when my son died, it was a totally different story. Mark is with me all the time. He's not at the top of the consciousness, but he's there. He's always there. Let me put it this way: it doesn't hurt anymore but you don't have your arm.

The connection that sprang up in Solomon's mind between playing music and the death of his son reminds me of an association I made. In 1975, at Easter, we had a family picture taken; just a few days later Travis was run over by a car. We didn't take another Easter picture again until 1980—and shortly after that, on May 3, Cari was killed. So I don't have family pictures taken at Eastertime anymore, and I doubt that I ever will—even though I, too, know that the one event did not cause the other. My rational mind knows that. My superstitious mind isn't willing to take another chance. I suspect that many mourners make similar associations. As long as the connections don't turn into phobias, don't worry about them. If they begin to interfere with your life, however, the problem needs to be addressed. Therapy is the best way to do that.

You might think that the presence of grandchildren would help a lot. Surprisingly, what little research there is on the death of an adult child indicates that that is not necessarily the case. Emerson L. Lesher, Ph.D., and Karen J. Bergey conducted a study of bereaved mothers between the ages of seventy-nine and ninety-six living in the Philadelphia Geriatric Center. They found that after the death of the child, 70 percent of those bereaved mothers felt closer to the grandchildren of their *surviving* children, whereas only 10 percent felt closer to the grandchildren of the deceased child. It's a striking statistic. Lesher and Bergey suggest that when the child dies, the parent may lose a sense of connection with the grandchildren, possibly because the tie they feel with their daughters-in-law and sons-in-law is simply not as strong as the tie they feel to their own children.

Nevertheless, even when there is conflict with in-laws, grandchildren can bring comfort. Dorothy Loring is an excellent example of that. Shortly after her twenty-eight-year-old son, Jack, was killed by a drunk driver, she and her son's ex-wife had a dispute (over life insurance) and Dorothy was denied access to the five-year-old grandson. Dorothy took it to court:

> Before my son's death I had my little grandson at least once a week and sometimes two or three times. My son lived with me and when he had his visiting time, I would have Ricky then. Two or three months after my son died, just about the time it was really hitting home, they stopped letting me see him. I had no legal right to see him and I had to go to court. We had to fight to get to see him. We had a case just like a husband and wife over visitation rights. The judge was not sympathetic at all. We have twenty-four hours a month, and any other time that we see him is left to her discretion.
>
> Being with our grandson is wonderful. One time when he was about seven, he got a crew cut which my son always wore.

Ricky was in the pool and all I could see was his head and it was like looking at my son. Jack was a really great kid and this kid is so much like him. Anything he does that reminds me of his dad—when he looks a certain way or gets silly like his dad used to—thrills me to death. As I grow older, I keep thinking, what would my son be like now? With this boy, I think that, if I live long enough, I will see how my son would have turned out. We have a piece of our son left.

MISCARRIAGE, STILLBIRTH, AND THE DEATH OF A BABY

Imagine what it's like to lean over the crib to pick up your healthy baby, and the baby is dead. In 1986 sudden infant death syndrome (SIDS) claimed 5,278 babies. Among infants between one month and one year old, SIDS is the top-ranking cause of death. Parents who suffer from this experience are racked with guilt, a feeling to which other people may contribute: What were you feeding the baby? Was there an air freshener in the room? Didn't you check on the baby? None of these questions have anything to do with why the child died, but because the causes of SIDS are still mysterious, mourners often blame themselves.

The grief that follows the death of a baby is intense, but many people may not recognize its depth or length. For although the death of a child is almost always acclaimed as the worst possible sorrow, that's less true when the child is an infant. In the popular mind, the loss of a child so young is considered a shame but not necessarily a tragedy. People often suggest that there must have been something wrong with the baby; they attempt to offer comfort by saying that you're still young, you can have another. And they seem to assume that since you didn't have the baby too long, you can't mourn for too long.

The anguish of the parents, however, is unmitigated by the age of the child. Laura Walter, a twenty-seven-year-old mother in Billings, Montana, is one of the close to 33,000 women whose babies are stillborn annually. She made these comments a few months later:

There are days when all I do is cry and think about Adam. There are days when I feel like I am going crazy because so many thoughts are going through my head. A lot of people think that since we didn't really have him with us, it shouldn't be this hard. My family and friends think I should be over this. But I carried him for eight and a half months and I knew him within me. I knew what times of the day he was awake and when he was sleeping. I knew he was alive as long as I carried him.

Parents who have lost a child through miscarriage, stillbirth, or death immediately after birth often find that the death is dismissed as unimportant. "My husband's parents never came to the hospital or to the funeral visitation," said one mother after her child was stillborn. "Two weeks later, one of his sisters asked, 'What are you still upset about?' His brother said, 'It was only a baby—don't let it ruin your lives.' His older sister was the only one who understood how sad we felt. It seemed the rest of them didn't care."

The temptation to grieve endlessly may be especially strong when a very young child dies, because the younger the child is, the less mark the child will have made upon the world. With an older child, there are others who remember: the child went to school, played with the neighbors, had a life in which other people participated. The child existed in the eyes of the community, and in however small a way, made some impression on others.

But when a baby dies, the child's greatest influence may have been the grief the parents feel. Other people may not even understand why the mother and father are so upset. Their grief—and perhaps *only* their grief—is proof that their child lived. They feel guilty if they're *not* grieving, as Beverly Harris of Eastlake, Ohio, did. After her second child, Daniel, was stillborn, her grief was profound. Five years later, she wrote, "I don't think about Daniel as much, and when I do, I feel guilty that I don't think of him more."

Miscarriages are barely recognized as losses at all. In part this may be because they are so common. Estimates of the number of pregnancies that end in miscarriage reach as high as 25 percent. Many of those are early miscarriages, but according to the National Center for Health Statistics, in 1986 there were 28,972 fetal deaths above the age of twenty weeks. Parents who mourn those losses often mourn alone. A seventy-two-year-old woman remembers, "I was pregnant six times. My daughter was the fourth child. Of the others, one was stillborn, one lived a couple of hours, one lived two days, and I had two miscarriages. People were not sympathetic. People thought that as long as you had not brought the child home with you, it was nothing." The same thing is going on today. "No one wanted me crying. They wondered why it bothered me," said a recently bereaved mother.

Many times, people try to forget the death by having another baby right away. Another child is wonderful. But it's imperative to grieve for the first one, for one baby cannot replace another.

Finding friends to share your feelings with is not always easy. Pennsylvania poet Marion Cohen, whose third child, Kerin, died at the age of two days on December 24, 1977, wrote about her mourning for her child in *An Ambitious Sort of Grief*. She told us how her friends reacted at the time of his death:

> Friends listened—not so much because they *knew* to (many had not had experience with tragedy) but because I *told* them to and they obeyed! But as time passed, most didn't know that grief over a baby continues—and continues. One friend, I particularly remember, seemed to think we should talk All About It the first time we met after the tragedy, but the second time we should talk about Other Things, as though It never happened. I simply *told* her, and she understood. I was lucky: my friends were true friends.

There are other steps you can take. With the death of an infant, it is important to be involved in funeral preparations, because that may be your sole opportunity for interaction. Many parents emphasize the benefit they gained from holding their dead children. One mother of a stillborn baby girl recommended doing even more: "I wish I had dressed her at the funeral home and washed her," said Kathy Tuttle, a special education teacher in Wisconsin. "I miss that, even though we held her. I wish I had done more mothering."

Naming your child is important—even if the death occurred some time ago. It's never too late.

Ask for a footprint. Save a lock of your baby's hair. And take photographs. Parents seem virtually unanimous in recommending that even with a stillbirth, pictures be taken. That little body can be wrapped in a blanket and photographed. The idea may sound ghoulish to some, but the reality is usually far less upsetting than the idea. In later years, you will be glad to have those mementos. It's important to have something concrete, and a photo is better than nothing. It really is. Beverly Harris lamented not having had pictures taken after her child was stillborn:

> I was offered some pictures of Daniel while I was still in the labor room. At that time, I didn't want photos. I was told that pictures would be taken and held in my file for six weeks in case I changed my mind. A week later, I asked for the photos. I was told that since I had said I didn't want photos, none were taken. I deeply, deeply regret not taking those pictures. I always will.

When a baby dies, people may suggest "putting it behind you and getting on with your life." The way you do that is to grieve fully. With an infant, it can be difficult because there is so little to remember. That's why it's helpful to create something tangible. In 1989, the Pregnancy and Infant Loss Center in Wayzata, Minnesota, sponsored a National Baby Memory Quilt, made of small individual quilts sewn by bereaved parents. Making a quilt to commemorate your own baby could be a way to act on your grief. It's also a wise idea to make an album of memories, even if the only things included in it are an ultrasound picture and a copy of the eulogy. And if the eulogy wasn't a very good one, write a new one now.

ABORTION

Not everyone mourns after an abortion. Some women absolutely do not want a child at that time, have no hesitation about having an abortion, and do not grieve. But many women choose abortion with reluctance, often because the circumstances do not seem conducive to having a baby. They may choose abortion primarily because they are afraid of what other people will think, or they may choose it without really considering all its ramifications. That can be a big mistake. Annette Brogan is a management consultant in Chicago, who had an abortion eleven years ago:

> I was about to get married and I'd been having an affair with a married man who I loved so much and I went to tell him that we mustn't see each other anymore. In that last passionate good-bye, I got pregnant. Five days after my wedding, I got a positive pregnancy test. When they called me and said it was positive, I burst into tears and my husband looked at me and said, "It's his baby, isn't it?" I burst into tears once again. I thought that, number one, if I had this child I would never get over the married man, it would keep me connected to him forever, and number two, it was unfair to my husband. I had the abortion in the hysteria of the moment, and that was the tragedy, I think for my husband also. If the clinic had been closed that Friday and we had had to wait till Monday, I don't think it would have happened.
>
> I began grieving almost immediately afterward when I came out of my bedroom and said to my husband, "Something's very wrong." He said, "What?" I said, "The baby's gone." I looked at him and he looked at me and I started cracking up. He was

traumatized. I remember, in my hysteria, wanting to blame everyone, hating myself. I was full of guilt: How could I do this to my husband? How could I do this to the man I'd been seeing? How could I do this to his wife? My horrible grief was in large part because of how much I loved this man. I lost the man; basically I knew this was the loss of my husband; and I lost the child. But the added thing, and this is what abortion is about, is that *you did it.*

The great wisdom came from my mother. Before I had the abortion, she screamed at me, saying, "Don't you realize how many women in history have had children that didn't belong to their husbands? That's not a reason to throw away a child. When are people in your generation going to learn some compassion? Don't you know there's no such thing as an illegitimate child?" I was amazed at her counsel. If only I had taken it.

There are cases where it could be argued you have a reason to have an abortion. I'm a well-known liberal democrat in this community, and I think it should be legal. But I would not do it again in a million years.

Many women who have abortions feel very ambivalent about it. They may feel both relieved and sad. Despite what many people think, those feelings can and do coexist. For those who do grieve after an abortion, it's important to honor that feeling and to act on it. Irene Coleman of Boston told us about her reactions to an abortion:

My boyfriend held my hand throughout the procedure. When it was all over, and the horrible sound of the machine was off, I burst into tears. I had the sensation of my uterus collapsing, being empty, and that was when it really hit me that I had lost a child.

About a month to two months after the abortion, I knew I had to say good-bye to the baby. I was alone in the apartment one afternoon. I got a big pillow and held the pillow in my arms as if I were holding my baby and spent hours sitting in a rocking chair and talking to my baby about the life that could have been. And then it came time to put the baby down. I put the baby down in the rocking chair and I sat on the floor and said why that was never going to be. Before I talked to the pillow, the depression was a solid weight. Talking to the pillow helped to break that up and helped some of the other feelings—the sorrow, the anger, the isolation—to begin to come out. I do remember that.

Particularly vulnerable times may be several weeks after the abortion and around the time when the baby would have been born. After an abortion, many people feel depression, anger, guilt, sorrow. Those feelings will fade but there's no point in pretending they don't exist. If there's one thing we know about grief, it's that ignoring it doesn't work.

CAN THIS MARRIAGE BE SAVED?

A child dies. A marriage falls apart. Many people worry that there's a cause-and-effect relationship between the two. They're right to be concerned. The stress of losing a child often turns out to be more than the marriage can carry. Maybe it's because bereaved parents look at their partners and are invariably reminded of the child. Maybe it's because things were falling apart anyway. In any case, the result is the same: on top of death, many bereaved parents have to deal with divorce. Video producer and director Robert Wilkinson of Austin, Texas, and his wife, Betsy, had a baby who was stillborn. Their marriage survived. But before that, he had another marriage that ended following a disastrous pregnancy:

> My previous wife and I also lost a child. It was a tubal pregnancy. The doctor said that if we had waited another two hours, my wife would have died because peritonitis set in. There was so much pain and neither of us had the skills to even begin to heal. I tried to fly above it because I didn't know how to cope with it. So she split a few months later, taking my adopted daughter with her.

How many marriages actually disintegrate? Educated guesses vary wildly. Research conducted by Lehman and Wortman suggests that, when death has come about through an automobile accident, the figure is around 20 percent. Other experts place the number as high as 90 percent. Of course, some psychologists point out that marriages only fall apart if problems already exist. That seems disingenuous. What marriage has no problems? This much is clear: in the aftermath of the death of a child, many marriages crumble.

Sometimes couples blame each other for the death. Perhaps one parent allowed the child to go out or forgot to pick the child up or didn't insist that the child wear a life jacket—and as a result, the child died. Rather than joining together in their grief, couples may turn against each other. But even when blame is not an issue, their emotional needs may be at cross-purposes. One seeks solitude; the other craves distraction. One wants to discuss it; the other doesn't. One cries; the other wants to avoid it. Shawn Wilson, music director at a secondary school in Spokane, Washington, had a two-month-old baby who died of SIDS. "On the day Caleb died, I experienced an extreme feeling of 'I can't believe this happened!' The day after the funeral, I cried at the drop of a hat. My husband voiced an acceptance of the crib death but worked out his grief totally differently," she said. "The day of Caleb's death, he washed every car that was driven to our home by friends and loved ones coming to offer their condolences."

Often, differences in grieving style are gender-related. Typically, the woman mourns openly, crying and wanting to talk about the child, while the man pulls away from his powerful and frightening emotions. Often, he may avoid his emotions entirely but nonetheless feels afflicted by a barrage of other maladies: headaches, backaches, insomnia, high blood pressure. Rather than allowing himself to mourn, he may immerse himself in work or in sports or in fixing up the yard. According to Pennsylvania psychotherapist Jeffrey Kauffman, "Men tend to discharge feelings through action."

When that happens, the woman can't believe it! She is grief-stricken, and he is running around the house or the office doing things! He, on the other hand, feels that she is wallowing in grief, dwelling on the loss, and trying to drag him back into the worst thing that's ever happened to him. He can't stand it. So they grieve at cross-purposes. "I did everything I could to keep extremely busy, especially at the office," said Richard Haboush a few months after his son died. "Being extremely busy in my business has helped my thoughts to not concentrate on those last moments prior to my son's death. My wife has not fared as well. She feels guilty leaving the house and cries on a daily basis."

Societal expectations reinforce this pattern, for the man is often counted on to be "strong"—which means he must suppress his emotions—while at the same time he is expected to provide emotional support to his wife. Robert Wilkinson remembers that, after his baby was stillborn, "There were times when people would express their sorrow by saying, 'Gosh, I'm really sorry to hear that your wife lost a baby.' I wanted to scream. I tried to say very gently, 'Yes, *we* lost *our* baby.' Then they would try to backpedal and apologize." "Men are so untended," says therapist Susan Faber-Brook. "People don't offer them support. They're not expected to have the same feelings as women do. Yet they are just as afraid of falling apart and being unable to cope." That may be; it doesn't always look that way, however.

As a result of these differences, parents feel isolated, lonely in their individual loss. They may lash out at each other. Or they may retreat into a pattern known as the "conspiracy of silence." It's what happens when people love each other so much they don't want to hurt each other. They turn away from every sad reminder, every possible disagreement. In other words, they stop communicating.

It is imperative for couples to recognize that grieving is a uniquely individual process. There is no right method. And your partner may be unable to help because he or she is equally overwhelmed. Remember that mood swings are part of mourning, and be kind to each other. Depression is normal; anger is normal. Don't storm out of the house. Don't make big decisions. Once the peak of mourning has passed, parents find that they can come together again. "What holds a marriage together is that the two people keep talking and are willing to get help," states Judy Tatelbaum, author of *The Courage to Grieve.* "The lack of talking is what creates the breakup—not the loss." When grieving parents make an effort to tolerate their differences, the marriage can survive.

Sexuality can also become a highly charged area. Often, one partner is anxious to make love, to seek comfort in that way. The other, horrified that the spouse can think such a thought at such a time, turns away. Or perhaps one of the partners is desperate to have another child while the other wants to wait. Nora Goodwin of Miami, Florida, discussed how her marriage was affected by these issues after the death of her teenage son:

> I didn't have any energy to be worried about my marriage. It was an effort just to get through the day. I wasn't interested in sex. That was one topic at Compassionate Friends. No one brought it up in the group but they discussed it afterward. It's that the men feel sexual, the husbands want to go to bed right away! And the women are repelled, horrified. The whole idea was revolting to me.
>
> At the same time, I very badly wanted to have another baby. John didn't. I only wanted to make love during my fertile period because otherwise it was a waste. He kept using birth control, and that became an issue.
>
> Finally, he said, "Okay, if you want to have another baby, go ahead." I realized that if I had another baby, it wouldn't be Seth. It would be a different child. I didn't want another infant—I wanted Seth! So then I went through a period where I felt that if I wasn't going to get pregnant, what was the point? Why bother having sex at all? It took six more months to get past that.

What can you do in a case like that? Be willing to compromise. Whether you choose to make love or not, remember the importance of physical affection. Find ways to touch each other in nonsexual ways. Do things that are enjoyable for you both. Allow for being apart without feeling betrayed. And keep in mind that seeing a counselor can help during such a stressful time.

Despite predictions of disaster, many couples make it through this crisis with their commitment to each other not only intact but strengthened. Oliver and Harriet Mann, for example, found that they became closer after their daughter Cindy shot herself. "My wife and I both turned to each other for support," Oliver said. "We have actually planned the remainder of our lives in this manner. I feel very close to her."

"HOW MANY CHILDREN DO YOU HAVE?"

"Every now and then someone will ask, 'How many children do you have?' and I never know what to say," a bereaved father said. "Usually I say, 'One.' Recently someone asked, 'How many children *did* you have?' I don't know why she phrased it that way but I said, 'We had two and now we have one.' The response is always, 'Oh, I'm so sorry.' People feel uncomfortable and embarrassed."

They certainly do. The idea of losing a child is such a terrifying one to most people that an honest answer to this ordinary question throws a real pall over social interaction. It's never clear what the answer ought to be. Before Cari died, I had three children. Now what do I say? For a while, I said I had two children. Then I got irritated and said I had three. Now I explain, when there is a need for more conversation, that one is dead.

Many parents end up making a different decision each time about what to say. It begins with a quick assessment of the person asking the question. Is this relationship going anywhere? Are you likely to become friends? In that case, it may be a good idea to tell the person—briefly—about your loss. If you've just been introduced to a person you fully expect never to see again, it's a different matter. You can explain later, if necessary, that one of your children died.

If you feel better including the dead child, by all means give the higher number. Particularly in the beginning, not including your child in this innocent exchange can feel like a denial of that child's existence. On the other hand, if it feels easier not to mention your deceased child, give the lower number.

This question is especially rough for people who have lost an only child. For them in particular, I think it is important to maintain their identity as a parent. When people ask if you have children, I would recommend saying that yes, you had one, but that child died. It's a horrible thing to have to say. All I can tell you is, it gets easier.

Your decision depends on where you are in your grieving, and it changes over time. One day three or four months after Cari died, while I was still selling real estate, I was driving along showing property to a couple with three children. They asked the dreaded question. I said, "I have three children." Then I started crying, and I said, "No, I have two." I couldn't stop sobbing. I looked at their three kids and I knew that I had only two. I pulled off the road and said, "I have three children. One of them is dead." That statement was so wrenching that afterward, I avoided situations where I would have to say it. I stopped doing real estate; I threw myself into MADD, where everyone knew in advance that one of my children was dead.

Today, I find that it is easier to respond to that question. I have talked about Cari's death so much that I can say it without being uncomfortable. People usually respond with "I'm sorry." Sometimes they ask what happened, and I'll tell them briefly. But I've talked about this issue with many other bereaved parents. No one has an easy answer.

A NEW SELF

Mourning a child is a journey that changes you. The grief diminishes gradually, reappearing on anniversaries, holidays, and all kinds of occasions that might have been significant, had your child lived. These flashbacks have been called "shadow grief." You may feel them for the rest of your life. But you will also feel pleasure in living again—as unlikely as that may sound.

"One day it just happened," Elisa Glatz reported. "Instead of waking up and saying that my child was dead, I looked at a blue sky and I actually thought that it looked like a pretty day. I started to whistle and sing again and I even laughed. I felt guilty for laughing. I had read somewhere that there comes a time when 'grief softens.' It didn't go away but it was not the harsh, cold feeling it started out to be." Eventually, the agony subsides. Parents become less obsessed with the death. They begin to feel energetic, to take an interest in other areas, to feel pleasure and purpose in living.

But they are changed. "I am a different person now—as completely after his death as I was after his birth," states Californian Deborah Ryan, whose older son was killed by a drunk driver. "I think much of my personal anguish is the birth struggle of that new person."

The new self is shaped by grief. People who have experienced a loss so immense, a crisis so major in its proportions, become larger, more empathetic people. They grow. Their values change. They change their priorities. They learn to appreciate the present. "My son taught me a lesson, and that lesson is that life is good. We should live it to the fullest, making every second count," said Wayne Montgomery of South Carolina, whose sixteen-year-old son, Richard, died of leukemia. "Not only did he teach me how to live, he taught me how to die. Still, the greatest lesson of all is that you don't know how much you love someone until they are not with you anymore." To live; to die; to experience the full sweep of love; that is a compelling gift for a child to leave a parent.

Bereaved parents feel weakened by a loss they had never imagined. Paradoxically, that grief can also make them stronger. "Once people survive this insult to their lives, this deadly wound, they can't sweat the small stuff. They're more direct. They know they have a right to be treated with respect. They believe in their own dignity. They become more forceful," states therapist Susan Faber-Brook. "In a strange way," said Malibu realtor Paul Grisanti after his baby died, "this has made me more powerful." That's because once you survive the death of a child, you feel you can survive anything.

CHAPTER 10 | Other Losses, Other Loves

By my bedside, I keep a picture of my sister and me when we were small. We were standing together with a mangy old dog. The two of us: there we were, all set for life. Boy, we didn't know what was coming.

—BENNETT SLOAN

Every death creates a community of mourners. But in the pantheon of grief, some mourners rank higher than others; some losses are considered worse than others. When a child, parent, or partner dies, everyone knows the loss is an important one. But the death of a brother or sister, aunt or uncle, niece, nephew, grandparent, grandchild, friend, or colleague is less readily acknowledged. People mourning those losses simply aren't expected to grieve in an equally heartfelt manner.

To a great extent that's because when a parent, partner, or child dies, the loss usually *is* more traumatic. But any death can affect us profoundly. What matters is the quality of the relationship we have with that person, not just now but in the past and not just in the mundane reality of our day-to-day lives but in our secret hearts. The more intense the relationship, the more intense the grieving.

Yet in their mourning, people who fall outside of the universally recognized categories receive relatively little recognition as grievers. No flowers appear at the door, no sympathy cards in the mailbox. No one may call. They receive no time off from work. At the funeral, they may have no role at all. They are second-tier mourners.

SIBLINGS

Check the shelves of a library or bookstore for information about grieving, and you will literally find more books about the loss of a pet than about the death of a sibling. Yet when a brother or sister dies, you can expect to experience the full spectrum of grieving. At any age, a sibling can be the most important person in your life. But that possibility is seldom considered.

Both for elderly people who lose a sibling and for young people, the loss is great. Young people are more likely to feel isolated in their grief, however, for few if any of their contemporaries may have endured a similar loss. Janice Watson, thirty, raises sheep and trains horses in addition to being the mother of two children. In December 1987 her brother Larry was critically injured in a mining accident and died eleven days later. She remembers feeling slighted in her grieving:

> We're the first in my circle of friends and my age group to lose a sibling. I had several good friends who did not even send a sympathy card, which shocked me and hurt me. I completely severed those relationships. I was very angry because they never contacted me and they never acknowledged his death. People would ask about Mom and Dad or Larry's wife, Greta, or his children. But they would avoid saying how are *you* feeling. One night I went to an annual dance that we'd always gone to with Larry and Greta. As soon as we walked in, I saw a brother and sister dancing together. It was the first time I had gone to the dance since Larry died and I missed him so much. I really wish he had been there to dance with.
>
> Later, at the dance, I said to a lady I know, "I'm having a really rotten time thinking about Larry right now." She walked off without comment and left me standing there with a bad taste in my mouth. I shouldn't be so resentful; I understand that people fear having to comfort somebody's loss. But I sure would have liked some support at that moment. I do believe that if Mom had made that statement, or if Greta had said it, either one of them would have gotten some comfort. But I'm just a sister. Oh, it's just a brother: I see a lot of that and that's an irritating point.

Even within the family, the grief that siblings feel may be dismissed. Valerie Clark is a thirty-one-year-old artist from Illinois whose brother Kevin died in an automobile crash at age eighteen. Her family discounted her loss:

My mother was absolutely devastated. I used to have fights with her about who grieved the most. It always came down to whose pain is more, and it's an understood thing that a mother's grief is always more—which is not necessarily the case. My brother was so important to me, but I let her win all the arguments. I'd start telling her about how I was feeling and then she would completely deny my feelings. She'd say, "You don't know. He was just your brother, but he's my son. You don't know until you've lost a child." My mother couldn't acknowledge that I really missed Kevin and had a lot of things I needed to deal with. She just couldn't comprehend it and so denied it.

Relationships between siblings are always complicated and ambivalent. Even if the age difference is vast, every sibling figured mightily in our childhood. Older brothers and sisters may have been role models; they also may have been people who tortured and snubbed us. A younger sibling may be the first person for whom we felt responsible—and also the first person with whom we felt in direct competition. The relationship between twins (or any multiple birth) is especially strong, for a twin is both an intimate and a direct symbol of the self. My aunt Alice McCarty has lost seven sisters and brothers, including her identical twin sister, Alicia, who died of cancer several years ago. I remember Alice telling me that when she looked at her in the coffin, she knew that that's what she would look like too.

Identification between siblings is strong. So is sibling rivalry. At once compatriots and competitors, siblings can be best friends and fiercest opponents, highly critical of each other—and astonishingly loyal. As children, our relationships are passionate, uncivilized, full of intimacy, alliance, anger, and envy. Although our behavior as adults may improve, those childhood feelings do not disappear. So when a sibling dies—no matter how old we are when that happens—feelings are intense.

In consequence, bereaved brothers and sisters often have to deal with guilt and anger that goes way back. Even if they are good friends as adults, it's not uncommon to feel remorse or anger over small remembered incidents of childhood—not to mention more recent issues, including jealousy over all the attention the sibling received while dying and guilt for feeling relieved that it wasn't you. When siblings are not close, the emotional distance between you may turn out to be a source of guilt (if you think it's your fault), hurt, or anger (if you blame your sibling).

Like the loss of a parent, the death of a sibling stirs our earliest memories and deepest emotions. The sense of loss is strong because brothers and sisters remember the child we once were. They share the deep roots of our childhood memories; they truly know the intricacies of the emotional and physical geographies that shaped us. In the secret games as well as the external dramas of childhood, our siblings costarred. So when siblings die, it's a major event—even if they have spent the last few acts offstage.

The memories that come flooding back are often very early ones. By stimulating the childhood bond, those unexpected recollections emphasize what we once had and what we have no more. After her brother's death, Janice Watson was surprised by memories:

> Larry and I used to dig worms when we were kids. This spring, I was out in the worm patch one day. I could smell the earth and feel it and the tactile sensations brought the memory back so vividly. I could see us sitting in the worm patch with our Matchbox toys. We were there for hours making bridges and roads and all sorts of things. I hadn't thought about that since I was six years old. It hurt. But I appreciate pulling that memory back because now I have it. Every time I go to the worm patch with my kids, I remember Larry.

Not all memories are equally gratifying. Despite the nostalgia many people like to feel for childhood, the memories that are stirred up when a sibling dies may not be so sweet, and the grieving may not be so easy. Looking back—recalling the parts of the relationship that were awful and the parts that were glorious and the parts that were simply shared—is an important part of grieving. Bennett Sloan recalled his relationship with his sister Irene:

> Beanie—that's what I called my sister—died when she was forty-one of complications arising out of a lifelong battle with juvenile diabetes. My earliest associations with her were not positive. I didn't enjoy being a child in the house I grew up in and my sister's illness was always there. I wanted to get away. It was only when I'd been away from her and my family that I was able to look more closely at what was there of value for me. My sister became of value.
>
> I got close to her in the last ten years of her life. We were best friends. We had a wonderful relationship that developed over the telephone. We'd have long conversations. She was so wise. I had an overwhelming sense of love and admiration for her because she was such a unique person. When she was about twenty-five, she went blind from diabetes and two or three years following that, she had to have a kidney transplant and my father gave her his kidney. She met her husband through a Braille function and she was the first kidney recipient to give

birth. Yet I never heard her complain or play victim to the fact that she had this disease. She was an inspiration, plain and simple. She was a great person.

After she died, I talked about her a lot. I shared with friends in different ways, telling stories, remembering what I considered to be her greatness. She was dealt a difficult hand to play in life and I think she played as well as anyone could. I was proud of her. She gave to people. She didn't take. I hope that some of who she was rubbed off on me.

Siblings, possibly the only people we know as adults who also knew us as children, share such intangibles as a sense of humor, a streak of sentimentality, a tendency to outrage, or a seldom-expressed yearning for a certain kind of life (or a certain type of rice pudding). Even when they do not look like us physically (and they may resemble us far more than we realize), they nonetheless share traits: the same hair, the same tendency to burn in the sun, the same gestures, the same laugh. No one else we know has those traits. No one. So even when we don't particularly identify with our sibling in other ways, we do identify when it comes to life or death. That's why the death of a sibling can stir up fears of our own mortality—especially when the sibling suffered from an illness for which there is a family disposition, such as heart disease or cancer. When a sibling dies, we imagine our own death.

In addition, the death of a sibling disrupts the structure of the family. Pamela James, one of Janice Watson's sisters, said, "We had been strong as a family and could handle anything, but with Larry's death, our foundation was being chipped away. We weren't sure we could survive anything anymore."

That worry about "surviving" can be quite literal. Like any death, the loss of a sibling makes life look more fleeting and more precious. It becomes easy to imagine all kinds of other deaths. Janice Watson explains:

> I have developed the fear of losing one of my children. That is one of the deaths I don't think I could cope with. And I often wonder, oh Lord, what if something happened to my sister Pamela? I don't know if I could handle something happening to Pamela. My husband and I have good life insurance. Our wills are done. But ever since Larry died, very often my husband goes to work and I say to myself, what if this is the day when he doesn't come home? What if I never see him again? Probably twenty out of fifty days I'll think that. He works with a lot of machinery. What if something happens to him? The "what if" game is definitely more prevalent since Larry's death.

OTHER FAMILY MEMBERS

The lack of recognition that is sometimes given the death of a sibling is slight compared to what generally happens with more distant relations. When Texas writer Mary Lynn Johnston-Davis was mourning the death by drowning of her step-nephew Anthony, she found that "some people could not understand the depth of my feelings for a step-nephew. The same thing happened to my mother. She was hurt when someone in her church said, 'At least it was not your real grandson.' My mom replied, 'Anthony was ours in love, not by blood. But he *is* my grandson.' "

Unlike what people suppose, there's no such thing as a "distant" relation if you are emotionally close. Third cousins can be as close as siblings; a great-aunt can feel like a mother; and nieces and nephews can play a role very similar to that of children. The death of a grandparent or a grandchild can be particularly devastating. What matters is the quality of the interaction—not the diagram on the family tree. Your grieving will reflect your relationship.

DISENFRANCHISED GRIEF

When the person who dies is a member of the immediate family, it's considered a legitimate loss. Other people may underestimate the depth of the grieving, but you can talk about it. At least you will be notified. At least you can go to the funeral.

But with certain types of loss, that's not the case. If you are having a secret affair with a married person, and that person dies, where will you grieve? And with whom? Even when such relationships are in the past, the death of that person affects you. Yet you may not get to talk with that person before the death. You may not get to attend the funeral. In your grieving, you may feel almost entirely without support and without recognition.

The emotional constellation that accompanies this type of loss is known as disenfranchised grief. "The essential concept of disenfranchised grief is that it's a loss not publicly acknowledged or socially sanctioned or recognized," states Kenneth J. Doka, Ph.D., professor of gerontology at the College of New Rochelle in New York, and an expert on disenfranchised grief.

That's how writer Stephanie Jones felt when a well-known actor with whom she had had a passionate affair passed away:

> I met him because I was asked to put together a book proposal with him. There was an instant attraction. He was so handsome!

He was also very married. One day he started kissing me and he told me that his wife was into nutrition and had gotten so skinny he was going to divorce her. I probably weighed 135 pounds and he loved it. He was everything I was looking for.

We split up after about a year. He didn't want to rock his marriage boat. He was my first married man. I would never become involved in that situation again, for moral reasons as well as practical ones. But I was swept along and by the time I realized he was not going to leave his wife, I was really in love.

After we split up, I didn't see him, but it gave me a pain in the heart because I would turn on the television and there he would be, all the time. One night I was at a friend's house and we were watching the news and I learned that he had died.

I had gotten over him but his death brought it all back. I felt totally left out. It's a lonely type of mourning. We didn't have mutual friends. I felt helpless. I didn't go to the funeral. I cried a lot at first. I went through a low-grade, diffuse depression that was affecting my work. I think it was because I felt so helpless in that relationship and ultimately so excluded. I probably didn't grieve the way I should have. I didn't visit the grave site. I didn't want to. I took a long time to get over him and I just couldn't reopen that wound. Maybe I will someday.

Similar problems of disenfranchised grief come up when a former spouse dies. "Those relationships are complicated and they vary considerably. Some may be quite cordial, others are disconnected, and still others are hostile. In any of these relationships, but particularly when it's a stormy and generally miserable one, people may not expect to experience a sense of loss. But in reality, there still may be a connection," states Dr. Doka. Unfortunately, there may be no opportunity to act on that connection. Instead, ex-spouses may even be barred from the funeral as Tina Vogel was:

I met my husband during Christmas vacation when I was a freshman in college. We fell madly in love. We dated for two years and got married in 1964. We got divorced in September of 1969 and he remarried in February. I saw him one time after they were married. I never resolved the reason we got divorced. I never understood what it was about our marriage that was missing or lacking. It was like I was the dinghy and he cut me adrift and left me out there in the ocean.

In 1980, my friend Ken told me that Craig was sick and I

said I'd like to see him. I was told absolutely not, under no circumstances are you to contact the family. His wife did not want me to see Craig; she absolutely forbade it. I decided I was not going to add to her misery. And then Ken called me when Craig died and said, "I know that you would probably like to come to the funeral, but please don't."

So I couldn't go to the funeral. I wrote his mother a letter. My husband, Jim, was supportive, but he doesn't handle death very well and so he listened, but without comment. My boss helped me a lot. She had recently lost a father and was helpful. But other than that I've been dealing with it alone.

The ex-partner who was not legally married may discover additional difficulties. Because the relationship was unofficial, the grieving may be underestimated or discounted in some way. That's what happened to Robin McCarthy of Connecticut. She was in her twenties when her boyfriend died in a motorcycle crash:

I was working in a bar and Bobby used to come in all the time and flirt with me. Finally, he asked if I wanted to go for a boat ride with him and I said, only if there are several other people with us. We went out on the boat and stayed for a day and a half. From then on, we were together every single day. It was intense from the beginning. It took me a long time to get to trust him, though. I used to have dreams that we'd go to California and then we'd break up and I'd be abandoned, far away from my family. Then we moved to California, and sure enough, that happened. He died on the Fourth of July—two years to the day from the first night we went out.

Bobby was in intensive care for four days before he died. His mother took over and when the neurologist wanted to speak with the family, I wasn't included. She said, "You can fall in love again, but I'll never have another son like Bobby." After he died, the only person outside of my parents who even acknowledged that he existed was my grandmother. She sent me a letter. Because I was Catholic and living in sin, no one else said a word. His family had a memorial service in Connecticut and I wasn't invited to it. I felt like everyone wanted me to pretend that nothing had happened. They didn't want to deal with it.

Disenfranchised grievers may also receive none of the recognition that comes from being named in a will. A woman we interviewed who was closely involved for many years with a man she did not marry described some additional losses she felt after he died:

> When the will was read, I didn't expect anything because Roger was angry at me in the last few years. His ex-wife, whom he was not close to, became a very wealthy woman. His sister and his mother, whom he could not stand, became very wealthy women. His daughter got most of it. I was named as executor for his daughter, which was appropriate. But otherwise I was not mentioned. I got nothing. It really taught me about marriage. I was a post–flower child who thought that marriage was no different from living together. I do not feel that anymore. I felt like I was punished for not having been his wife.

Sometimes, when people inherit money, they feel guilty about having benefited from the death of someone they loved. When they don't inherit, however, which frequently happens in disenfranchised relationships, mourners may feel anger and resentment. It's not easy to make that complaint publicly without being accused of all sorts of base motives: but then, many varieties of anger are difficult to express following a death. With disenfranchised relationships, anger can be widespread because there is often a history of hidden feelings, including anger at the nature of the relationship.

FRIENDS

A good friend, chosen voluntarily—what Cicero called "a second self" —can be closer than family. While most friendships are pleasant, full of gossip and shared activities, the rare ones are more than that. They are heady elixirs, brewed of an admiration and recognition so strong that in certain ways they are more like love affairs.

When a friend of the heart dies, a person with whom we have shared a complicated history, a person to whom we have revealed the intimate details of our lives, the loss is immense. Los Angeles psychotherapist Barbara Brighton describes her complicated relationship with a close friend who died in her early thirties:

> I met Ruthie when we were twelve or thirteen. Ruthie was very fat and we became immediate friends. We'd hang out at the Jewish Center smoking cigarettes. In ninth grade I wanted to hang out with the cool kids and she was too fat and I abandoned her. In twelfth grade our friendship rekindled itself. We grew up together.

She was a great singer. I'd play the piano and she'd sing. Her mother wanted Ruthie to be thin and Ruthie got back at her by staying fat. They sent her to Czechoslovakia to a fat farm, to North Carolina for the rice diet. She would be the one who'd find out where the candy store was. She was going to write a book called *Losing Weight Around the World*. She was a very funny woman.

After I got a divorce, we moved in together and it was a disaster. We didn't speak for a year. Then we reconnected. She got in this diet program and lost about a hundred pounds. This fat ugly girl became this beautiful, sophisticated, talented person. Her singing career was taking off.

Then one day, she told me she'd been having stomach pains and vaginal bleeding. She had to have a D&C and then she called and said they wanted to do an exploratory. But Ruthie was a terrible hypochondriac. So I wasn't worried.

Next thing I know, Ruthie went into intensive care and they did surgery. There was cancer everywhere. They removed everything. Afterward, she was at her parents' house and during that time, I went to Palm Springs for four days. When I came back, Ruthie was back in the hospital. I went into intensive care and there she was, almost bald.

After that, I was with her every day. The last two weeks she was in the hospital with a morphine drip and people chanting *Om Ngoho Renge Kyo* outside the door. A couple of times she came to life and looked at me and said, "Can you believe this is happening?" One time she showed me the colostomy bag and said, "What the hell is this?" One time I said, "Ruthie, just let go." She died within a few days. I got there within fifteen minutes after she died.

It was so painful, so unbelievable. I cried and cried. I functioned. But I could not get it out of my mind.

That mixture of love and anger, guilt and sorrow, is not uncommon. The difficulty is in resolving those complicated feelings. Many people look to the friend's family for help with their grieving. When there is recognition from the family, it can provide a special solace. The acknowledgment that you were an important part of your friend's life is definitely reassuring. Pat Huffman is a registered nurse in Claremont, California. After her best friend committed suicide, she found comfort with her friend's family:

My friend's husband had left her and she was anguished beyond her endurance. She had a history of depression for about fifteen years. She had a great deal of psychotherapy and had taken steps to keep herself alive at the time of separation from her husband. Finally, entirely overwhelmed, she decided to go to a remote place and die by carbon monoxide in the family car.

She was missing for two weeks. I knew of her suicide plan and suspected she was probably dead, but when I received word that she was in fact found dead, I wanted to scream. I paced a lot. I felt anxious. Then the grief muted and reappeared as depression. I knew I would survive the feelings of loss and knew no regrets for having invested so deeply in the friendship. My one regret about my own behavior was that I wished I could have been available for my friend at her death. I wish I had called her in the morning before she left home. But I could not keep her alive.

Her relatives—sister, cousin, aunt, and mother—all acknowledged our close relationship. And it helped that her identical twin sister was comforted by the fact that I had been her sister's close friend. Our mutual sharing helped us both deal with the loss.

But mourners do not necessarily find comfort within the friend's family. The family may find it hard to reach out to friends, because friends may be a painful reminder. Your grief may upset them; or they may feel that, as family members, their grief is necessarily greater than yours. And let's face it: the family may not even like the friends. They may have felt in competition with the friends; they may see the friends as people who took their loved one away from them and into some other life. In those instances, many mourners turn to the other friends. Barbara Brighton found comfort with Ruthie's other friends, and after the death, she devoted more time to them than she had previously:

All the friends came around. The night Ruthie died, we all went out for Chinese food and we laughed and talked about Ruthie and cried. We all had Ruthie stories. At the funeral, people spoke about Ruthie and we all sang a song she liked: "Lay Me Down and Roll Me out to Sea." We spent time together, a lot of time. We were very connected and we kept in touch.

Ruthie was neurotic and selfish. She did stupid things but I loved her so much. Her life changed me. Her death changed me. Her death has made me live my life much more completely. I wish I had talked to Ruthie more about how much she meant to me. When my friend Randy got sick, I was there.

I went to the doctor. I made myself available more directly. I wanted to be there. I've consciously made the decision to tell my friends now, in this moment, how much they mean to me.

Sometimes there really is no one to share your grief. Maybe you did not live in the same part of the country. Maybe you didn't share the same social circle. Perhaps the friend was a colleague with whom you ate lunch several times a week—for years. A loss like that is absolutely major. But you may not know the person's family or even their other friends. You may not even be contacted.

Emily Gould's friend Lydia was a fellow teacher at the high school in New Jersey where they both taught. For many years, they ate lunch together every day. Their friendship continued after Emily's retirement. "She called me every Monday on her first prep period and said, 'How could you have done this to me? How could you have retired and left me?' She missed me and I missed her too." Then Lydia took a sabbatical and seemed to disappear. Emily couldn't locate her. Her phone calls and messages went unreturned:

> For ten days, I called every day. I was really worried. And then her niece called and told me Lydia was dead. Lydia had made her promise not to tell me she was sick. Imagine: she was in the hospital and I couldn't telephone her! I talked to her every day when I worked with her. I had all her confidences. Another friend of mine died recently and at least I tried to help her. But with Lydia I felt like I abandoned her! I am mad that she didn't call me. She wasn't facing it herself. I feel terrible because I didn't get to say good-bye. I didn't get to tell her how much I liked her.
>
> I went to the funeral. The mass was in Spanish and I didn't understand a word that was said. That was very depressing. One of Lydia's sisters sat with me and cried with me and her brother put his arms around me and cried. Two people came from our school for the funeral. They talked to me but they didn't really know her. I didn't talk to anybody who enlarged my knowledge of Lydia. Finally, a couple of weeks later, I had a long talk with another teacher because she knew Lydia too. I talked with her and she understood. It was such a relief. It always helps when you talk—no matter what the problem is.

When someone we love dies, whether friend or relative, the relationship does not simply evaporate. We remember that relationship, and by doing so, we internalize it. We imagine our loved one's responses; we speak to their images within ourselves. With friends in particular—the people we love on a strictly voluntary basis, the people who are so frequently reflections of ourselves or of the selves we wish to be—that process has a special poignancy. "Even the deaths of friends will inspire us as much as their lives . . . ," Thoreau wrote. "For our friends have no place in the graveyard." Alas, that's not literally true. Friends do die. But they also live on within us.

AIDS

In many, many ways, AIDS is still a disenfranchised death—despite predictions by the U.S. Public Health Service that by 1992, 365,000 people will have been diagnosed with the disease, and of those, a whopping 263,000 will have died. Yet even as the number of dead and dying rises, even as the extent of the disease's spread becomes more obvious and appalling, there is still shame and fear attached to the plague of our time. Many sufferers from AIDS, and many people who have lost loved ones to the disease, are still afraid that if they tell the truth, they will be stigmatized. And they may be right. As the years of the AIDS epidemic mount, as more and more people, including admired public personalities, succumb to it, and as the disease moves beyond the boundaries of the homosexual community and into the population at large, the death becomes less stigmatizing. But it would be naive to think that that stigma has disappeared. It has not.

Maureen Wells is a Minnesota social worker who leads both bereavement groups for men who have lost their lovers to AIDS and support groups for women with AIDS. "When someone dies of leukemia, it's like an act of God. It's one of those things that happen, who knows why," she states. "But AIDS is something you get from other people. You get it from sex, you get it from drugs. You get it from things that are not talked about in nice society. There is a lot of stigma attached." That stigma affects everyone, from gay men, to the parents of AIDS victims (or people with AIDS—PWAs—as they prefer to be known).

AIDS is also a political issue, a fact many people grow to realize as they thread their way through a bureaucratic and financial maze in search of the basic medical care they need. Often, those services just plain aren't there. "Los Angeles City is one of the top three places for AIDS and it has virtually no public services," states attorney Carolyn Fank, former chairman of the board for the Los Angeles Shanti Foundation, the purpose of which is to provide emotional support to persons with life-threatening illness. "More people have died from AIDS than died in Vietnam, and the numbers are going to increase, and yet on the federal, state, county, and city levels, there is virtually no response. It makes you feel insignificant and powerless."

That powerlessness, along with a growing sense of unthinkable and untimely loss, is part of the mourning. As one man confided, "So many of my friends have died, I want to scream." Many people share that feeling.

For gay men in particular, the grief connected to AIDS-related death is complicated in the extreme. Anger, guilt, depression, and feelings of abandonment vie with fears of their own possible death from the same cause. According to Maureen Wells, thoughts of suicide are common, especially among those who have tested HIV positive. Without question, within the gay community there has been a rallying-around and a coping with the reality of death, on both a practical and a spiritual level, that is nothing short of extraordinary. Yet even gay men may find it difficult to express their grief, because the topic is so highly charged. Lawrence Hunt, for instance, is a Delaware-born writer who discovered that when his friend Bill died, he had no place to grieve:

> I haven't even told my parents because I don't want to increase their worries about me. I haven't been able to talk about him with anyone. The only one of his friends I know well has a very strong philosophy that I don't agree with, so it's difficult to relate to him in terms of grieving. At work, there's no one. Partially that's so because Bill died of AIDS but also in general I keep my relationships at work very work-oriented. My partner Nigel—who wasn't nearly as close to Bill as I was—was able to cry. I comforted Nigel when he cried. But I felt cheated. I wanted to be comforted and instead I responded to him and ignored my own needs. I really haven't grieved.

Outside the gay community, mourning presents other difficulties. Friends are ignorant of the disease and often judgmental and afraid; many parents feel guilty and others can't cope. Entire communities turn away. For parents, losing a child to AIDS is fraught with shame and blame. "With AIDS, not only do you have to share the fact of disease, you have to share the life-style issues, and the perception is that those reflect on oneself. As with child suicide or adolescent suicide, the survivors share a sense of stigma," states Dr. Doka. "Whereas with cancer and accidents, they don't have that same sense. In working with parents whose children have died of AIDS, we have found that they don't feel they get the same support as other parents."

Beverly Barbo and her husband can attest to that. They own a printing business in a small town in Kansas. In November 1986 their twenty-seven-year-old son, Tim, died of Kaposi's sarcoma, an AIDS-related cancer. During the grieving that both preceded and followed his death, Beverly felt the weight of public disapproval. It was a struggle she had described movingly in her book *The Walking Wounded*. She told us about her experiences:

How can one feel losing a child to AIDS? Losing a child is the most terrible thing that can happen to a mother, but when that child is considered one of the "throwaways of society," by many people, and the church, it is devastating. This situation is so isolating. You don't know who to trust, who to share your grief with during your child's dying process—who will love you and your son without judgment? My baby was dying and I couldn't talk about it to anyone.

Within the family, my sister-in-law wouldn't let us in the house after we had been with Tim, but otherwise, everyone was wonderful. During my trip to Minnesota, I watched my family demonstrate the meaning of unconditional love and later in the hospital I felt the same way. I am angry at how people with AIDS are treated. I am angry at how families are treated when a member is living with or dying of AIDS.

Within our community and church, we said Tim was dying of cancer (which technically was true). We weren't ready to say AIDS. We weren't ready for any more rejection. Even the clergy didn't help. They couldn't validate my grief because Tim was a homosexual. I am very angry at the church for the lack of response.

The least support we had was from the very religious. There were no casseroles or other gifts of food for our family when we came home after Tim's memorial service. My husband had been left alone for six months while I stayed in California to care for Tim, and only one family from church invited him for a meal. There is another family in town who lost their son to AIDS. Someone in our very conservative church asked them, "Was Michael gay?"

"Yes," the mother replied.

"Then you will never see him in heaven."

After Tim died, Dave and I decided that people needed to be educated, so we came out of the closet, so to speak, and told the truth. Very few parents in Kansas are out of the closet, so Dave and I started a support group for Families of Gays, with or without the AIDS issue.

Support groups can be vital for those whose lives have been shattered by AIDS. "It helps to go to a grief group where other people have been through the same thing," states Maureen Wells. "It gives them a place where it's totally acceptable to be who they are, to talk about all those things they're uncomfortable talking about: their guilt, their anger, their personal health fears, their fears about dating. In a regular grief group, you have to spend too much time explaining and justifying." A bereavement group may be the only place where grievers feel relaxed enough to talk honestly.

Beyond that, there are other things you can do too. Beverly Barbo makes these suggestions: "During the death process, love and affirm your child/partner/friend. Do not blame him for being sick with this 'unacceptable illness.' Give him/her permission to leave and then let go, knowing he/she will be in a better place. Find a faith community that can love you and validate the person's life and your grief. This is not a time to stick with a stiff-necked, unforgiving congregation."

In the aftermath of such a death, anger is common. "I feel angry toward the disease, the government, other nonsupportive families, most of society for their apathy, and comedians who make jokes about AIDS," said Barbara Cleaver, whose son died of the disease.

Like many other mourners, she struggled with guilt. "Why didn't I have the courage to tell the truth about his condition?" she asked. Yet because AIDS is so stigmatized, it is often difficult to admit to it. During the dying, people may not always call the disease by its name. They'll call it cancer or pneumonia—both of which are frequently elements of AIDS. But afterward, this reticence may feel like a betrayal of their loved one, and they feel guilty and cowardly.

Because these feelings are so strong, it can be intensely healing to take action. For many people, both heterosexual and homosexual, this often involves coming out of the closet and admitting the truth about what happened. After her son's death, Barbara Cleaver cofounded Mothers of AIDS Patients (MAP). But you don't have to found an organization to find the relief that comes from banding together with others who have similar concerns. It helps to do *something*, whether that means participating in local fund-raising endeavors, contributing to an organization such as the American Foundation for AIDS Research, or volunteering your time at a counseling center. People with AIDS have suffered more than the horrors of the disease. They have also had to live with ostracism and hatred. Reaching out to other people is one way to help counteract those forces. It's one way to make sure that your loved one will not have died in vain.

Finally, just as many people have been moved at the site of the Vietnam Memorial in Washington, D.C., people whose loved ones have died of

AIDS have found some comfort and catharsis in viewing the Names Project, or the AIDS quilt—a gigantic collection of patchwork pieces, every one of which commemorates a person who died of AIDS. In October 1989 the quilt was exhibited in its entirety in Washington, D.C.; now it's too large to be shown in any one place. But portions of it will continue to be exhibited. Participating in the creation or the viewing of a personalized memorial like that is a surprisingly effective grieving tool. Maureen Wells discussed the impact of that quilt:

> A lot of ritual has grown up around that quilt because it's a way that friends can do remembrance. It's something concrete you can do. People come together to work on a quilt piece and design it. We had a complete showing of the quilt in the Hubert H. Humphrey Metrodome, better known as the Hump. Here was the whole quilt all laid out, and the place was full of people who were alone. It was like walking into a church. When you walk through it, looking at the quilt, you look for the people you know. I was wiped out. When my AIDS group met, people talked about the quilt. One man said after he had finished his lover's piece, it was hard to let it go. He laid it on his lover's bed and looked at it, and giving it up was like giving up another piece of his lover. But it was important to make it a part of the whole.

What else can be done? With AIDS, as with other forms of death, you can expect powerful, tumultuous feelings; and you can expect those feelings to shift. It helps to "realize the value, the gift, the positive from the person and the experience," said Los Angeles realtor David Sheridan after his lover died of AIDS. "We don't have a choice but to go on. It may as well be in a positive, beneficial way, both for ourselves and the one we loved. The stone cannot be polished without friction; we learn through adversity; and we must work to get results."

That work involves facing your emotions honestly—and gently. Find a place to mourn. Don't be hard on yourself about why it happened or what you should have done. Have compassion: for your loved one. And for yourself.

PETS

As every pet owner knows—and close to 60 percent of all households in the United States include a cat or a dog—animals can be more loyal, more cuddly, and infinitely less critical than people. Our relationships with cats and dogs can also last twenty years or more—longer than many marriages—and during that time, our pet loves us unreservedly. Aldous Huxley observed that "to his dog, every man is Napoleon; hence the constant popularity of dogs." And it's true: only in the eyes of a pet can ordinary mortals become conquerors for the ages. It's no wonder that the death of a pet can be so upsetting. But only another animal lover may understand your feelings. Non-animal lovers seem to believe that grieving for a pet is making a big deal out of nothing. It is not.

Grieving for a pet follows the same essential patterns associated with any other kind of grief. Shock and numbness are part of the initial mourning. There may also be relief that the animal's suffering is over, along with some guilt, especially if the owner has had to assent to euthanasia.

When a pet dies, there is the usual jumble of emotions. After all, you live with a pet. Daily rituals such as feeding them, walking them, holding them, talking and singing to them in private, may be a large part of your life. When that animal dies, the loss is a big one. Unfortunately, it's also one that other people may discount. Margo Carruthers of Maine described what happened when her ten-year-old dog Shane died:

> Shane was a purebred golden retriever and he had the lack of IQ to prove it. When he was nine years old, he got a tumor. They removed it, and he was supposedly okay. But a couple of months later, he broke out in hundreds of tumors the size of marbles, all over his body. They said they'd never seen anything like it. I called my family on Saturday and said Shane was dying. Two days later he died having a seizure while I was holding him. I felt the life go out of him: I was just holding him, really tight, and all of a sudden he was gone.
>
> We got a pet bereavement card from the people in my husband David's office. "On the Death of Your Pet," it said. They all signed it. I thought that was wonderful. They understood. But I didn't hear from anybody in my family for a week. Finally I called. Their attitude was, "It was just a dog—it's not like it was a person or anything." They were totally rude about it.
>
> That whole week and then periodically afterward, something would remind me of him and I would start crying. I had a lot of dreams where I was trying to save him. I'd have my arms around his neck and I'd be trying to drag him out of the water and then I'd wake up and feel what it was like to have my arms around him and give him a bath. I really missed him. My other dog was very freaked out too. In a lot of ways, Shane was a better companion than anyone in my family. Dogs are unconditional: they love you! You don't have to beg!

Although the grief when an animal dies is similar to the grief over a person, there is a difference. Because the relationships we have with our animals are relatively straightforward, unmarred by complicated ambivalence, unfathomable expectations, weird double messages, or guilty manipulations, the mourning tends to proceed at a faster pace. Laurie Winston of Annapolis, Maryland, reacted strongly after her beloved cat ran out into the street and was hit by a car. "The first day, I felt absolutely awful. At the animal hospital, my husband put his arms around me and let me sit for a long time. I cried and cried." But several days later, much of that pain was gone. It's not uncommon to be upset several weeks or even months later. But it seldom takes longer than that.

At the same time, it is sometimes hard to find resolution for the death of a pet, because the loss may not be considered worthy of grief. Pet owners may feel that other people discount their sorrow, but they also may suppress it themselves, particularly if the death of the pet is overshadowed by another death. When my cat Michelob died of natural causes in the backyard, I was already grieving; it was May 1, 1985, almost five years after the day that Cari was killed. I felt sad about Michelob but it certainly wasn't the focus of my feelings. On the other hand, I remember when my cat Kahlua (mother of Michelob) died. I had her for seventeen years, and then I had to put her to sleep. I sobbed for days afterward.

It helps to have some kind of funeral. When an animal dies, there is frequently no funeral at all. The beloved creature simply disappears forever. Margo Carruthers remembers the ceremony she and her husband had for their dog Shane:

> David dug a hole in the backyard and we buried the ashes. He bought flowers with a little ribbon that said Shane on it and we put it over the spot. We told him that we'd miss him. Shane's birthday would have been on Christmas, so in December we planted our Christmas tree over his ashes. After that, I'd find David out there, just hanging out, and my other dog, Amber, would be there too. I am certain that Amber knows. He's been peeing on that tree ever since.

When Kahlua died, I paid to have her buried on a farm where there was a pet cemetery. A week later, I got a lovely card from the people there. It made me feel better.

What about getting a new pet? It's not a bad idea, but it is important to grieve first, to reach some sense of acceptance about the loss of your animal companion. Give yourself some time to cry over the loss, to reminisce, to adapt to your pet's absence. Think about whether a new animal would make you feel better or just remind you all the more of the one you lost—and remember that even if you get the exact same breed, it won't be the same wonderful animal you once had. That's why it's better, as a rule, to wait a while before getting a new pet. When you do get one, do it in the knowledge that the new little creature, however fuzzy, however adorable, however warm and funny, will not replace the one who is gone but will, instead, present a whole new universe of animal behavior.

With all the losses talked about in this chapter, community support is often lacking; mourners may feel imprisoned by sadness. As much as they need to give sorrow words, it's not easy to do when there's no one in your life who shares your grief. Whether you choose to visit the cemetery, write in a journal, or make a contribution to a worthy cause in your loved one's name, it is essential to find a way to acknowledge the loss you have suffered and the love you have experienced. It is comforting to know that the feelings of loss will fade. The feelings of love will not.

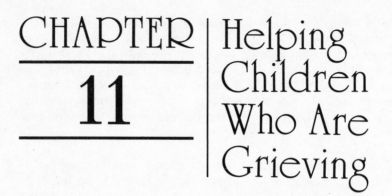

CHAPTER 11 | Helping Children Who Are Grieving

I never knew my dad. I never knew what he was like. I just have visions and photographs and stories.

—ALEXANDRA COUSTEAU

Death is a crisis for everyone, but children encounter special difficulties. Lacking the life experience and emotional skills that help adults muddle through trying times, they are vulnerable and poorly equipped to deal with the bewildering flood of feeling that accompanies death—especially if they are also too young to have a rational understanding of death. The change in circumstances that accompanies a death in the family can be equally difficult for them. The idea that children are more adaptable, that death is less traumatic to them, is a myth. The fact is, children are in many ways *most* affected by a death, for unlike adults, whose identities are formed, they must brave a further challenge: growing up in the face of loss. Whether the death takes place during their infancy or their adolescence, whether the person who dies is a relative or a friend, the impact can last for the rest of their lives.

After a death, children may feel profoundly abandoned, confused, and afraid. They worry about who's going to die next. Their sense of security is undermined, for in addition to the loss itself, a death in the family creates a ripple effect of other losses. Chief among these may be parental attention. Anguished adults, anxious to protect their children from further pain, may withdraw into the circle of their sorrow or try to hide their grief. Bereaved parents may feel so drained, so emotionally annihilated, so worried, or so obsessed with thoughts of the person who died that the child receives only cursory consideration.

Practical problems also arise after a death. That's especially true with the death of a parent. Perhaps the remaining parent has to sell the house or find a new job and hence cannot stay home with the child; occasionally, a child is even sent to live temporarily with someone else, thus losing a home as well as a loved one. Unavoidable changes disrupt the child's world and may prevent the parent from giving children the intimate attention they need. Without it, their grief and yearning can linger for a long, long time. And that can be true even when the child is too young to remember the person who died. Alexandra Cousteau, for example, was three years old when her father died; shortly thereafter, her mother gave birth to another baby. Alexandra was thirteen years old when she described her experience and the feelings she has now:

> My father died when I was three. He was working for the Cousteau Society, for my grandfather. He crashed into the ocean in his plane and they buried him at sea, off the coast of Portugal.
>
> I was used to him being away because he was always off on expeditions and sometimes I would go with him and sometimes I wouldn't, but I guess I thought that this expedition took a little longer than it was expected to. I remember asking where was he? And why wasn't he home? I was told, your father's not coming home. I was waiting a long time for him to come home. My mom was pregnant at the time with my little brother and she was really sad. She was crying a lot. Right after that, my brother was born and I felt kind of kicked out. He got all the attention. And sometimes I just wish I had more attention than I did.
>
> I don't think I realized what had happened until I was old enough to comprehend death, when I was around five. I get angry at God. I don't understand why it was him and not somebody else. I look at other people's fathers and I wonder what he would be like, if he would be the same or whether he would be different, what he would do, how he would act. And a lot of times I wonder where we would be or what would we be doing if he were here. Would I horseback-ride? Would I live on the Calypso? I wonder about those things. We have two golden retrievers, and sometimes I think how much he'd love them. I certainly wish he were here.

HOW CHILDREN MOURN

In the past, psychologists have argued about whether children grieve at all. Today, based on the work of psychiatrists such as John Bowlby and Beverley Raphael, the belief is that children do grieve—but their repertoire of responses is limited.

Under the age of six months, infants barely react to the death of someone other than the mother. After her husband's sudden death less than three months after the birth of their son, a young widow said, "The baby didn't seem to have any reaction and went through the whole ordeal untouched. He is a very happy fellow." Infants respond to the death of the chief caregiver, presumably the mother, just as they do to other separations: they cry and show distress, a reaction that diminishes when someone whom they trust takes over the responsibility for their care. If their care is provided for, they adjust quickly.

Above the age of six months and up to about two years old, according to John Bowlby, the initial reaction is protest. Children cry and scream, desperately hoping for the parent's return. When that doesn't happen, they may sink into despair, losing interest in everything around them. If no substitute caregiver is found, if they are deprived of the nurturing they need, they may shift from despair to detachment. Because children this young lack language skills, it is essential to anticipate their needs, which include vast quantities of hands-on attention, affection, and consistent, devoted caregiving. Like other children who have no comprehension of death, they may wonder for a long time: "When is Mommy coming home?" But at least children who are verbal have a way of expressing that thought and getting a response. Children who are pre-verbal do not.

The grief of children is colored by fear. When a parent dies, they may worry that the other parent could die too. They fear abandonment. When a sibling has died, they may worry about their own possible demise. "After my baby was stillborn, my six-year-old son was very hurt and confused," said Jodie Wilson. "He had waited a long time to be a brother and the loss manifested itself a few months later in great fears of sleeping or of being out of our sight." Children may state their fears or they may manifest them physically, complaining of terrible stomach cramps or headaches or various other aches and pains, often in imitation of the symptoms of the deceased.

In response to these fears, children, particularly beneath the age of five, often cling. They may become very demanding. Often they regress, wetting the bed and acting in ways you thought they'd outgrown. Young children may feel angry and hurt because they secretly believe that if Daddy really wanted to return, he could. Children of any age may feel angry at you, at the world, and at the person for dying, as Serena did.

The week after Cari died, their softball team played a game, the theme of which was "Let's win it for Cari." They won too. However, the next game they played, they lost. Serena came running home that day, threw her bat on the floor, cursed and screamed at Cari for dying, and stomped off into her room. I was very concerned, so I called up my former therapist and told him what had happened. He said, "Good, I'm glad to hear it." Her outburst of anger was entirely appropriate—not a cause for worry—as I found out.

Children also feel guilty because, egocentric little creatures that they are, they readily conclude that Mommy isn't returning because of something they did. Their guilt involves not just their behavior but their thoughts. They are major practitioners of what psychologists call "magical thinking"; they remember their negative thoughts (I wish you were dead!) and they may believe that their wish caused the death. In their minds, it's a logical connection: they wished the person would go away forever, and since it happened, it must be their fault. They may not share these thoughts with you, however; they bear their grief silently.

Children, like other mourners, also feel intense yearning for the deceased. Young children may search, generally in the places where that person used to be. They may run to the front door when they hear a car pull into the driveway, hoping that, at last, it's Daddy—as it once would have been. This is another place where magical thinking can intrude, for children sometimes have the idea that if they behave in a certain way—if they're extra good, or if they sleep on their right side every night, or if they wish upon a star—the person who died might come back. Sometimes their yearning is so strong that they create fantasies in which the person lives. That is especially likely to happen when the family does not talk about the death. If their feelings are not addressed, the grieving happens largely inside their minds. This was the case with Pat Huffman of Claremont, California. She is a nurse whose mother died from polio when Pat was five years old:

> On Thursday she did not feel well. She did not eat with the rest of the family. On Friday I watched my mother cry when my father brought her lunch and she was unable to eat sitting up. Very soon the doctor arrived and started the preparations for her to be hospitalized. I sat on the porch next door, watching my mother walk to the car that was to take her to the county hospital. I remember telling myself that she had been to the hospital to have my brothers and she always came back. During the night, she died.
>
> Throughout elementary school, I cried daily in the classroom over some event or something said, but I did not connect the

weeping to the loss of my mother. I felt different from other children and assumed that, without a mother as interpreter, I would not be understood by others. By the age of nine I began to fantasize each night as I fell asleep that my mother was alive. I would talk to my mother as she sat sewing or rocking.

Although the initial grief reactions, including behavioral changes, tend to diminish after a year or so, children can only handle so much grief at a time. So while adults may immerse themselves in the process, children have to spread it out over time. They grieve intermittently, and often invisibly. As they grow, new developmental stages can revive their grief and cast it in a different light; the role that a deceased parent or sibling has in the mind of a fifteen-year-old, for instance, differs from the role that same person may have had in the child's mind at age five or ten. The process of identifying with and thinking about the deceased undergoes many shifts throughout the course of a lifetime. Feelings may ebb for several years; then, during times of transition, they come flooding back. Pat Huffman recalls that her feelings of grief for her mother were especially strong at three different times: at puberty; when she began having children of her own; and finally, "I knew the full experience of grief when I reached the age my mother was at her death." Like adults, children grieve over time. Even for very young children, the effects of grief can be long-term.

TELLING THE CHILD

The way a child is told about the death lays the foundation for the way that child will adjust to the loss. Telling the child is so painful, however, that people sometimes postpone it to what they imagine would be a more propitious time. There is no benefit in that. Children should be told as soon as possible. Waiting spares the child no pain, for children inevitably know that something is wrong, just as they sense that someone is lying to them. A child who is not told is forced to figure it out alone and to grieve in isolation, without the support of other family members. It was some time before Pat Huffman learned about her mother's death:

I heard the family, especially my grandmother, tell people that "Helen died of infantile paralysis," but no one told me. The family was quarantined and the children given gamma globulin. I didn't go to the funeral. My dad let a cousin of my mother's take me home with her, 150 miles away. I stayed there for several months. About six months after my mother died, my dad took an opportunity when I was already crying to tell me that my mother was never coming back. He began to cry. I stopped crying.

The adults in the family seemed to repress and avoid confrontation. In adulthood, my brother, who was two and a half, said he knew right away that Mother had died. My other brother, who was nine months old, did not seem to know anything was missing from the family. And we have never talked about it.

Ideally, the child should be told by the parent and in familiar surroundings; the security a child derives from the presence of a parent and from a known environment provides an unspoken message of safety and continuity. More often than you might expect, that doesn't happen. In a 1974 study of Boston widows, almost a third of the women did not notify their children themselves. At the initial moment of loss, the moment when the bottom drops out of their world, children who hear the news from others, including people they know slightly or not at all, may not receive the reassurance—and the love—that they need.

When Cari died, my children were both told by neighbors because I wasn't home. They knew before I did. Travis, who was spending the weekend with his father, was playing football with some neighborhood children:

> The neighbor told me that my sister had been hit. That's how I found out. I went running door to door trying to get a hold of my dad to tell him what happened. I didn't know what was going on. My friends and I were just little kids then, and we decided to pray for her. As soon as we sat down, Carla, the girl who was walking with my sister when she got hit, drove up with her parents. I asked what was going on and they said Cari was dead.

Serena learned of her twin sister's death in a similar manner:

> I was in a neighbor's backyard and there was a phone call and the mother of the children there became hysterical and said that Cari had been hit by a car. We ran down the street to find out what had happened. When we got there, she was shielded by paramedics, who shuffled us away. They said things like, "She's going to be fine, maybe she has a broken leg, she won't be able to play softball. Don't worry about it." We didn't know any differently; we believed them.
>
> I walked to the school where we played softball because that's

where we were supposed to be that day. I wanted to be alone.
I was sitting on a bench and my neighbor's husband, Basil,
walked up to me and touched me on the shoulder. I was startled.
He said, "Let's go home. I have to tell you something." So we
got in the car, and I said, "How's Cari?"

He took a deep breath and he said, "She didn't make it. She
died." He had tears in his eyes. I didn't know what to say. So
we drove home, didn't say a word, and I got out of the car and
went straight into my house.

I am thankful that my children were told in a clear and direct manner
by someone they knew. That doesn't always occur. Young children,
especially, are frequently told lies and evasions, sometimes purposely, by
adults who don't think they can handle the truth, and sometimes inadvertently, by adults whose own fear of death makes them instinctively
shun words like "dead" and "died." Rather than saying that Grandma
died, they say that she's "gone to heaven" or "is on a long trip" or "passed
away." Because the language they choose is neither concrete nor straightforward, they fail to convey the reality of what has happened. Everyone
knows except the child. One widower was concerned about the way his
grandchildren were informed of his wife's death; although it was done
with care it was also done with euphemism:

> The older two girls were told the next morning that their grand-
> mother had gone to be with Christ. The little one had just
> turned two. She knew there was something wrong and she broke
> down and cried. It broke our heart. She couldn't eat—and her
> daddy was getting after her because she was misbehaving. I said,
> "You have to understand that this little girl knows that some-
> thing has happened." It was hard to see. For a long time, the
> little one would say, "Where's Grandma?" I said that Grandma
> had gone to be with Jesus.

The younger the children are, the more likely they are to take these
phrases literally and apply their own peculiar logic to them. To a small
child, being "with Jesus" may in no way imply being dead. Euphemism
doesn't work for children. A child who has been told that a loved one is
"away" or "in heaven" may await that person's return; after all, the person
left home many times before and always came back. All of these terms
fail to make the most important point about death, which is that it is
permanent.

With very small children, however, even the clearest, coldest language
may not communicate the message. Children under the age of five often

lack a basic comprehension of death; they may think of it as a temporary, reversible state. So they need specific, concrete descriptions: they need to hear that Grandpa can no longer move, breathe, think, eat, or indeed do anything at all. They need to be told repeatedly that death is forever. Sylvie Guicher-Vizard emphasized that when she told her two-and-a-half-year-old son about his father's death:

> When I came home from the hospital, I told Jean-Mathieu that his father was not going to come back; he was dead. I was pretty concrete. I'm not religious so I didn't say he'd gone to heaven. I said that he would never come back, that he couldn't move, that he was not alive. He would not come back. He would not come back. He would not come back. I think he understood that there was something definite about the death.

Although being specific in that way may sound harsh, ultimately it is kinder because it can help the child realize that death *is* definite and forever. Attempts to make death more palatable don't work. Drawing an analogy between death and sleep, for instance, can cause children to dread sleep. Announcing that the deceased has traveled to "a better world" can make the child want to go there too. And telling a child that "the angels took him" can be terrifying: whom might they decide to take next?

Even biological explanation must be made carefully. Saying that someone died "because he was sick" is inadequate if a child is not old enough to know the difference between a terminal disease and the sniffles. The distinction between ordinary and fatal illness needs to be clarified so that the child doesn't become terrified when chicken pox, measles, headaches, or tummy aches strike. They need to be reassured that people who get sick don't usually die; they need to hear that death is not contagious; and they need to know that just because one person died does not mean that anyone else they know (including you and including themselves) is going to die in the near future. They need to be reassured that death is a rare event.

Finally, for children as well as adults, death raises difficult philosophical questions. When those subjects arise, take the opportunity to discuss them on whatever level is appropriate. If you have strong opinions about life after death, by all means let your children know your beliefs. You may want to describe some of the myriad beliefs of other people. Just don't make the mistake of telling them something you basically think is a lie, with the idea that you'll tell them what you really believe when they're older. No matter how pretty a picture you paint, making up a story will not bring comfort if they sense a discrepancy between your words and your feelings. It will only confuse them. When children ask unanswerable questions about death, you can tell them, honestly and sincerely, that death is a great mystery which you do not understand. No one does.

THE FUNERAL

Many parents, afraid that the funeral will traumatize their children, leave them home on that momentous occasion. Yet by and large, professionals agree that attending the funeral is useful, even for small children. Not only does the funeral emphasize the reality of the death, it offers the children the comfort of knowing, in later years, that they participated. "My own philosophy is that anybody who is old enough to die is old enough to go to a funeral," states Maryland psychologist Dr. Dana G. Cable, a grief counselor for seventeen years. "I have never seen a long-term negative effect on a child who has gone to a funeral. I have, however, seen it in those who have not, who years later are angry because 'I never had a chance to say good-bye' or 'I wasn't there. I wasn't part of it.'"

Although parents usually make the decision to leave their children home because they want to shield them from further pain, Dr. Cable points out that there may be additional motivations for not bringing the children. "The reality is that adults don't want the children to see them cry and they don't know what to say to them," he notes. It's fine for children to see you cry; after all, they *know* you're upset. And the issue of what to say is simple: give them clear explanations about what happened and what is going to happen.

As much as possible, this should be done in advance. Tell them that the minister or rabbi will speak, that there will be music and flowers, that the family will sit in the front and other friends and relatives will be there too. Describe the arrangement of the room, where the coffin will be, and what it will look like. Tell them about the hearse and the limousine. Tell them what to expect at the cemetery. And tell them how other people may act. Prepare them for tears. You can't anticipate everything. But if you are fairly confident that, say, Aunt Tricia is going to pass out or try to throw herself into the grave along with Uncle Otto, warn your kids about these possibilities. Also let them know that there may be moments when people's tears turn to laughter, whether in remembrance or out of nervousness.

With small children, it's wise to ask an adult the child knows well to accompany your child. That way, someone will be available to pay full attention to the child and if, perchance, the child does become upset, that person will be able to take him or her elsewhere.

Children also need preparation regarding their own behavior. Tell them that you might cry and they can too. You might discuss with them ways to respond to people who offer condolences ("Thank you" goes a long way). And be sure to give them the chance to ask questions. Older children may feel awkward because their queries seem trivial in the light of the incredible thing that has happened. Nonetheless, they need answers. When Leslie Gilman's father died, for instance, she was uncertain of what she ought to wear:

> I remember the first crazy funny thing that happened. My father was going to be buried near his parents, so my mother and I had to fly to New York. We were packing, and I came into her room and asked, "Should I take my dressy things?" and she said, "No! What do you think, you're going to a party? This isn't a party! Your father died!"
>
> So I showed up at the funeral with loafers, knee socks, and school clothes, and I felt very out of place. It was very important to fourteen-year-old me because I never forgot it, and later it struck me as totally weird that she had said that when all I was thinking was that I should probably be dressed in my good clothes—and I was right!

Children are very conscious that funerals are important occasions, and they want to act appropriately. That's why it's a good idea to let them know what is appropriate, not only at the funeral but afterward. That's something Serena was insecure about:

> After the funeral we all came back to our house and we had a wake. Tons of people were there and there was food and I remember feeling like it was a party. I didn't know whether I should go make jokes and act happy or if this was the kind of party where you just are solemn all the time. I remember being really confused about that.

I had no idea, of course, that this was a question in her mind. Today, I know it's common for children to be concerned about such issues. Discussing in advance the discomfort that everyone feels around death can help to allay their anxieties. Remember too, children are still in shock even though they may be functioning reasonably well. It takes a while for all the feelings associated with grief to surface. Just because they're not expressing them now doesn't mean they won't be feeling them later.

VIEWING THE BODY

Looking at the body in the coffin can be upsetting, but as with adults, there are benefits to be gained—assuming that the child is prepared for the event and is not *forced* to look at the body. Seeing the body can help children accept the reality of the death, which makes them less likely to fantasize that maybe the person is still alive, or maybe the wrong body was in the casket, or maybe the casket was empty. Seeing the body erases doubt. It also offers an opportunity to say good-bye not just in the formalized way of the funeral but in a personal, face-to-face manner. Children need to be told that the person will not look alive, that their eyes will be closed and that they will not move. If they are going to be encouraged to touch the body—and under no circumstances must they be forced to do so—they should know what it will feel like: they should be told that the skin will feel firm and cool to the touch.

Children often have surprising questions, especially if they are very small. Because an open casket is generally closed below the waist, children frequently wonder what happened to the legs. They may also want to know what it means to be embalmed, what happens to the body after it's buried, and so forth. It's a good idea to answer such questions, however morbid they may seem. Questions like these are the kind that adults learn not to ask. Children, who still possess an active sense of curiosity about the world, ask.

And again, keep in mind that children have bizarrely literal minds. Dr. Dana Cable reports:

> A friend of mind tells an interesting story about a child. The grandfather had died and the parents offered the child the chance to go to the funeral. The child said, "I don't want to go." Absolutely refused.
>
> The father said, "You're going."
>
> They got to the funeral home and the child didn't want to look in the casket. Finally, he looked, his eyes got bright, and he said, "Grandpa has his head."
>
> The father said, "What do you mean?"
>
> And the child said, "Everybody's been talking about Grandpa's body being at the funeral home. I thought that when you died they must cut your head off and I didn't want to see that."
>
> Now, who would have ever thought of that? The problem is that we think as who we are, as adults; we don't think as kids do.

WITHDRAWAL

After a death, parents usually expect strong reactions—tears, fears, anger, and so on. What they may not anticipate is withdrawal. Yet this is a common behavior. The child goes on playing as if nothing had happened. It may look as if the child doesn't care. Yet even when bereaved children hide their grief, you can be sure it is very much there.

Children who withdraw need to know that their feelings—including fear, anger, and guilt—are perfectly acceptable to you. They also need to know that these feelings will diminish over time. They may be afraid of the strength of their own reactions; their attempts to act unaffected are often motivated by fear of losing control. They need to know that they will be taken care of, that there is someone they can trust, before they give in to their feelings. If the child is sent away after the death, or if the other parent falls apart, the child's world is so thoroughly threatened that shutting down emotionally may seem the only solution. Those repressed feelings don't disappear: they emerge later on, often in adulthood. Here's how Pat Huffman ultimately dealt with the death of her mother:

> While I was growing up, denial was the predominant response of my family. I experienced anger, guilt, depression, and acceptance much later in my life. I felt the anger usually as a migraine headache triggered often by sad movies which depicted the loss of love. One outstanding headache came from seeing *Beloved Infidel*, in which F. Scott Fitzgerald dies and Sheila Graham yells in the street. It was only as an adult that I could express the guilt as "I wasn't important enough for her to stay." And I had a fair amount of depression. My husband and I were in group therapy for about seven years. For me it was essential, even though for a period of time I cried when the word "mother" was uttered and had the subsequent migraine headache.
>
> I no longer have those headaches. In many ways I have adjusted well, but it has been difficult not to view my most important descriptor as "My mother died when I was five."

In families in which the adults subscribe to the stiff-upper-lip theory of grieving (something which they may deny utterly but which is evident in their behavior), children may likewise feel compelled to hide their sorrow. They may become extra helpful around the house or devote themselves to their schoolwork. They may, in short, do all the things you normally want them to do. It is unwise to be too impressed by such reactions, for children may be using those activities as a way to deny their grief. After the death of his day-old son, Malibu realtor Paul Grisanti noticed that the two oldest children in his family, fifteen-year-old Ashley and eleven-year-old Scott, reacted just that way:

> Ashley was artificially cheery, trying to help the others. She didn't seem too upset but we found out later that she hid it from us. Scotty was brave and said he tried not to think or talk about it. He was deeply disappointed because of his strong desire for a brother, and in a macho type of compensation, became a more exemplary child, working harder in school and so forth.

Finally, children, and adolescents in particular, may suppress their mourning in a misguided attempt to help their parents. When that happens, it's a good idea to talk with them about it. After Cari died, I worried about Serena because I never saw her cry. One day, she and I went to the grave and I asked if she ever cried. She said she did. I was relieved to hear it. I also told her that feeling guilty was normal.

She continued, however, to keep her feelings from me. A year later, I asked again if she was grieving for Cari. She told me then that she had gone to the cemetery several times. She would sit on the grass and tell Cari what was going on in her life: school, boys, everything. I think she hadn't brought the subject up because she didn't want to see me hurt. Like many children, she tried to protect the parent.

Children who feel pressure to make that parent happy or to take care of that parent may act prematurely "grown-up," perhaps even taking on additional responsibilities—a hitherto unimagined behavior. At times they are specifically given the message that they must be strong, perhaps even that they have to take on the roles of the deceased. Comments such as "Now you're the man in the family" can cause children to feel a responsibility that is not in fact theirs. Children who hear such statements—and even if you don't say them, other people probably will—feel overburdened and inadequate, yet they may nonetheless attempt to perform the role that is cast upon them. As a result, their own strong need to grieve and to be comforted goes unfulfilled. Leslie Gilman recalls her feelings after her father died:

> On the way to the funeral, my mother was weeping, weeping, weeping, weeping, and starting to lean on me. That role started to develop right away. And I remember my mother holding me in the bed. It was so horribly sad that I removed myself from the situation. I became like an observer watching this child with her mother, and seeing this horrible thing had happened that I couldn't do anything about. I felt responsible. There were just the two of us. I was the little girl and on the other hand,

I was a substitute mate: I was both adult and child. It gave her a sense that she wasn't alone. She would say, "You're my whole life." That's a heavy thing to throw on somebody. She said that a lot and for a long time.

A bereaved child may also feel prompted to ease the parent's pain by attempting in some way to replace the deceased. Julie Osburn's brother died when she was sixteen years old. This is one way in which she attempted to cope with the loss:

I felt like I needed to live his life also. I needed to fill his shoes. I was now the oldest and I felt like I had to become the older brother. My parents were mourning the fact that Mike was gone. They didn't ask me to be Mike. But in some crazy adolescent way, I thought that might be one way to ease the sadness. I thought maybe they wouldn't notice so much if I did all the things he did.

When a sibling dies, the pressure to replace that person may be internal, but it may also be external. Parents and other people may encourage it in subtle ways. In the case of twins, that pressure is especially strong. Serena felt it from Cari's friends. "Her friends were really nice to me. I didn't realize it at the time, but they kind of wanted me to replace her."

Needless to say, that's an impossible demand to fulfill. And yet, in certain ways, Serena did take on some of Cari's traits. I suspect that the fact that she did so much of her grieving in private was an important part of the process for her. Serena recalled:

One of my most prominent reactions after Cari died was the realization of how much I depended on her. I really had no idea. She was very together, and I wasn't. I always leaned on her for support; she was a real tough cookie and in the back of my mind, that relieved me of something. So when she died, I had to stand on my own two feet and make decisions and choices all by myself.

I kind of pulled back and started looking at the things around me. I had never really noticed them before. I started realizing a lot of things, I started making my own judgments. At the end of the school year, my health teacher told me, "I cannot believe the change in you. Your eyes have opened to what's been going on around you." It was true. Before Cari died, I was off in my own little world. I had no idea what was going on around me.

But Cari always did. Cari was a good listener. If you had a

problem you'd always go to Cari, and she'd say, you need to be open and communicate and discuss this—just like my mom. I picked that up over the years. I didn't have it before. I always liked that quality in her and just maybe never had the energy for it, but I'm definitely more like that now.

ACTING OUT

If some youngsters become model children, others turn into monsters. They become irritable and aggressive, either right away or a few months later. They can be angry at you, at the person who died, at the doctors, at God. Their anger, hurt, and sorrow spill out everywhere. Sean Boyriven, Mariette Hartley's son, was six years old when his best friend died suddenly from an allergic reaction on a camping trip with his father. Sean was thirteen when he talked about his initial shock and subsequent behavior:

> I came home from school, and my mom was on the phone, crying hysterically. It made me want to cry just looking at her. So I asked her, "Mom, what's wrong?" She said, "Chris is dead." I was speechless. I didn't cry. It was like I was dead but alive. I was kind of teary, so I ran into my room. My mom came in and we played a game of Monopoly.
>
> I went to school the next day and no one said a word to anybody. Finally, the teacher said, "Listen, we are all very sad about Chris' death." I didn't know that everybody else knew! I thought I was the only one who knew. We all felt bothered by what had happened and we didn't want to think about it, we didn't want to be a part of it, we wanted to get it out of our minds.
>
> But so many things proved that I was still thinking about him. I did things that weren't good. We had a pet rat in class—ugly, white head, red eyes, one of those. We used to play hot potato with the rat. I kept on throwing the rat high in the air, and he hit the ceiling and then he hit the ground. I couldn't catch him. And of course he broke every bone in his body. So he died and then I got all the guilt from the class. It was like, "Yes, I am the idiot of the class. I killed the class rat." Why I killed it, I don't know. I didn't even think about Chris at the time.
>
> I felt like a murderer. I felt like a killer. We went into the backyard of the school and we buried the rat and a few weeks

later, I unburied it. There were bones and a little bit of hair, and I put it in a jar, and I took it home with me. I seem to remember that I buried it in my own backyard in the ivy. It was very secret to me.

After Chris' death, I began to steal from my friends. I stole two little Matchbox cars and I stole a watch. My emotions about his death have gone back and forth between not thinking about it at all and then thinking about it but not really thinking about it. Your body is telling you, and you act up.

Behavioral problems are frequent with adolescents who are simultaneously dealing with issues of independence. Initially, they are likely to behave well. But that initial compliance later can turn to rebelliousness—a natural enough chronology, but a distressing one. They may fight, become sexually active, engage in life-threatening activity such as using drugs or driving recklessly, or—at the very least—talk back to you. Beneath the tough exterior, there usually lurks a broken heart and perhaps a guilty conscience.

After a death, everyone is so sensitive that the normal tensions between parents and teenagers are exacerbated. In the years following Cari's death, Serena and I did not get along, partially because I became overprotective. Like many bereaved (and nonbereaved) teenagers, Serena turned to her friends:

I migrated toward my friends and they became my life. I built a wall: my friends were my first priority, and then there was my family. All through high school, that's how it was. My mother and I fought all the time. I was constantly grounded over stupid things and I hated her. I thought she was extremely overprotective and we had huge fights about that. She didn't want me going out of the house. I couldn't take it. I thought, how dare you ruin my high school years. Cari was my sister, and I was just as sad as she was. I felt like she was punishing me. And I really hated her for that.

I don't need to tell parents how painful that is. It's important to recognize that acting out has its roots in feelings such as anger, guilt, and fear that the child may be unable to express in other ways. Those feelings may be a result of the death, but they may also be a consequence of your own behavior, which may have altered significantly since the death. Some parents, for instance, may expect the child to take over a parental function or to be unreasonably well behaved because things are so hard now. Yet in addition, they may ignore the child far more than they realize, because their attention is focused on the person who died. Acting out is one way in which a child who feels ignored may try to get your attention.

Acting out is also a way to express inadmissible feelings. Grieving involves far more than love and longing, yet those may be the only feelings children are allowed to voice. That simply isn't fair. Parents who reprimand their children when they express other emotions inadvertently encourage acting out. Children have to know that their feelings are normal and acceptable to you.

It is imperative, after a death in the family, that children be reassured, through actions as well as words, that you love them, are interested in everything they do and think, want to be with them, and trust them in the world. It is important that you take care not to project your own fears onto them. Many parents succumb to the temptation to keep their children safe, by their side, at home: or, to look at it the child's way, in prison. It's a formula for rebellion.

At the same time, it is true that teenage rebelliousness eventually simmers down. When I moved to Texas, Serena stayed in California to finish high school. Our relationship improved tremendously:

> I would always call my mom because I loved her advice. Whether I took it or not, I knew it was always good advice, and it was always good to hear what the right thing to do was, even if I wasn't going to do it! It was kind of comforting. We just talked, gossipy things, and we weren't fighting. We got a lot closer. By the time I moved to Texas, two years later, I moved in with her and we got along great. The fights were over more legitimate things—like coming home late and not calling.

ISOLATION AND EMBARRASSMENT

Despite the fact that by age fifteen, one out of every twenty children has lost a parent, bereaved children feel isolated and set apart from their contemporaries. Davida Singer discusses her reactions after her father died when she was thirteen years old:

> Right after I found out that my father had died, one of my closest friends came over and we went for a walk. That was probably the first moment I felt of isolation. I felt different from this friend. I felt her looking at me like an alien in some way, and I think it wasn't paranoia; there was now a gap between us. I had lost a parent. This alien feeling did not go away. I was the only one in school who had a parent who died, and

there weren't many divorces in those days so it was unusual. I was very active, I was very popular, I was a leader. And all of a sudden there was this wall, this distance.

Often, a lot of attention comes their way because of the loss, but it is not necessarily attention they relish. Indeed, teenagers may feel oddly embarrassed by the loss because it makes them feel different. Sometimes, they don't even want other people to know what happened—partially because they feel intimidated by the extent of their own grief and may not want to confront it. Sixteen-year-old Ashley Hayward was very hesitant to discuss her baby brother's death:

> I want to forget about it because it's so sad. I didn't want the whole world to know but eventually they found out. Even now, when someone says, "I heard your little brother died," I feel like saying, "I don't want you to know about this." It's not that I'm ashamed of it. It's just really personal. I just want to close all the doors. I want to feel safe.

DEALING WITH CRUELTY

Children who have experienced a death in the family face difficulties in school and within their peer group that adults never hear about. Children don't generally volunteer the information that a classmate has taunted them about the death but it happens often. Only recently did I learn, when Nancy interviewed my son for this book, that this had even happened to him. "Right after Cari died, there was this kid who was new to our school. He was a grade higher than I was and I didn't even know him," Travis said. "One day I was walking by his house and he started laughing and saying, 'Ha, ha, your sister's dead, ha, ha, ha.'"

Because adults live in a more civilized world than children do, these interactions seldom happen to us; but they do occur in the lives of our children. One high school student told us that when the famous musician father of a classmate died, the bereaved daughter was jeered at by a fellow student who said, "I'm glad your father died. I hated his music." Nor are such interactions limited to the months immediately following the death. The death of a parent or sibling is frightening to other children —and the bereaved children are the ones who take the brunt of that fear. Alexandra Cousteau suffered through several of these experiences in the decade since her father died:

> A boy in my class took this book with a rotting skull on the front and he came up to me and he said, "Look. I found a

picture of your dad." And, oh! I felt so bad! I didn't say anything. I ran out and went to the bathroom. That happened last year.

Another time, I was arguing with a girl in my class about something little, and she said, "Well, at least I have a dad."

I looked at her and I said, "What do you mean?"

And she said, "Your dad's dead, isn't he?"

I said, "Yes, he is. What does that have to do with what we were talking about?"

And she said, "Well, I'm so much luckier than you, I'm so much better than you, I have a dad."

I just walked away. I didn't feel like finishing the conversation. This was a long time ago. I was in fifth grade. When I look back on it, I think how stupid it was. That was a dumb thing to say. I don't let it bother me. The one with the skull, I still think about that a lot.

In a death-denying society, most people are uncomfortable talking about death. Children need to know that; they need to know that other people are so fearful that someone they love might die that they may ignore the person who reminds them of death (a typical adult experience) or strike out at that person (an experience many children suffer in silence). Those people don't really mean the cruel things they say; they just have no other way of expressing their anxieties. So they lash out or use ridicule. The best way to respond to taunts and jeers is to ignore them.

It's important to explain to your child why other children make these remarks. And keep in mind that children are remarkably resilient. "Kids bounce back faster than adults," states Dr. Cable. "They feel pain, but I have never yet seen a child who doesn't recover faster than an adult does. Often a little bit of talking with the child is sufficient; a week later it's long forgotten. It's only when we don't do anything about it or when we do the opposite and make a big issue of it that it can become a problem."

PROVIDING STABILITY

For children, death upends the basic structure of their lives—often the only structure they have ever known. They need reassurance both in words and in actions. Stay with them. Touch them and hug them frequently. And talk to them about your plans: you might even consider telling them what would happen to them if you died (and the extreme unlikelihood of that event occurring anytime soon needs to be stressed). The word "orphan" is a terrifying one to children. Dickensian scenarios live in their minds; they fearfully imagine having to live in an "orphanage" or being forced to forage for food in the woods or in the garbage cans. They need to know that nothing like that will happen; they need to know they are safe.

A stable environment can help provide that security. It is not a good idea to move after a death. When I moved to Texas for MADD, Travis came with me. Not only did he lose his sister, he lost his home and his other sister and all his friends. In Texas his grades were poor and his friends were not the ones I would have chosen for him. Moving was a big mistake—not so much for me but for my son. It is so easy for adults to ignore the wishes of their children and to assume that children can adapt. But children have fewer resources than we do. They are largely powerless in their own lives, and it is up to us not to take advantage of that. After a death, they need stability. They need reassurance. And they need love.

ALLOWING YOUR CHILDREN TO GRIEVE

I recently heard a discouraging story about a couple whose oldest child, a nine-year-old boy, died of leukemia after an excruciating struggle that took over a year and a half. He was in and out of the hospital many times, and he submitted to a painful bone-marrow transplant that the child himself knew was an attempt to save his life. The parents never spoke with their dying son about his impending death, although the child seemed to know what was happening. They also never spoke of the imminent loss to their younger child; their rationale was that if the younger child knew, she would tell her brother and he would be upset —despite the fact that the dying boy was already distressed and angry about the obvious disintegration of his body (and the admitted failure of the "lifesaving" bone-marrow transplant). Silence reigned. When the boy died—very close to the time that had been predicted—his sister was unprepared. Afterward, the parents couldn't speak of it: they referred to their son's death as "the incident."

In situations like that, children grieve in isolation; they are emotionally abandoned. While their parents are coping with an expected death, the children are dealing with the greater shock that comes from an unanticipated death—and they're doing so in circumstances that allow recognition neither of feelings nor of facts.

That's why it's so important to allow your children to express their feelings. Most of the time, this doesn't happen. Elyce Wakerman, author of *Father Loss*, and Holly Barrett, Ph.D., conducted a study among women whose fathers died before they were eighteen years old. Seventy-five percent of those women reported that at the time of the death, they were not encouraged to express their emotions.

To help your children express their feeling, you have to be willing to discuss your own. "If you can be honest and direct, the child will adjust much easier," states family therapist Jerri Smock, Ph.D., of Sacramento. "A child takes his cue from the adult. You need to handle your own emotions—anger, hurt, grieving, tears, whatever—and you need to be vulnerable and you need to be able to express and identify your feelings so a child can do the same with his or her own feelings."

Children respond to the way the parent grieves. If silence rules in the house, they may become distrustful and afraid. If the parent grieves actively and openly, they may feel free to do that as well; on the other hand, if the parent's grief seems excessive, if they are frightened by it, they may feel the need to repress their own. Their individual reactions combine with the reactions of the parent. Sometimes it's a combustible mixture. When her husband died of a cerebral hemorrhage, Sylvie Guicher-Vizard, a French psychologist living in Los Angeles, had an infant and a two-and-a-half-year-old son, Jean-Mathieu. She describes her husband's death and the ways her older boy's reactions intersected with her own:

> In the middle of the night, John had this terrible headache and he said he had to go to the emergency. I had the kids, so he drove himself to the hospital and came back the next day. The day after that, the hospital called and said something was on the scan and they wanted a spinal tap. I drove him to the hospital and he had the spinal tap at seven in the evening and Jean-Mathieu and I brought him some tea and cake. John was alert and normal and knew he would need an operation. That night, he went into a coma and he died the next morning. I was stunned. I couldn't believe what had happened.
>
> During the first five months, it was pretty hard. Jean-Mathieu was very, very attached to his dad, and he became very clinging. He had a strange game where he would pretend to be something else; he would say he was a dog. I don't know what that was about. During the first couple of months, he slept in a bed in my room. For maybe two months, he had problems sleeping. Both of us, though, went more into anger than depression. He was very irritable. He would scream and hit, he would run into his room and throw things, sometimes he would bite himself; that was usually a reaction to my own anger. I often burst into anger at him. It was inappropriate, but that was what I did. I said I was sorry for being angry and that it was not at him.

Being open with your children does not mean you should weep and wail and tear your hair out in front of them. Nor does it mean that you should confide in them your deepest fears of emotional breakdown, bankruptcy, or homelessness. It's important to avoid putting your child in the position of adult, friend, or therapist. But you can say, "I'm sad because I'm thinking about your father" or "I'm upset because I can't seem to do this as well as your mother did, and I miss her." By doing that, you make it possible for them to express their own emotions.

The ideal way to mourn a death in the family would be to grieve together. It seldom happens. My kids and I did not grieve together, and many people find it uncomfortable. Adults may fear that expressing their feelings will terrify their children, depriving them of the sustenance that comes from a parent's reassuring constancy; or they may be afraid that they will be unable to handle their child's emotions. Unfortunately, just because an emotion is unexpressed does not mean it is unfelt. Repressed feelings grow in influence.

The best occasions for talking about the loss are ordinary daily ones. If your children look sad or distracted, and you suspect it's due to the death, you might simply say, "Are you thinking about Grandpa?" If they're not, fine: if they are, your question can open a door. But be prepared: some children may not want to talk about the deceased. It might be too much for them to handle. In that case, you might try reading to your children or giving them a few books to read on their own. Books such as photojournalist Jill Krementz' *How It Feels When a Parent Dies* are sad but reassuring.

You might give your child something that belonged to the deceased. Children are often forgotten in the distribution of the loved one's possessions. But an object given to your child (and you might want to put it aside until they're older) is something they will cherish their entire lives. Moreover, they will mourn its absence if they are given nothing. "The divers stole my father's watch when they went down to get him, and I wish I had it," said Alexandra Cousteau. "I'd be happier if I had something that belonged to him, like an article of clothing."

Those objects mean as much to children as they do to adults. After I got divorced, my dad was like a father to my children. When he died, I let Serena pick whatever she wanted from the jewelry he'd given me. She chose a ring and a beautiful silver cross with a blue gemstone in the center, both of which she wore to the funeral and has worn frequently since. Travis was the recipient of the flag that was draped across my dad's coffin. He also received a less formal memento. One night, shortly after my father's funeral, it was cold, and I asked Travis if he wanted to wear a sweater of my dad's. It's not a style much favored by teenage boys. Nonetheless, for several weeks after my father died, Travis wore it every day.

As time goes by, children may have difficulty remembering the deceased. Forgetting is a normal way of reacting to pain. But just because memories have faded doesn't mean the pain has disappeared. Children worry about forgetting the person who has died, and that may cause them to grieve more. As they grow, the depth of the loss may increase in their minds. That's something Serena has mentioned about Cari:

> When I got out of high school, the more mature I became, the more sad I became about it. I realized that I kept forgetting things about her childhood and I didn't want to forget things. I'd think, this is terrible, five years have gone by and it's getting very hard to remember things that we did, things that we talked about. It was almost like a past life, and I felt really bad about that.

This can be a particular problem for children too young to have really known the deceased. Children want to know about the person who died—even if they don't remember that person. Telling them stories about the deceased in which they figure can give them lasting memories. Making a scrapbook of memorabilia can help them to create an object they will treasure when they are older.

WHEN TO SEEK HELP

It's not always easy to judge when professional assistance is required, because the difference between normal grieving and problematical grieving is a matter of degree. Children need to express the anger they feel after a loved one has deserted them by dying. But if anger is ongoing, if it is affecting their relationships at home and at school, if it seems uncontrolled and inappropriate, that is a good reason to talk to a professional—preferably a child psychologist who has had experience with bereaved children.

The same is true with other reactions. Withdrawal, acting out, or difficulties concentrating at school are normal, as long as they occur within reasonable bounds. But if such behavior continues without signs of abatement, it can't hurt to consult a professional. It can also help to find a bereavement group for children, such as those at the Fernside Center for Grieving Children in Cincinnati, Ohio, where children are encouraged to talk freely, share experiences, and express themselves through puppets, art, music, and writing.

Normal grieving reactions cover a lot of territory; it's even normal for children to yearn for the person who died so intensely that they express a desire to die—to "join" that person. That's a reaction I would not want to ignore, normal though it may be.

Some signposts that indicate help may be required include tears that won't stop even after several weeks, extreme regression, depression, or denial, and any other major behavioral change. When a good student starts getting F's, that deserves attention, and the same is true when a child who was previously a troublemaker turns into an angel. That child may well be terrified, and it can't hurt to investigate. A child who is setting fires, hurting animals, or acting in self-destructive ways needs help. If your child is having difficulty sleeping, is not eating, and is unresponsive, preoccupied, and full of rage or self-hatred, talk to a professional.

Children who have also suffered other major losses may need help more than most. Other deaths fall into that category, but so do losses linked to divorce, disease, and moving. And it's most important, when the death has been an extremely traumatic or violent one, to find counseling—the sooner the better. Be prepared, though: many therapists consider behavioral problems a family problem, not simply a problem of the individual, and they may want you to participate too. Dr. Jerri Smock worked with the new family of a five-year-old boy named Tommy whose divorced mother died of a drug overdose in circumstances that were exceptionally upsetting:

> The little boy was with the mother for twenty hours when they found him. The father was informed about the mother's death and brought the boy back with him. He and his wife knew immediately that this child would need counseling.
>
> Tommy had tried to wake his mother up and when she wouldn't wake up, he went downstairs to knock on the neighbor's door. It was at night, and he was so afraid. He walked down a dark stairway, inch by inch, knocked on the door, and got no response. He stood there in the dark—a five-year-old child. Then he went back upstairs and sat next to his mom, trying to wake her up, for hours. He didn't knock on the neighbor's door again because at five years old, developmentally, if they're not there, they're not there.
>
> As a result, Tommy had nightmares and bed-wetting. He couldn't go up and down stairs by himself. He felt guilty too. He thought, if only he had stayed up longer, Mommy wouldn't have died. If only he hadn't been watching TV, he would have seen her lie down and he would have awakened her. And he had so much anger. At the first sessions, this little boy kept kicking and screaming. He had a lot of fear about his father's dying. He often asked, "Is Daddy going to die?"

His father and stepmother, who took custody of the boy when his mother died, were wonderful. They got him into a counseling group, they got him into therapy, they got him into soccer. They talked about grieving and dying and so his fears were out on the table. About eight months later, they sent him to see his aunt. He went back into bed-wetting and the fear of the dark shadows on the wall. It was too soon. His stepsister was with him but it wasn't enough protection. He came back a week later. The memories were too strong for him still.

I saw him every week. I would see him alone, with his stepsister, and with his whole family together. That's the way I work. Now these things are pretty much resolved. I see him every two or three months and he's doing great. He can talk about his mother, but it isn't with tears, it isn't with as much longing, it isn't with the pain. That's when you know someone is healing. If someone is grieving and you feel the emotion and the tears and the trauma behind their words, a lot has to be worked through. When a person can talk in a lighter way about the loss, you know the healing is happening.

GROWING UP WITH LOSS

No matter how much time has passed, no matter how quiescent the grief becomes, it can spring to life at any moment. When your bereaved children graduate from high school, they will miss their dad. When they get married, their happiness may well be mixed with sorrow, for their sister will not be in the wedding party. For the rest of their lives, there will be times when they want more than anything in the world to talk to their dead parent, grandparent, sibling, or friend.

These feelings can be bittersweet; as they grow up, children who have been able to grieve will also be able to remember with fondness. At moments of accomplishment, they will be able to imagine their loved one's pride. At moments of joy, they will be able to picture their loved one's pleasure. And at the inevitable moments of sorrow that accompany life on earth, they will know that they have already suffered one of the hardest blows of all—a death during childhood—and they have survived. They have been both scarred and strengthened.

CHAPTER 12 | Coping with Grief

Do everything you can to understand that everything you experience is normal, healthy, appropriate. Forgive yourself. Engage in life-supporting activities, and when grieving, grieve full out.

—BYRON CALLAS

Mourning is the most intense process that most people ever go through. Grief is complex, unpredictable, and primal. Many people are frightened by it—frightened by feeling it, frightened by seeing it in others. Fortunately, there are ways to move through it, and those ways all involve expressing your feelings. If you act upon your grief, you will make room in your life and in your heart for hope and happiness. If you suppress it, it sticks around forever. However unpleasant or disturbing some of those feelings may be, there is no benefit in trying to ignore them.

I know this well, because for a long time I didn't do it. Maybe it's a family problem. My aunt, Hazel Haydon, didn't do it either, and I believe she has suffered as a result. She talked about the death of her mother four decades ago and how it has affected her. Hers is a cautionary tale:

> I made arrangements to come back for the funeral but I just went to pieces and I wasn't able to go. I wasn't able to function at all. I grieved more for my mother than I did for anybody else. I think it was because I had just been married for the second time and we had moved to Annapolis and I didn't know a living soul there. My husband, Stan, thought it was better not to talk about these things. And so I didn't have anyone to talk to. We didn't even have a telephone. I tried to shoulder it all by myself.

I still miss the talks my mother and I used to have. She was my best friend and a woman I could tell anything to, my hopes and dreams and everything under the sun. I miss that so much. We always were so close. I think I grieved about forty years for her. I'm not over it yet. I'm really not.

Grief is not simply an additional punishment, some horrible sequel to the death. Nor is it merely a process of adjustment. There will be times for the rest of your life when you will yearn for the presence of your loved one. But those feelings can also be accompanied by pleasure in remembrance as well as by satisfaction and pride in the present. Grief is, in a sense, a gift that the dead give to the living, their final legacy. From the grieving process, we can gain empathy, wisdom, an appreciation of life. We gain something of what they were, we incorporate their values, and we continue to be influenced by them—in our actions, in our values, in the ways we treat others, in the ways we see the world, and in our memory. Death changes the living. Grief is the journey you take from the person you used to be to the person you will become.

To ease that transition, there are specific steps you can take.

• **Let yourself experience not just sorrow and loss, but anger, guilt, even triumph.** Many people are afraid that if they admit their real feelings or give in to them, they may go crazy or lose control. In fact, it works the other way around: by expressing feelings, we release them. The love never disappears; but the stuck feeling, the feeling that you will forever reside in darkness, can vanish entirely.

So let yourself cry. Let yourself scream. When Ed de Blasio's friend Leo died, he was not contacted. "I found out about six weeks after the fact. A friend told me that if I was feeling incomplete about not having attended the funeral as an official farewell gesture, I should do what the Indians used to do upon the death of a companion: go up to the hills and howl. It was good advice."

If you're angry, rather than taking it out on other members of your family, kick a pillow, slam a towel against the floor, yell at a photograph of your loved one, or scream in the safety of a parked car. Bereavement specialist Dr. Sandra L. Graves recommends pounding on pillows or tearing up paper. Those actions may sound silly and artificial but they perform an important symbolic function by providing a means to express anger vigorously. And they really do make you feel better, even when you are not aware of being angry. It's better to attack the bedding than scream at the people around you. And if your loved one was the victim of a crime, by all means join a political action group.

If you're depressed, it is important to maintain activity along with some semblance of a schedule. Set goals for yourself, but make them small ones that include getting out of the house every day, talking to someone every day, and treating yourself with kindness. And take some solace in the fact that your feelings—shock, numbness, denial, confusion, depression, anger, guilt, anxiety, emptiness, hopelessness, and all the rest—are normal, natural, and, given expression, will someday fade.

• **Discuss your feelings with other people.** It's not sufficient to recognize them yourself; it's better to share them. Spend time with supportive people, not only because it helps in reducing loneliness but also because those people can help put your feelings into perspective. Talking about your feelings with someone who is willing to listen can be enormously consoling, especially if that person has experienced a death similar to the one you are grieving. Knowing that we're part of a community of mourners brings a bitter comfort but a comfort nonetheless.

• **Take care of your body.** This is extremely important, especially if you are worried about your health or suffering some of the physiological effects of grief such as weight loss. Get a checkup, just to make sure that there is nothing organically wrong with you.

Insomnia is a common problem among grievers. Lying in bed with your eyes closed, even if you're awake, increases the possibility of sleep. Sipping a cup of hot milk or chamomile tea can also help, as can relaxation exercises. But if you're so wired that sleep is nowhere on the horizon, find quiet activities such as leafing through magazines or writing in your journal. Insomnia usually strikes in one of two ways: either you can't fall asleep when you go to bed, or you wake up in the middle of the night. If you tend to wake up a couple of hours after you fell asleep, it's helpful to keep a book by the bed. When Cari died, I used the California Vehicle Code, because it is truly boring, and invariably I fell asleep over it. When my dad died, I read best-selling novels. Other people prefer the Bible, poetry, or metaphysical literature. Stay in bed if at all possible. On the other hand, impressive feats of housekeeping have been achieved by mourners who finally gave up on sleep entirely at three in the morning and decided to wash the kitchen floor or straighten their bureau drawers. One woman even used the predawn hours to garden. It's not a good idea to begin with such active tasks, because they tend to energize you. But if sleep is really not in the cards, you might as well use those extra hours productively.

There are also a few things you can do during the day to increase the likelihood of sleep at night: don't take naps; avoid coffee (including the decaffeinated varieties), tea, cola, and chocolate, all of which contain caffeine; prepare for bed at the same time every day; and begin to slow down prior to the appointed bedtime. An hour before bed is not a good moment for active tasks, such as vacuuming the house, or for upsetting ones, such as paying bills.

Massage is something that can be very useful during the grieving process, especially for people who feel touch-deprived. "We bereave in our hearts, we bereave in our minds and our psyches, and we grieve in our bodies," states licensed massaged therapist Cindy Stark Reid. "Touch has been used for thousands of years to comfort the bereaved." If you're tense (and having difficulty sleeping), it can help relax you. If you're all bottled up, it can help release your feelings. After his partner died, David Sheridan said, "I got a lot of deep tissue massage work on a weekly basis." When you're grieving, pampering yourself that way is appropriate and helpful. Other body work such as polarity therapy or acupressure, both of which seek to balance the various energies within the body, can also be beneficial.

Nutrition is also a major factor in how you feel, although healthful eating for many mourners seems like an unachievable goal. It's important to try to maintain a healthful diet, one that includes vegetables, fruit, carbohydrates, and protein every day. It can be difficult; many mourners find it painful to cook because it reminds them of the person who is not there to share the meal. But whatever efforts you can make in that direction will serve you in good stead. Although you may be tempted, it's important to resist the urge to smoke more, drink more, or eat a lot of sugar, because all three habits are hard on the body and ultimately difficult to kick (sugar included). A multivitamin pill and some vitamin C, on the other hand, can't hurt.

Exercise is vital. Many mourners who were interviewed for this book said that exercise was the most helpful thing they did for themselves. Olive Paulson, whose husband, daughter, and mother all died within a fifteen-month period, was one of those people. "I started a water aerobics class at the Y," she said. Other people ran, jogged, walked, bicycled, swam, took aerobics classes, joined gyms. In the beginning, heavy exercise may be more than you can do. If the very thought of running around the lake or taking an aerobics class sounds vaguely akin to climbing Mt. Everest, at least do some light exercise, such as taking short walks. Keep in mind that not only is exercise good for your body, it also improves your mood through the release of endorphins, a chemical compound in the brain that acts as a painkiller and a relaxant.

Other chemical compounds are less useful. Many people look to anything at all to numb the pain, including tranquilizers, sleeping pills, and mood-elevators prescribed by physicians. If there's a way to avoid drugs, if you can possibly function without them, do so. Drugs either prolong, postpone, or suppress what is a natural hard time in your life. In addition, it is easy to become dependent on them for the longer you take them, the more attached to them you become. "After my son Matthew died, I needed my sleep and wasn't able to get any. I called my internist and asked him to prescribe a sleeping pill. I was given Halcion. If my husband, Stan, hadn't died five months later, I would have been off it sooner," said Harlene Marshall. "I continued taking it for probably eight months and then had to work up the courage to stop. I was afraid of being awake, alone in the middle of the night with morbid thoughts. I'm glad I took it. I'm glad I stopped."

Not everyone is successful at finding that courage. "I have one patient who has been on medication for over a year, and every time I try to suggest tapering off, it's a crutch and I meet with total resistance," states Dr. Heather Allen. "My patient is convinced that she'll be totally depressed again." That's why, if you possibly can, it's better to deal with the feelings at the time they arise rather than masking them through drugs.

On the other hand, it's important to note that many mourners have found drugs to be useful. "My husband's doctor talked to me and gave me a prescription for ten sleeping pills because I was losing so much sleep," said Carolee Rake. "So far, I have only taken three and I was given the prescription eight months ago. He doesn't want me to get into the habit and I don't believe I will. But they do help." This seems like a very reasonable use of drugs. Used occasionally and under a doctor's prescription, sleeping pills have their place. But the fact of the matter is, grief is a natural process and being awake in the middle of the night with morbid thoughts is just part of it. "Grief is the way the psyche rights itself. All the screaming, all the pain, is what we have to go through to get to the other side, so I'm very leery of prescriptions of psychiatric drugs," states Marianne Williamson, the founder of the Center for Living in Los Angeles and Manhattan. "The time to have a broken heart is when your heart is breaking."

• **Keep a journal.** Writing your feelings down can help in getting locked-up emotions out. Forget literary aspirations: write as fast and furiously as you can. When you get angry, when you feel sad, write it down. One of the many journal-writing techniques useful during grief is to write an imaginary dialogue with the dead. Writing can be especially useful in the middle of the night, when there's no one to call and you're wide awake and your mind just won't stop. It also provides a useful and reassuring record, because when you reread your journal, you will be able to see your progress. A journal provides a record of change.

The benefits of this are primarily psychological, but according to Bernie S. Siegel, M.D., author of *Peace, Love and Healing: Bodymind*

Communication and the Path to Self-healing: An Exploration, they can also be physiological. He reported that college students and business executives who wrote in journals actually had more active immune systems and got fewer colds than they had before they started writing.

If giving sorrow words is difficult for you, try giving it pictures instead. Dr. Sandra Graves recommends keeping a visual journal in which you don't write: you scribble. "Get a blank book, and whenever you're feeling anything and you're not sure what it is . . . scribble. Doodle. Quit trying to put it into words." This has two major benefits: It offers a way to express feelings that you can't quite articulate. And it provides an excellent excuse to buy art supplies. Artistic expression of all sorts open other avenues of expression, regardless of your level of talent. After her brother Ted died, Rae Ecklund said, "I painted a portrait of him (and cried on the watercolor) and it helped."

• **Write letters to the deceased.** It's one way to say some of the things you didn't have the opportunity, or the courage, to say in life. If you're angry at the deceased, if they hurt or disappointed you, you can tell them in a letter. You can also tell them how much you love and miss them, and how much you have been affected by the death. Kay Pappas, a poet and professor, lost a close friend to AIDS. Although the friend had been ill for some time, he didn't share that information with her, and she was shocked by his death. Isolated in her grief, with no one to talk to, she found relief in letter writing:

> Rob was HIV positive for three years before he died but he didn't tell anyone. I didn't even know he was sick, and then I found out he was cremated. I had no place to deal with it. My husband said the right things and was supportive but Rob was not someone he was close to. So here I was—and no one in my life knew this person! When I called my friend Ingrid, she said, "You have to write about this."
>
> I said, "I can't. I'll fall apart." I was overcome. Ingrid said, "You have to speak directly to Rob."
>
> I started writing him letters and it was like opening a floodgate. Writing to the person invokes them. I wrote to him every day for months, pages and pages and pages. I stopped at about forty or fifty pages. It was a way of keeping him alive. Eventually, I wrote a poem and sent it to Ingrid. I realized that I was finished with one stage of the grieving; I was over the shock.

David K. Reynolds, Ph.D., author of *Playing Ball on Running Water* and other books, is a leading practitioner of Japanese Morita therapy, which stresses the importance of action. When he was interviewed for this book, he suggested that mourners write two letters to the person who died and read them aloud, either at the grave site or in front of a photograph of the deceased. Here are his recommendations:

> One is a letter of gratitude or at least a letter of thanks for specific things that person who died did for them during each ten years of life they had together. If their mother died when they were forty years old, there'd be four specific, concrete things in that letter: thank you for the yellow striped pinafore dress you got me on my fifth birthday; thank you for the time I had strep throat, when you sat by my bed. . . .
>
> The other letter should be a letter apologizing for specific things the grieving person did that caused trouble: Dear Mom, I'm sorry that I stole money out of your purse when I was nine years old, I wanted to buy a licorice; I'm sorry when I was fourteen years old. . . . What these letters do is make sense of the grief one is feeling. It makes sense to be grieving for someone who did positive things for you and whom you hurt.

Dr. Reynolds' suggestions can be particularly useful both for those who may be feeling guilty, because it allows you to apologize in a specific way, and for those who are feeling a great deal of resentment toward the deceased, because this method encourages you to seek positive memories.

• **Give yourself simple pleasures.** Grief is such a profound emotional state that it may sound ridiculous to recommend taking a bubble bath, going to a ball game, or investing in a VCR so you can watch movies at home. Simple pleasures offer no major solution; no one claims otherwise. And yet, they do provide relief. They really can make you feel better, because they carry messages to the interior—messages that say that, even alone, you matter. Kindnesses you do for yourself reinforce that message. That's why it's important to treat yourself with a little forbearance, especially when you're depressed.

Laughter helps. Funny movies help. This is no longer just folk wisdom either. Scientific research confirms that laughter improves respiration, affects muscle tone, and helps produce endorphins. Laughing may seem like a betrayal but it's not: it's an affirmation of life.

Other forms of escape also provide some temporary relief. "Mostly I spend a day reading when I'm depressed. I read historical novels and murder mysteries. By the time the day is over, I'm tired of reading and I feel better," said one widow.

"While my mother was dying, I didn't drink or take tranquilizers.

But I'd go to the movies. That I found was solace," said Rachel Ballon. "Going on walks was helpful. Looking at the ocean was helpful. After she died, I was emotionally drained so I did nothing. I watched TV. I couldn't read anything deeper than *People* magazine. That's all I could do."

Another widow reported that "I bought a nice stereo and have been collecting tapes and records." Music that you associate with the deceased may be difficult to hear, but it might also comfort you by reminding you of something that person enjoyed. "My father loved James Galway's flute-playing, and so we made a tape and played it at his funeral," said Karen Shannon of Woodstock, New York. "The first time I listened to that music after the funeral, it brought tears to my eyes right away. But since then, it has brought me pleasure." Music can provide a life and a distraction. It can also be tremendously evocative and many people find welcome catharsis in it. Other people find music too emotionally stimulating and avoid it for a while.

Travel can also be helpful. "I went to Sante Fe for about ten days," said David St. John. "The spiritual dimension of the landscape and the peacefulness were really recuperative. The tension and pressure of the couple of months before began to slip away, and I could think about the fact of his absence and what that meant."

After his thirty-one-year-old son died of cancer, Richard Haboush also praised the benefits of travel. "I forced my wife and my youngest son (who is twenty-eight) to go on a skiing trip for four days. We also took our dog and it was a lifesaver, especially for my wife. The change of atmosphere and being away from the house helped."

With travel, there is only one caveat: remember that you can't run away from grief, no matter how far you roam. Travel—especially to visit friends or family—can certainly provide a good break, but eventually you have to return.

It is true, however, that there are benefits in a change of scenery. Another way to do this is to change something in your house. Moving is not a good idea in the beginning, because moving is stressful in and of itself. But painting a room, putting up some new pictures, buying some new sheets, or rearranging the furniture can make it easier when you are at home. Like other small changes, it reinforces the fact that your life is moving forward.

• **Be open to the paranormal.** Seeing or hearing the deceased or sensing the presence of that person is a remarkably common experience, but one that is seldom discussed. A widow twice saw her deceased husband outside the kitchen window dashing toward his car. A bereaved son reported that his deceased father came and sat in front of his desk at work and told him he was happy and in a good place. My aunt Alice McCarty said,

"When I went to bed the night my brother Bobby was killed, I was crying and carrying on something terrible. I heard somebody say, 'Alice.' I looked up and his face was in the window and he said, 'I'm all right. I'm fine. Now stop crying.' "

And Andrea Sherman, who was widowed two times, had after-death encounters with both her husbands:

> My second husband came back several times. The first time he appeared, I was in bed asleep and I was awakened and looked up and there he was! He was sitting cross-legged on his side of the bed, fully clothed and saying, "Wake up." I'm sure that the words were not spoken; it was probably in my head. And he was giving me advice, which he always did. That happened twice. I was glad to see him. I was sorry when he left.
>
> Another time, his son, my two children, and I were playing in the kitchen. It was late at night and all of a sudden the cat started wailing and the hackles on his back went up. He was looking right up in the corner of the room. I felt something strange too. The kids stopped and we all felt his presence. We all felt it was him.
>
> After my first husband died, I felt his spirit continually for a period of a few weeks. Every time I would come to the parking lot where I worked and walk from my car to the office, I saw the same bird. And it sang to me and would follow me. And I thought that very definitely was his spirit.

Other mourners, too, have talked about birds—a mythological symbol of the soul. "My sister's bird hadn't sung for months and months while my mother was ill," one woman told us. "It began to sing again the day she died."

Most people are silent about such experiences. Who can blame them? Many people sneer at such stories, including professionals, who routinely discount experiences like these as products of wishful thinking, manifestations of denial or "searching" behavior. I do not discount them. I take them seriously—as does Louis LaGrand, Ph.D., distinguished service professor of health science at the State University of New York in Potsdam, and former president of the board of directors of Lawrence Hospice at St. Mark's Valley. "My guess is that probably forty to fifty percent of the people who have close, intense relationships with somebody who died have some sort of paranormal experience," he said. Some researchers have disagreed with that estimate, reporting smaller but still impressive percentages. In the United States, according to one study, 27 percent of the people surveyed reported such encounters.

The fact that these experiences are common may not prove a thing, scientifically. To many people, these experiences suggest that there is indeed some form of existence that continues after death. Obviously, it's impossible to prove that, but one thing is certain: the vast majority of people who have had such experiences came away consoled and with an overwhelming sense that their loved one was doing just fine.

• **Expect changes in your sexuality.** This is another aspect of grieving that is hardly ever mentioned, even though many people experience such changes almost immediately after the death. Some people become totally uninterested in sex. "It was just repulsive," said one woman whose child died. "It reminded me too much of the birth, which reminded me of the death. I felt numb. I didn't want to be touched." Many people feel similarly; for them, sex at such a time is something they can't even imagine.

But other people feel the opposite way. The night Cari died, something happened which mystified me. After everybody left except for my friends Cheryl Hart and Nancy Lemmon, I was sitting with them in the family room, and suddenly I felt an incredible wave of sexual desire. I was embarrassed. I could not understand these feelings and wondered how in the hell on the day my daughter died I could in any way want sex or lovemaking. It was a strong, distracting feeling that I couldn't ignore. I looked at my friends and said, "Gee, this is really awkward."

"What's the matter?" they asked.

"I feel so horny," I confessed. Their responses were instant.

Cheryl said, "Well, don't look at me."

And Nancy said, "Don't look at me."

We all started laughing. They suggested I call Wayne, an old boyfriend of mine who had just left. Of course, I didn't do it. But I was momentarily tempted.

The incident weighed on my mind and the next day I told my psychiatrist about it. I was disturbed by my feelings. How could I feel sexual at a time like that? It seemed unnatural. He reassured me immediately. He told me that my reaction was a normal, life-affirming reflection of the human need for comfort. I felt relieved. Since that time, I have discovered that many people in similar situations feel the same way. At the worst moment, the moment of greatest loss and shock, sexuality can reassert itself. Another mourner who experienced such sensations is actress Mariette Hartley, whom I got to know when she starred in the 1983 movie *Mothers Against Drunk Driving: The Candy Lightner Story*. As she discussed in Chapter Six, Mariette was in her early twenties when her father committed suicide:

> I was aware of a real sexual urge. I don't think it lasted very long but it sure was there in the beginning. I think it may

happen more than people realize. It's such a verboten subject —sex and death! I think it's a tremendous life surge, it's re-creation again, it's your body telling you, you've got to live, you have to live. What better way to remind yourself that you are a procreator. Every antenna is out.

In a curious way, it's like the theater—you become very sensual when you're working on a part that opens you. In theater, there's a creative surge that just kind of splatters out, and I'm sure that happens in grief.

Byron Callas had a similar reaction after his wife died of cancer in 1984, when he was thirty-five years old:

Would I have liked to go to bed with somebody the night my wife died? The straight answer is yes. It's not like, oh I need to right now jump into bed with somebody. But it would have been wonderful, wonderful, to hold somebody. It's a large emotional gestalt; it isn't just sexual, but it includes sexual. I wasn't going to go knocking on doors, but if somebody had suggested it, I wouldn't have needed any coaxing

When the urge arises, it's important, whether you choose to act on it or not, to recognize it for what it is: not a sign of disrespect, certainly not an indication of lack of love, but a positive impulse, a proclamation of the urge to live, and just another part of the complicated process of grieving.

• **Prepare to cope with the material side of death.** The will is a large part of that. Wills have their own strange histories. Seldom is the reading of a will the dramatic act it is in the movies. But in their absence as well as in their presence, wills can wreak havoc. "People are upset by wills all the time, even when they are written with the best of intentions," states New York attorney Sharon Bronte. "The slightest difference between siblings causes incredible pain. You leave it equally to all the kids, but you leave your silver to Jessica and they all have a fit."

Unfortunately, wills are not always written with the best of intentions. "People making their wills can be vindictive," Bronte reports. "They're fully capable of saying, 'I'm doing this because my daughter needs it more than my son,' and an hour later they'll say, 'My son never comes to see me anyway.' It's a 'vengeance is mine' type of thing." Two sisters, for instance, were shocked to learn that their mother had willed her house to their brother—who was, among other distinctions, the wealthiest of the three children. They wondered why she hadn't willed it to all three of them, to split equally. Was she confused? Was she coerced? Was she angry at them? And, if so, why? Questions that may never be answered can make the grieving process more difficult.

With the settling of an estate, many mourners, especially if they have children, may find themselves dwelling on their own eventual demise. If you haven't done it before, making out your own will at such a time might seem a bizarre form of punishment. It is not: it can instead give you an increased sense of power and control by proving that you really are a competent adult.

If you do it right, you can also help ensure that your own death won't be immediately followed by a family fight. "I did one will for a lady who knew she was dying. She had cancer and the entire family sat around the table while we did the will. Every time I looked at the husband's face, pure agony was written across it," Sharon Bronte states. "But she did something I really approve of; she did the will with the family there." Everyone in the family should also be informed about any changes that are made. That way, no one is surprised.

People of ordinary means often think they have straightforward, un-complicated estates. But once a house, savings accounts, life insurance policies, personal debts, and highly valued objects are considered, a will can become remarkably complicated. For that reason, the choice of executor can be a crucial one. "In certain situations, a family member should be appointed because they are more likely to know about the affairs of the deceased," observes Patricia Trent, an estates planning attorney in Las Vegas, Nevada. "However, if there are problems with the beneficiaries, it might be a good idea to designate a third party just for the purposes of keeping everybody honest." That way, the executor of the will doesn't have to walk the line between self-interest and a just distribution. A neutral executor can help reduce paranoia and resentment on the part of the inheritors.

The settling of an estate includes far more than dealing with finances. When a loved one dies, a universe of mundane tasks descends upon the mourner. Not the least of these may be cleaning out the person's pos-sessions. Going through these things can make people feel like archae-ologists in their own lives. The past is revived. Objects that were completely unremarkable may now seem packed with meaning. In her memoir of her mother, *A Very Easy Death*, Simone de Beauvoir describes this phenomenon: "As we looked at her straw bag, filled with balls of wool and an unfinished piece of knitting, and at her blotting-pad, her scissors, her thimble, emotion rose up and drowned us. Everyone knows the power of things: life is solidified in them, more immediately present than in any one of its instants." That crystal fruit bowl you always loved and that red hat you always laughed at become greater than themselves: they become mementos of an entire relationship. That's why sorting through those items can be an intense and cathartic experience.

• **Act upon your relationship with the deceased.** Visiting the cemetery to talk with your loved one is one way to do that, but it can also be done in small ways. Framing a few snapshots, for example, is a tiny way in which you can memorialize the person who died.

Many people find comfort in gestures intended to perpetuate the memory of their loved one, such as planting a tree, sending money to an organization whose work you admire, or donating library books in that person's name. It's particularly meaningful to do something that reflects your loved one's life. For instance, Honolulu attorney Carolyn Nicol and her brother and sister commissioned two stained-glass windows in memory of their mother and father for their parents' church in Briarcliff Manor, New York; not only was the church very important in their parents' lives, but the designs of the windows featured various flowers indigenous to the region where they had lived.

Marty Winthrop makes an annual donation on behalf of her father. "My father had a dog and two cats and he would take food to a little animal shelter and he fed the birds. So every year around Christmas I contribute money to the animal shelter in his memory."

David St. John's father was commemorated with an athletic scholarship. "My father was a basketball and track coach and he had been a star tennis player at Cal State Fresno. He won more matches than anybody who had ever been there. So they started a tennis scholarship that will be given each year in his name. A friend of his who's the basketball coach there was able to make it happen. That was important to me and to my mother. It was really gratifying."

And I can tell you for a fact that acting to correct a wrong—whether that wrong is drunk driving or inadequate research into a disease—can make a tremendous impact not only on your own state of mind but on the world. Beverly Barbo, whose twenty-seven-year-old son, Tim, died of AIDS, felt better when she started speaking out. "I have been in fourteen states telling our story. I put a face on the homosexual and take the unreasonable fear out of the disease. It changes people's perceptions. I am healing because I am doing something that makes my son more than a statistic."

• **Create a private ritual of commemoration on the anniversary of the death.** It doesn't matter how small that ceremony is. "I lit a candle at a local shrine where I sometimes pray in extreme cases, as I did when my father died," Giles Slade said. "It makes me feel self-conscious, and I am not a Catholic, but it helps." Solomon Berg found another way, on the anniversary of his son's death:

> One year on the anniversary of his death, I was the president
> of the Ethical Society, and the guest on that occasion was the

poet Mary Cheever. I recited a Spanish translation of a poem by Walt Whitman which begins this way: "When lilacs last in the dooryard bloom'd, And the great star early droop'd in the western sky in the night, I mourn'd—and yet shall mourn with ever-returning spring." I felt it was very fitting because it's about mourning, and my son died in the spring. Reading that poem was my own private way of acknowledging the date. No one else there knew why I read that particular poem. But it made me feel better.

• **Don't ignore holidays.** It's imperative that you have something to do or someplace to go on those days. But doing the things you did when your loved one was alive may be tremendously painful, so you may want to create a new tradition, to celebrate in a different manner. Many people find that it helps to travel someplace new, where they won't be constantly reminded. If you always hosted a Christmas Eve dinner at your house, you might consider going out that night—to someone else's house, to the opera, or even to a children's hospital or a shelter for homeless people where volunteering your time might ease someone else's loneliness. Instead of having the extended family over to Christmas dinner, you might consider making them brunch instead or inviting a few new people. They won't make up for the person who died, but they can bring a fresh quality to the holiday season that you may enjoy.

It's a good idea on these occasions to include the deceased by doing something in recognition of the love you feel for them. Many bereaved parents, for example, put a Christmas ornament on the tree in memory of the child who died. Trying to get through a holiday by pretending you don't remember doesn't work; it's better to acknowledge your memories. "A boy who was very much a part of our life and had been at our Passover table since he was a little boy was killed when he was thirteen and a half, right after his bar mitzvah," said Rabbi Laura Geller. "His name will always be mentioned at our Passover seder."

Take time to reminisce; take time to cry; and make a concerted effort to do something enjoyable, however much you have to force yourself. Keep in mind, too, that holidays can be hard for everyone. The Norman Rockwell image of a happy family sitting around a holiday table laden with food is an archetypal myth, not a reality. Even people whose families are intact can feel the tug of sadness on holidays.

• **Seek understanding.** Many people find solace in the rituals, literature, and beliefs of their religion. Even people who were not religious prior to the death are often drawn to their church or temple as a place where they can find comfort, understanding, and wisdom.

Other people discover that whatever religious feelings they may have had are wiped out by the assault of the death. Furious at God for allowing such a thing to happen, they turn away from their religion. The death precipitates a real crisis of faith (a crisis addressed in Harold Kushner's now-classic work, *When Bad Things Happen to Good People*). Ruth Kieffer remembers her feelings after her child was stillborn:

> I think the most anger I felt was at God. How could He let this happen to us? Where was our miracle? I screamed at Him, I swore at Him. I did not return to church for a year and I refused to talk to our pastor. Now, four years later, my faith is starting to return but I don't know if I will ever regain the trust I once had.

Many people today find spiritual sustenance in nontraditional places: in Transcendental Meditation, in Native American healing rituals, in ideas of the afterlife written about by Elisabeth Kübler-Ross and Raymond Moody, in books that take an Eastern approach such as *The Wheel of Life and Death*, by Philip Kapleau. Death, more than any other event in life, stimulates the search for philosophical or spiritual understanding. If you have interests along this line, this is the right time to pursue them.

• **Recognize the ways in which your loved one's life has influenced you.** That influence is lifelong and ever-changing. Aspects of your loved one's personality may seem to grow within you. Things they loved may come to mean more to you now than they ever did. For instance, my mother was Lebanese, which did not interest me at all while I was growing up. Nor did it immediately interest me after she died. But in the years since, I have become fascinated by that heritage and committed to the cause of peace in the Middle East. It's a form of homage to my mother.

And recognize, too, that your loved one's death can influence you in positive ways. Life is never the same after the death of someone we love; we are never the same. But we are not diminished. We are expanded, both in understanding and in experience. By grieving fully, we gain the capacity to transform ourselves and to help others who are in pain. In doing so, we reach new levels of resolution, of acceptance. But acceptance is not some final goal, some ribbon to crash through, after which you're done grieving once and for all. Rather, mourners accommodate to the loss tentatively, slowly, fitfully. Accommodation doesn't come all at once: it comes in moments, moments that occur over the rest of your life.

• **Take steps to create a new life for yourself.** Once you're past the initial period of mourning, however many months that turns out to be, look for ways to add to your life. Pursuing a new interest, taking courses at an extension university, donating your time to an organization or cause you support, meeting new people, getting a new assignment at work, or even finding a new job (especially if you have been unemployed) can open new vistas to you, as Dotty Graf of Riverside, California, discovered. She is a retired office worker whose husband died of a heart attack at age seventy-three:

> When my husband died, I had to fight depression: fifty-two years of habit, and all of a sudden the house was so empty. Every Saturday morning, I used to take him to Carl's Junior for breakfast in his wheelchair and with his crutches. We'd sit and people-watch. When he died, the whole thing was shot. So one day I started looking for a job. I went to Hallmark, to Alpha Beta, to the candy store. I got to Carl's Junior, and the manager said, "Dotty, I just lost my brother, and I know what you're going through." He hired me to work every day for two hours, from 11:30 to 1:30. I loved it. It enabled me to get my feet on the ground. I met a lot of people and I'd be smiling and happy and then when I got back home, I'd fall on my face. Carl's Junior was my salvation! I wasn't sitting there having a meal and going on my way—I was working!
>
> Also I went to modeling school. My daughter said, "Mom, you always wanted to be a model. Nordstrom's is tired of twenty-year-olds." I forced myself to go every Monday for thirty-two weeks. I graduated and had my picture in the *Enterprise* as a model. I was over seventy years old. I wasn't sure if I wanted to go to Hollywood and go on TV. Maybe I could be another "Where's the beef?" lady and make a fortune.
>
> But I was still depressed. Even if we were fighting, at least that was something! I started thinking about the Peace Corps. The feeling got strong and I called. I don't know if I'm going. But I know it's vitally important to me to do for others and to stay active. So I started volunteering at the Salvation Army, where I have been counseling teenagers. When I come home, I take a half-hour walk up Canyon Crest and when midnight comes, I fall into bed. On the way to sleep, I'm thinking about what I'm going to wear tomorrow. What can I put together that looks smart? Next thing I know, it's six o'clock in the morning. It's the first day of the rest of my life, and I'm ready to live.

SEEKING OUTSIDE HELP

Many people find comfort in support groups for those in mourning. The number of such bereavement groups has ballooned in recent years; today, hundreds of such groups exist around the country. The most useful groups consist of grievers whose losses are similar to your own, such as the Widowed Persons Service run by the American Association of Retired Persons, groups offered through MADD, the Compassionate Friends, a self-help group for people who have lost a child, or SHARE, a self-help group for parents who have experienced a miscarriage, stillbirth, or death of an infant. Groups such as these, which meet on a weekly or a monthly basis, offer guidance, support, and a place to express feelings. But their usefulness depends totally on the group and on the leader. "I joined a group at the YWCA and it didn't do anything," one widow said. "Then I tried this group at the Calvary Presbyterian Church. Jo, the leader of the group, is a marvelous person who creates an atmosphere of trust. We can talk openly. I've made friends with people who were acquaintances before. We go out to dinner and lunch and we call each other and we go to the movies and the symphony. There's a friendly closeness, and it's helpful to be with people to whom you can talk freely without being a burden."

Bereavement groups can provide knowledge about the process of grieving, understanding friends, and reassurance. But problems can arise, as Sara Grisanti found after her baby died. "I went to a self-help group and the first time, I cried and I cried. We all cried. But there was a sense of who was the worst, who was the saddest, who has the most pathetic story. And then I went home and I felt wrung out and my husband said, 'These people are in a competition to be the saddest parents in the world.' I don't want to be in competition for that." That's the chief difficulty; while it is inspiring to see people who have suffered a similar loss and found some inner peace and happiness, it is discouraging to see people whose loss may be much less recent than your own and who are nonetheless still stuck in the heart of darkness.

Another problem is that while groups can provide useful transitional help, some people turn the group into a substitute for the loved one. They become addicted to the group; they need the group in order to function. Six or seven years after the death, they're still religiously attending. That's too long.

The key factor is the facilitator. When the person in charge of the group is untrained, you take a risk. Sometimes these people are highly skilled, intuitive group leaders. Sometimes they're not. The same is true with professionally trained counselors, but your chances are better of getting someone who can lead you through the process and turn the group into a truly supportive and positive network.

The best way to judge if a group is right for you is to attend a meeting. If it doesn't feel right, try another group. If you're also uncomfortable in that one, it may be that a group isn't right for you. You might prefer to work with a therapist or a clergyman, or simply to talk with a good friend.

Therapy, too, is an individual choice, one that I and many other people have found tremendously helpful. "Going for counseling and learning to care for myself emotionally was the most important thing I did," Alyce Birkett told us. Therapy is a useful tool that shouldn't be discounted simply because you think it might imply that there's something wrong with you. Therapy is called for when your grief is excessive, and therein lies the problem: it's not easy to judge what is excessive and what is not. You certainly can't trust other people to tell you; many people are so uncomfortable with grieving that they think *any* real expression of emotion is excessive. You have to try to assess your own levels of grieving, and it's not easy to do that. But if many months have passed and you simply are not functioning—if your tears won't stop, or you are waking up night after night with nightmares, or your feelings of anger or guilt are unrelenting, or you are often thinking about ways to kill yourself— seeing a therapist is the best thing to do. The same is true if your marriage is in jeopardy, if you're alienating other people, or if your performance at work is seriously undermined. A good therapist, preferably one trained in grief therapy, can help guide you through the process. (To find one who has experience with mourners, contact the Association for Death Education and Counseling, listed in the appendix.) And if you're not sure whether a therapist would help, you might make an appointment and see whether it looks like a good avenue for you. It can't hurt.

LOOKING FOR HELP IN ALL THE WRONG PLACES

Unfortunately, the very people who might be expected to have the greatest understanding are often the ones from whom grievers receive the least attention. Friends might be forgiven; after all, they may have had no experience with death. But professionals ought to know better. Doctors and members of the clergy—people who deal with death and dying as a regular part of their professional lives—are often sadly remiss when it comes to helping the griever. Doctors, with whom you may have spent a great deal of time during your loved one's illness, frequently disappear after the death. And members of the clergy who were empathetic and kind during the week of the funeral may never be heard from again. Of all the people interviewed for this book, it is astonishing how few received any significant help in dealing with their grief from these two sources.

No doubt there are reasons for this, as the professionals we interviewed were quick to tell us. Doctors, we were told repeatedly, are overworked and have to give their attention to the living. They are committed to saving lives; their focus is on cure, not consolation. Nevada oncologist Dr. Heather Allen described some aspects of the problem that she has observed both in her personal life and as a physician:

> I'm in oncology because when I was in high school my mother died of ovarian cancer. I would ask how is she, and the doctor would say, "Her white count's up, or her fever's down." They were focused on did she eat or what her potassium level was. So when I asked questions, that's what they would tell me. Those weren't the questions I needed answers to; I wanted to know how she was. I didn't care about her white count or potassium level. I thought at the time that if I ever was in medicine, I would never forget that. I've been on the other side of the stethoscope and I think about that a lot when I'm with families.
>
> In medical school and in the training programs, the emphasis is on the physical aspects, not the psychological. What you realize when you're trying to teach medical students, residents, and fellows is that you have a short period of time and you have to start making priorities. What are you going to do?

The training that physicians receive in dealing with depression and other manifestations of grief is shocking in its absence, especially when you consider that grief is known to have significant physiological components. Even psychiatrists receive little or no information about grief. "Training about the effects of grief was notoriously absent during my medical education," states New York psychiatrist Dr. Barry Kerner, M.D. "During my psychiatry rotation, as part of the didactic course, they went over it very quickly, along with a lot of other topics. They didn't spend a day on it. I finished my medical training in 1978 and there was nothing in my residency or internship on it. And in four years of post-M.D. training in psychiatry, there was no specific seminar on it. Nobody said anything about it. I had to learn about grief on my own, through my own studies and networking with other professionals who counsel specifically around issues of bereavement."

There is a reason why grieving receives so little attention from the medical profession. It has to do with why people choose to become doctors in the first place. "A lot of people who go into medicine do it for counterphobic reasons; that is, their own fear of death, which they sublimate, causes them to go into a profession where they'll have some victory over it. By saving people from death, they're subconsciously attempting to master their own fear," states Dr. Kerner. When they don't save someone from death, they often look upon it as a sign of personal failure. No wonder so few of them are at ease with the topic.

The absence of training and the tendency of doctors to not want to think about death are real problems. Fortunately, there are real solutions. The first has to do with the training of physicians. No matter how over-worked they may be, there still needs to be time devoted to the study of grieving within the medical curriculum. Grief is not, after all, a rare condition; it eventually afflicts virtually every human being on earth. Its absence within medical training programs is a bizarre omission that needs to be corrected. There is some indication that this is changing. Indeed, Dr. Kerner believes that "within the last few years, there's been a more humanitarian movement in medicine. Fifteen years ago, if you went into medicine, you could make a fortune. But as the economics of medicine have changed, with decreased reimbursements and the inability to make as much money, the kind of people who have been attracted to it are more humanitarian. They are doing it for the right reasons."

The hospice movement has done important, ground-breaking work with the dying. In addition, every hospice provides a program for those who are in mourning. Centers such as the Saint Francis Center for Bereavement in Washington, D.C., do excellent work with grievers, and branches of national and international groups already exist within many communities. At the very least, mourners need to be informed about this vast network of resources. But many doctors know nothing whatsoever about such services and fail to refer mourners to them.

A few hospitals, such as the Brotman Medical Center in Los Angeles, have addressed the problem by incorporating bereavement programs within the hospital itself. All hospitals need to have such a program, staffed by professionals. Few do.

In addition, hospitals ought to have viewing rooms, where mourners can spend time with the body immediately after death. They need to have a room where grievers can cry. Many hospitals do have chapels, but everyone knows that in a chapel one is expected to pray in silence. Grievers want to cry. They want to scream. They ought to be able to do that in a comfortable, soundproof room within the hospital itself. But more than anything else, they need a little attention, some kind words, a few recommendations, and a couple of follow-up calls or visits from the hospital itself.

The clergy is sometimes no better. Their problems are similar to those of doctors. "A high percentage of clergy go into their jobs because of their fear of death; this has been researched in all churches," states Father William Wendt of the Saint Francis Center for Bereavement. "It isn't just the church. It's the whole of society. But I think the churches probably have the most difficult time. I did a workshop for the hospice movement in New England and the director told me that one of the hardest tasks for his volunteers was taking people back to church. People don't want to hear that god-awful expression, 'It's God's will.' "

Once again, the problem is that members of the clergy are inadequately prepared to help people cope with grief. "When I got out of the seminary, I had almost no background whatsoever in dealing with grief. We learned how to celebrate funerals and weddings, and we read Elisabeth Kübler-Ross, but very little time was spent on grieving per se," states the venerable Hartshorn Murphy, Jr., of the Episcopal Archdiocese of Los Angeles.

"There are very few seminaries that have courses in death and dying or grief and bereavement, so you come out of the seminary very unexposed," Father Wendt observes. This, too, has got to change, and there are signs that it is. Many conferences, such as the 1989 conference on Growing Through Loss, sponsored by the Institute for Religion and Wholeness at the School of Theology in Claremont, California, have addressed these issues, suggesting that perhaps awareness is improving. Many religious leaders, including Rabbi Harold Kushner, have written useful books on the topic. But the clergy needs to take advantage of these resources. All seminaries, regardless of denomination, need to teach the kind of courses that Father Wendt suggests—and those courses ought to be required. Beyond that, individual clergy need to be sensitized to the issue. They need to know some of the specific problems encountered by bereaved parents, widows and widowers, those who have lost a parent, and so forth. Until they receive that education and begin to act upon it, they will continue to fail to bring comfort to those who need it the most. They need to know that their responsibility should not end with the funeral.

THE GIFT OF GRIEF

Death takes away. That's all there is to it. But grief gives back. By experiencing it, we are not simply eroded by pain. Rather, we become larger human beings, more compassionate, more aware, more able to help others, more able to help ourselves. Grief is powerful alchemy. It plunges us into sorrow and forces us to face the finiteness of life, the mightiness of death, and the meaning of our existence on this earth. It does more than enable us to change: it demands it. The way we change is up to us. It is possible to be forever bowed by grief. It is possible to be so afraid of one aspect of it that we become frozen in place, stuck in sorrow, riveted in resentment or remorse, unable to move on.

But it is also possible to be enlarged, to find new direction, and to allow the memory of the beloved person we have lost to live on within us, not as a monument to misery but as a source of strength, love, and inspiration. By acting on our grief, we can eventually find within ourselves a place of peace and purposefulness. It is my belief that all grievers, no matter how intense their pain, no matter how rough the terrain across which they must travel, can eventually find that place within their hearts.

EPILOGUE | Ten Years
_____ | Later

When I was very young and confused, I thought that when I reached my thirties I would finally be all wise and knowing, my values would be intact, and my life would be complete. Instead, my marriage ended, I began to question my values, and Cari died. So then I looked forward to my forties. Yet by the time I was forty, I was no longer selling real estate, I was no longer with MADD, my children had left home, and I did not know what I was going to do when I grew up. The future was a blank to me, but before I could move ahead, I had to look back. I had to grieve.

If there is one thing I have learned from working on this book and talking with experts as well as other mourners, it is that we all grieve in our own ways and on our own schedule. When I interviewed psychologist Dr. Jerri Smock for this book, she told me that you know you've made significant progress when you can go to the cemetery, you can look at the pictures, you can talk about that person without feeling overwhelmed by pain or sadness or tears. I've finally reached that place with Cari.

I came to this realization for the first time last year when I moved into a new condominium, this time across the street from the ocean, and decided to put up some photographs around my new home. Looking through my old albums, I picked out pictures of my children Serena and Travis, my parents, my grandparents, my aunts and uncles, my sister Kathy and her family, and myself as a child. And for the first time since her death, I put up pictures of Cari.

I will probably always miss my daughter. But I am no longer afraid of photographs of her. Looking through them, I didn't cry and I didn't feel pain; I remembered special moments. Of course, I felt some sadness, some nostalgia, but the unbelievable heartache wasn't there. I made a project of those pictures. I pulled out photographs that particularly appealed to me, shopped for frames, and spent several hours arranging the framed pictures until the display was just right. As I incorporated her pictures into my home, I began incorporating Cari back into my life.

On my wall now, I have a whole collection of photographs, including baby pictures of Cari and Serena together, their faces lit with smiles; an adorable picture of them at age seven wearing blue and white dresses; and the last picture ever taken of the girls together. It was a snapshot from their yearbook. After Cari died, I called the school to see if I could have a copy. They couldn't find the negative so we duplicated the picture from the yearbook. It's a grainy reproduction, one that wouldn't win any prizes, but I love it because it shows the girls leaning against each other laughing, sisters and best friends.

I also put up Cari's eighth-grade graduation picture. It's a formal studio shot in which a front view and a profile are superimposed on the same background. I had ordered a few copies of that picture shortly before she died, and after her death, I called up the photographer and said I'd like some more. He duplicated them for free and sent me as many as I needed. That picture is particularly moving to me; when I look at it, I remember Cari and the graduation ceremony she never attended, and I remember the photographer's kindness to a distraught stranger. It also reminds me of how far I have come and how much I have learned.

I again recently noted my own progress when I visited my dad in Sacramento and went to the cemetery where Cari is buried. Two friends, Linda and Michael Siegle, joined me, and as we sat and chatted, I cleaned up around Cari's tombstone. They asked if it bothered me to do that, and for the first time ever, I was able to say no. And I meant it. It took nine years to reach that turning point in my mourning for her.

Today, I don't dwell on *how* my daughter died. I don't seek out opportunities to say, "My daughter was killed by a drunk driver." And I don't avoid them. My focus is no longer on the past, no longer on drunk driving. I'm relieved to be able to say that.

Most people think that MADD was my tribute to Cari. It wasn't. MADD was my reaction to her death. This book is my tribute to her life, along with that of my mother and father.

When I started MADD ten years ago, I had suffered the unexpected deaths of my mother and my thirteen-year-old daughter. My father was diagnosed as terminally ill in November 1989. As this book progressed, so did his illness, and the irony was not lost on me. I realized how much I had learned about grieving when it came time to deal with his terminal illness and then death from cancer at age seventy-three. I reread the chapter on anticipated death just before he died and realized how important it was for me to say good-bye and also to talk about the future. I learned that from our mourners. When Dad was first diagnosed as terminal, in November of 1989, I thought that sudden death was preferable to anticipated death. But after I said good-bye, I realized how fortunate I was to be able to tell him how much I loved him and what he meant to me as a father. How I wish I had had that opportunity with Cari.

My grief for my dad is much different from my grief for my mom or for Cari. In many ways, my dad was the man of my life, loving me unconditionally, always supportive and always there for me. My sister and I were his girls and we were his life. We came first. When my ex-husband made the decision to abdicate his role as an active father in our children's lives, my father stepped in. He was Travis' male role model, the one who took him shooting, the one who discussed the facts of life with him. If my daughter needed advice or money, she could call not only on me but on my dad, and he never failed her.

When I was told my father's diagnosis, I didn't experience denial; he had been sick for so long that deep down I knew he would not live much longer. After he died, my anger was very short-lived, and my depression happened much sooner. I am now an orphan, and I am also the matriarch and patriarch of our family. All of a sudden, I aged. I didn't feel old after Cari died—just battered. Grieving for my dad hurts; but I know something about the process now and it doesn't scare me. I feel grief for my dad, and at the same time, I am enthusiastic about the direction I am taking in my life.

I have realized that for me, finding fulfillment means being committed to an issue. Although I will always care about the issue of drunk driving, I've become very concerned about the issue of victims of violent crime during the last three years. Blaming the victim once a crime has occurred is something that happens both in society and in the courtroom. Victims are not only blamed, they are virtually ignored, their needs dismissed, their presence in the court process discouraged. They are not notified of arraignments, trial dates, sentencing, and parole hearings. Their rights, if any, are limited and depend solely on the goodwill of the district attorney and judge. This must change. Violence happens around us every day, and when it does, the impact is horrendous—and made more so by the criminal justice system. The plight of the victim must be brought to public attention, and that's why my next book will focus on the need for victims' rights.

I also have other interests. I'm concerned about the stereotyping of Arab-Americans, about discrimination against them, and about peace in the Middle East. I'm very proud of my Lebanese heritage and I work with various organizations on these issues. I also stay involved in the political arena, lending my name or time to causes I feel are worthy, such as various propositions on the ballot in California. I still travel, speaking at conferences and schools. I write, and I'm involved in several projects. Though I am always busy, I've learned the importance of taking weekends off. I make time for myself, for friends, for visiting my daughter in New York or seeing her here, and for helping my teenage son through his latest crisis.

Yes, there is life after MADD. It's in Southern California by the sea. It's in taking time to know my children better and developing relationships based on who I am and not what I do. Ten years ago I could barely make it through the day. Now I look forward to the future.

RESOURCES

Because the number of bereavement groups and other self-help organizations has ballooned in recent years, the list that follows is perforce a partial one. To the best of our knowledge, every organization on this list can help mourners find appropriate support groups in their local area within the United States, or can at the least refer them to other groups that might be able to do so.

Accord, Inc.
1930 Bishop Lane STE 947
Louisville, Kentucky 40218
502-458-0260
800-346-3087

Aiding a Mother Experiencing Neonatal Death (AMEND)
4324 Berrywick Terrace
St. Louis, Missouri 63128
314-487-7528

AMEND offers one-to-one support and referrals for parents who have lost a child to miscarriage, stillbirth, or infant death.

American Association of Suicidology
2459 South Ash Street
Denver, Colorado 80222
313-692-0985

Association for Death Education and Counseling (ADEC)
638 Prospect Avenue
Hartford, Connecticut 06105
203-232-4825

Center for Living
1550 N. Hayworth, Suite 1
Los Angeles, California 90046
213-850-0877
213-850-0878 (outreach program)

Center for Living
704 Broadway, 3rd Floor
New York, New York 10003
212-533-3550

Both the Center for Living in New York and the one in Los Angeles provide support groups and outreach programs for people with life-threatening disease and their families and friends.

Center for Loss and Life Transition
3735 Broken Bow Road
Fort Collins, Colorado 80526
303-226-6050

Center for Sibling Loss
1700 W. Irving Park
Chicago, Illinois 60613
312-883-0268

Centering Corporation
Box 3367
Omaha, Nebraska 68103
402-553-1200

Children's Hospice International
1101 King Street, #131
Alexandria, Virginia 22314
800-24-CHILD

CHI provides a support system and resource bank for health-care professionals, families, and organizations that offer hospice care to terminally ill children.

Compassionate Friends
Box 1347
Oakbrook, Illinois 60521
708-990-0010

Nationwide self-help support group for parents who have experienced the death of a child from any cause at any age.

Dougy Center
3909 S.E. 52nd
Portland, Oregon 97206
503-775-5683

A nonprofit center with nationwide affiliates for grieving children who have lost a parent or sibling by death.

Elisabeth Kübler-Ross Center
South Route 616
Headwaters, Virginia 24442
703-396-3441

A nonprofit, nonsectarian organization that offers workshops allowing participants to express past pains, evaluate results, and develop new patterns of living.

Grief Recovery Institute
8306 Wilshire Boulevard, Suite 21-A
Los Angeles, California 90211
800-445-4808

Life with Cancer Program
Fairfax Program
3300 Gallows Road
Falls Church, Virginia 22046
703-698-2841

Support program for children between five and fourteen who face the impending or recent death of a parent or other family member. Participation is not restricted to children with a family member who has cancer.

Miscarriage, Infant Death, Stillbirth (MIDS)
c/o Janet Tischler
16 Crescent Drive
Parsippany, New Jersey 07054
201-263-6730

Support group and referrals for parents who have experienced miscarriage, infant death, or stillbirth.

Mothers Against Drunk Driving (MADD)
669 Airport Freeway, Suite 310
Hurst, Texas 76053
817-268-MADD

Some chapters offer group support for victims of drunk driving.

Mt. Vernon Center for Community Mental Health
Grief Program
8119 Holland Road
Alexandria, Virginia 22306
703-360-6910

National Association of Military Widows
4023 25th Road North
Arlington, Virginia 22207
703-527-4565

Provides military widows with support and referrals in personal and legislative matters.

National Funeral Directors Association
11121 W. Oklahoma Avenue
Milwaukee, Wisconsin 53227
414-541-2500

This organization sponsors an arbitration program for disputes that arise over funeral costs.

National Hospice Organization
1901 N. Moore Street, Suite 901
Arlington, Virginia 22209
703-243-5900

National Organization for Victims Assistance (NOVA)
717 "D" Street N.W.
Washington, D.C. 20004
202-393-NOVA

National Research and Information Center
1614 Central Street
Evanston, Illinois 60201
800-662-7666

Through the Funeral Service Consumer Assistance Program, this center provides consumers with information on funeral services and attempts to resolve any disputes concerning contracts.

National Self-help Clearinghouse
25 W. 43rd Street, Room 620
New York, New York 10036
212-840-1259

For information on support groups, send a letter describing your circumstances with a self-addressed stamped envelope.

National Sudden Infant Death Syndrome (SIDS) Foundation
10500 Little Putuxent Parkway, Suite 420
Columbia, Maryland 21044
800-221-SIDS

National Victim Center
307 W. 7th Street, Suite 1001
Fort Worth, Texas 76102
817-877-3355

Nonprofit organization that serves as a central resource agency for seven thousand victim-service and criminal justice programs.

National Victims' Resource Center
Office of Victims of Crime
633 Indiana N.W., Room 1352
Washington, D.C. 20531
202-724-5947

Parent Care, Inc.
Health Sciences Center, University of Utah
50 N. Medical Drive, Room 2A210
Salt Lake City, Utah
801-581-5323

Parents of Murdered Children
100 E. 8th Street, B041
Cincinnati, Ohio 45202
513-721-LOVE

Pet Loss Support Hotline
c/o Human-Animal Program
School of Veterinary Medicine
University of California
Davis, California 95616
916-752-4200

The hotline is open Monday through Friday from 6:30 P.M. to 9:30 P.M. Pacific time. Information and referral to other services is also available.

Resolve, Inc.
5 Water Street
Arlington, Massachusetts 02174
617-643-2424

Provides support and referrals to parents who have lost a child to miscarriage, stillbirth or infant death.

Saint Francis Center for Bereavement
5417 Sherier Place N.W.
Washington, D.C. 20016
202-363-8500

Nonsectarian, nonprofit organization counseling people with life-threatening illness and people who are bereaved.

Share
Saint Elizabeth's Hospital
211 S. 3rd Street
Belleville, Illinois 62222
618-234-2415

Nationwide and international support group for parents who have lost a baby, particularly (but not exclusively) due to miscarriage, stillbirth, and newborn death.

Society of Military Widows
National Association of Uniformed Services
5535 Hempstead Way
Springfield, Virginia 22151-4094
703-750-1342

National nonpartisan group of widows and widowers of career members of the uniformed services whose purpose is to provide companionship, sympathetic understanding, and helpful advice.

Sudden Infant Death Syndrome (SIDS) Clearinghouse
8201 Greenboro Drive, Suite 600
McLean, Virginia 22102
708-821-8955

Survivors of Suicide
c/o Advent Christian Church
905 E. Edgelawn
Aurora, Illinois 60506
708-897-5531 (administrative offices)
708-897-5522 (24-hour crisis line)

Teen Age Grief, Inc.
P.O. Box 4935
Panorama City, California 91412-4935
805-254-1501

Program that trains professionals and school personnel to lead support groups in secondary schools and youth organizations.

THEOS Foundation (They Help Each Other Spiritually)
1301 Clark Building
717 Liberty Avenue
Pittsburgh, Pennsylvania 15222
412-471-7779

International self-help group for widows and widowers.

Widowed Persons Services
A Program of AARP (American Association of Retired Persons)
1909 "K" Street N.W.
Washington, D.C. 20049
202-728-4370

Provides outreach, talk groups, information, and referral services to widowed persons.

BIBLIOGRAPHY

Agee, James. *A Death in the Family*. New York: McDowell, Obolensky, 1957.

Albertson, Sandra Hayward. *Endings and Beginnings: A Young Family's Experience with Death and Renewal*. New York: Ballantine Books, 1980.

Alderman, Linda. *Why Did Daddy Die?: Helping Children Cope with the Loss of a Parent*. New York: Pocket Books, Simon & Schuster, 1989.

Alvarez, A. *The Savage God: A Study of Suicide*. New York: Bantam Books, 1973.

Angel, Marc D. *The Orphaned Adult: Confronting the Death of a Parent*. New York: Insight Books, Human Services Press, 1987.

Ariès, Philippe. *Western Attitudes Toward Death: From the Middle Ages to the Present*. Translated by Patricia M. Ranum. Baltimore and London: Johns Hopkins University Press, 1974.

Barbo, Beverly. *The Walking Wounded*. Lindsborg, Kans.: Carlsons', 1987.

Beauvoir, Simone de. *A Very Easy Death*. Translated by Patrick O'Brian. New York: Warner Books, 1964.

Berrill, Margaret. *Mummies, Masks, and Mourners*. Illustrated by Chris Molan. New York: Lodestar Book, E. P. Dutton, 1989.

Bowlby, John. *Loss: Sadness and Depression*. New York: Basic Books, Harper Torchbooks, 1980.

Brockman, Elin Schoen. *Widower*. New York: Bantam Books, 1987.

Brooks, Anne M. *The Grieving Time: A Year's Account of Recovery from Loss*. New York: Harmony Books, 1985.

Caine, Lynn. *Being a Widow*. New York: Arbor House, William Morrow, 1988.

———. *Widow*. New York: Bantam Books, 1974.

Campbell, Scott, and Phyllis Silverman. *Widower: When Men Are Left Alone*. New York: Prentice-Hall Press, 1987.

Centering Corporation. *Dear Parents: Letters to Bereaved Parents*. Omaha, Neb.: Centering Corporation, 1989.

DeFrain, John, Leona Martens, Jan Stork, and Warren Stork. *Stillborn: The Invisible Death*. Lexington, Mass.: Lexington Books, D. C. Heath & Co., 1986.

DeSpelder, Lynne Ann, and Albert Lee Strickland. *The Last Dance: Encountering Death and Dying*. Palo Alto: Mayfield Publishing Co., 1983.

DiGiulio, Robert C. *Beyond Widowhood: From Bereavement to Emergence and Hope*. New York: Free Press, Macmillan, 1989.

Doka, Kenneth J., ed. *Disenfranchised Grief: Recognizing Hidden Sorrow*. Lexington, Mass.: Lexington Books, D. C. Heath & Co., 1989.

Donnelley, Nina Herrmann. *I Never Know What to Say: How to Help Your Family and Friends Cope with Tragedy*. New York: A Ballantine/Epiphany Book, Ballantine Books, 1987.

Donnelly, Katherine Fair. *Recovering from the Loss of a Parent*. New York: Dodd, Mead & Co., 1987.

Dunne, Edward J., John L. McIntosh, and Karen Dunne-Maxim, eds. *Suicide and Its Aftermath: Understanding and Counseling the Survivors*. New York: W. W. Norton, 1987.

Enright, D. J. *The Oxford Book of Death*. Oxford and New York: Oxford University Press, 1987.

Freud, Sigmund. "Mourning and Melancholia." In *General Psychological Theory*. New York: Collier Books, Macmillan Publishing Co., 1963.

Gaffney, Donna A. *The Seasons of Grief: Helping Your Children Grow Through Loss*. New York: New American Library, 1988.

Ginsburg, Genevieve Davis. *To Live Again: Rebuilding Your Life After You've Become a Widow*. New York: Bantam Books, 1989.

Gorer, Geoffrey. *Death, Grief, and Mourning*. New York: Doubleday & Co., 1962.

Grof, Stanislaw, and Christina Grof. *Beyond Death: The Gates of Consciousness*. London: Thames & Hudson, 1980.

Grollman, Earl A., ed. *Concerning Death: A Practical Guide for the Living*. Boston: Beacon Press, 1974.

Haraldsson, Erlunder. "Survey of Claimed Encounters with the Dead." *Omega* 19, no. 2 (1988–89): 103–13.

Ilse, Sherokee, Linda Hammer Burns, and Susan Erling. *Sibling Grief*. Wayzata, Minn.: Pregnancy and Infant Loss Center, 1984.

James, John W., and Frank Cherry. *The Grief Recovery Handbook: A Step-by-Step Program for Moving Beyond Loss*. New York: Harper & Row, 1988.

Johnson, Sherry. *After a Child Dies: Counseling Bereaved Families*. New York: Springer Publishing Co., 1987.

Juneau, Barbara Frisbie. *Sad but O.K. My Daddy Died Today: A Child's View of Death*. Nevada City, Calif.: Blue Dolphin Press, 1988.

Kalish, Richard A. *Death, Grief, and Caring Relationships*. Monterey, Calif.: Brooks/Cole Publishing Co., Wadsworth, 1981.

Kapleau, Philip. *The Wheel of Life and Death: A Practical and Spiritual Guide*. New York: Doubleday, 1989.

Klein, Melanie. *The Selected Melanie Klein*. Edited by Juliet Mitchell. New York: Free Press, Macmillan, 1986.

Knapp, Ronald J. *Beyond Endurance: When a Child Dies*. New York: Schocken Books, 1986.

Kohn, Jane Burgess, and Willard K. Kohn. *The Widower*. Boston: Beacon Press, 1978.

Krauss, Pesach and Morrie Goldfischer. *Why Me? Coping with Grief, Loss, and Change*. New York: Bantam Books, 1988.

Krementz, Jill. *How It Feels When a Parent Dies*. New York: Alfred A. Knopf, 1981.

Kübler-Ross, Elisabeth. *AIDS: The Ultimate Challenge*. New York: Collier Books, Macmillan Publishing Co., 1987.

————. *On Children and Death*. New York: Collier Books, Macmillan Publishing Co., 1983.

————. *On Death and Dying*. New York: Macmillian Publishing Co., 1969.

————, ed. *Death: The Final Stage of Growth*. New York: A Touchstone Book, Simon & Schuster, 1975.

Kushner, Harold S. *When Bad Things Happen to Good People*. New York: Avon Books, 1983.

Lehman, Darrin R., Camille B. Wortman, and Allan F. Williams. "Long-term Effects of Losing a Spouse or Child in a Motor Vehicle Crash." *Journal of Personality and Social Psychology* 52, no. 1 (1987): 218–31.

LeShan, Eda. *Learning to Say Good-by: When a Parent Dies*. New York: Avon Books, Macmillan Publishing Co., 1988.

Lesher, Emerson L., and Karen J. Bergey. "Bereaved Elderly Mothers: Changes in Health, Functional Activities, Family Cohesion, and Psychological Well-being." *International Journal of Aging and Human Development* 26, no. 2 (1988): 81–89.

Levine, Stephen. *Who Dies?: An Investigation of Conscious Living and Conscious Dying*. New York: An Anchor Press Book, Doubleday, 1982.

Lewin, Tamar. "Aging Parents: Women's Burden Grows." *New York Times*, Nov. 14, 1989: 1.

Lewis, C. S. *A Grief Observed*. Afterword by Chad Walsh. New York: Bantam, 1976.

Lindemann, Erich H. "Symptomatology and Management of Acute Grief." *American Journal of Psychiatry* 101: 141–48.

Lukas, Christopher, and Henry M. Seiden. *Silent Grief: Living in the Wake of Suicide*. New York: Scribner's Sons, New York, 1987.

Margolis, Otto S., Austin H. Kutscher, Eric R. Marcus, Howard C. Raether, Vanderlyn R. Pine, Irene B. Seeland, Daniel J. Cherico et al. *Grief and the Loss of an Adult Child*. The Foundation of Thanatology Series, vol. 8. New York: Praeger Publishers, 1988.

Moffat, Mary Jane. *In the Midst of Winter: Selections from the Literature of Mourning*. New York: Vintage Books, Random House, 1982.

Monette, Paul. *Borrowed Time: An AIDS Memoir*. San Diego: Harcourt, Brace, Jovanovich, 1988.

Murrell, Stanley A., Samuel Himmelfarb, and James F. Phifer. "Effects of Bereavement/ Loss and Pre-event Status on Subsequent Physical Health in Older Adults." *International Journal of Aging and Human Development* 27, no. 2 (1988): 89–107.

Myers, Edward. *When Parents Die: A Guide for Adults*. New York: Penguin Books, 1986.

Nudel, Adele Rice. *Starting Over: Help for Young Widows and Widowers*. New York: Dodd, Mead & Co., 1986.

Parkes, Colin Murray. *Bereavement: Studies of Grief in Adult Life*. 2nd American ed. Foreword by John Bowlby. Madison, Conn.: International Universities Press, 1972.

Penny, Nicholas. *Mourning*. The Arts and Living Series of the Victoria and Albert Museum. London: Her Majesty's Stationery Office, 1981.

Peppers, Larry G., and Ronald J. Knapp. *Motherhood and Mourning: Perinatal Death*. New York: Praeger Publishers, 1980.

Pincus, Lily. *Death and the Family: The Importance of Mourning*. New York: Schocken Books, Random House, 1974.

Prichard, Elizabeth R., Margot Tallmer, Austin H. Kutscher, Robert DeBellis, and Mahlon S. Hale, eds. *Geriatrics and Thanatology*. The Foundation of Thanatology Series, vol. 1. New York: Praeger Publishers, 1984.

Quackenbush, Jamie, and Denise Graveline. *When Your Pet Dies: How to Cope with Your Feelings*. New York: Pocket Books, Simon & Schuster, 1985.

Rando, Therese A. *Grief, Dying and Death: Clinical Interventions for Caregivers*. Foreword by J. William Worden. Champaign, Ill.: Research Press Co., n.d.

———. *Grieving: How to Go on Living When Someone You Love Dies*. Lexington, Mass.: Lexington Books, D. C. Heath & Co., 1988.

Raphael, Beverley. *The Anatomy of Bereavement*. New York: Basic Books, 1983.

Reynolds, David K. *Constructive Living*. Honolulu: A Kolowalu Book, University of Hawaii Press, 1984.

Rosen, Helen. *Unspoken Grief: Coping with Childhood Sibling Loss*. Lexington, Mass.: Lexington Books, D. C. Heath & Co., 1986.

Saint-Exupéry, Antoine de. *The Little Prince*. Translated by Katherine Woods. San Diego: Harcourt Brace Jovanovich, 1971.

Schiff, Harriet Sarnoff. *The Bereaved Parent*. New York: Crown Publishers, 1977.

———. *Living Through Mourning: Finding Comfort and Hope When a Loved One Has Died*. New York: Penguin Books, 1987.

Schmidt, Judith Sara. *The Thought-a-Week Guides: How to Cope with Grief*. New York: Ballantine Books, 1989.

Schoenberg, Bernard, Arthur C. Carr, David Peretz, and Austin H. Kutscher, eds. *Loss and Grief: Psychological Management in Medical Practice*. New York and London: Columbia University Press, 1970.

Schoenberg, Bernard, Arthur C. Carr, David Peretz, Austin H. Kutscher, and Ivan K. Goldberg, eds. *Anticipatory Grief*. New York: Columbia University Press, 1974.

Seskin, Jane. *Alone—Not Lonely: Independent Living for Women Over Fifty*. Washington, D.C.: American Association of Retired Persons, and Glenview, Ill.: Scott Foresman & Co., 1985.

Silverman, Phyllis. *Widow-to-Widow*. New York: Spring Publishing Co., 1986.

Simon-Buller, Sherry, Victor A. Christopherson, and Randall A. Jones. "Correlates of Sensing the Presence of a Deceased Spouse." *Omega* 19, no. 1 (1988–89): 21–29.

Simpson, Michael W. *The Facts of Death*. Englewood Cliffs, N.J.: Prentice-Hall, 1979.

Singer, Lilly, Margaret Sirot, and Susan Rodd. *Beyond Loss: A Practical Guide Through Grief to a Meaningful Life*. New York: E. P. Dutton, 1988.

Stannard, David E., ed. *Death in America*. University of Pennsylvania Press, 1974.

Staudacher, Carol. *Beyond Grief: A Guide to Recovering from the Death of a Loved One*. Oakland, Calif.: New Harbinger Publications, 1987.

Stroebe, Wolfgang, and Margaret S. Stroebe. *Bereavement and Health: The Psychological and Physical Consequences of Partner Loss*. Cambridge: Cambridge University Press, 1987.

Tatelbaum, Judith. *The Courage to Grieve: Creative Living, Recovery, and Growth Through Grief*. New York: Harper & Row, 1980.

Tittensor, John. *Year One: A Record*. Victoria, Australia: McPhee Gribble Publishers, Penguin Books, 1984.

Truman, Jill. *Letter to My Husband: Notes About Mourning and Recovery*. New York: Penguin Books, 1987.

Upson, Norma S. *When Someone You Love Is Dying.* New York: A Fireside Book, Simon & Schuster, 1986.

Victim Information Pamphlet. Mothers Against Drunk Driving.

Wakerman, Elyce. *Father Loss: Daughters Discuss the Man That Got Away.* Foreword by Holly Barrett, Ph.D. New York: Henry Holt & Co., 1984.

Weizman, Savine Gross, and Phyllis Kamm. *About Mourning: Support and Guidance for the Bereaved.* Foreword by Phyllis Silverman. New York: Human Sciences Press, 1987.

Wortman, Camille B., and Roxanne Cohen Silver. "The Myths of Coping with Loss." *Journal of Counseling and Clinical Psychology* 57, no. 3 (1989): 349–357.

Zisook, Stephen, ed. *Grief and Bereavement.* The Psychiatric Clinics of America, vol. 6, no. 3. Philadelphia: W. B. Saunders Co., Harcourt Brace Jovanovich, 1987.